The Ethnological Imagination

Contradictions

Edited by Craig Calhoun, Social Science Research Council

The Ethnological Imagination

A Cross-Cultural Critique of Modernity

Fuyuki Kurasawa

Contradictions, Volume 21

 University of Minnesota Press

Minneapolis

London

Published by the University of Minnesota Press
111 Third Avenue South, Suite 290
Minneapolis, MN 55401-2520
http://www.upress.umn.edu

Library of Congress Cataloging-in-Publication Data

Kurasawa, Fuyuki.
    The ethnological imagination : a cross-cultural critique of modernity / Fuyuki Kurasawa.
        p.   cm. — (Contradictions ; v. 21)
    Includes bibliographical references and index.
    ISBN 0-8166-4239-7 (alk. paper) — ISBN 0-8166-4240-0 (pbk. : alk. paper)
        1. Ethnology—Philosophy.   2. Ethnology—Methodology.   3. Marxist anthropology.   4. Structural anthropology.   I. Title.   II. Contradictions (Minneapolis, Minn.) ; 21.
    GN33.K87 2004
    305.8'001—dc22
                                                                          2004003692

Printed in the United States of America on acid-free paper

The University of Minnesota is an equal-opportunity educator and employer.

12 11 10 09 08 07 06 05 04   10 9 8 7 6 5 4 3 2 1

D'où venous-nous?
Que sommes-nous?
Où allons-nous?

Paul Gauguin, 1897

Contents

Preface

This book addresses Western social theory's seeming exhaustion or inadequacy when dealing with the pressing matter of cross-cultural thinking, which is all the more urgent today because of the increasing recognition of cultural pluralism and difference in our global age. I suggest that one of the routes out of this impasse lies in the rediscovery of what can be termed "the ethnological imagination," a theoretical countercurrent that has created mythical representations of non-Western societies in order to interpret and radically put into question Euro-American modernity's constitutive particularities. The ethnological imagination has inverted the intercultural gaze to "anthropologize" Western societies, that is, to defamiliarize, denaturalize, and situate their customs, beliefs, and institutional arrangements through juxtaposition to a series of non-Western alter egos. If it has generated problematic and flawed understandings of many peoples and societies, the ethnological imagination has equally fostered a powerful self-critique of the modern project in the North Atlantic.

I thereby retrace the ethnological imagination's presence at the heart of Western social theory by focusing on six of its key contributors: Jean-Jacques Rousseau, Karl Marx, Max Weber, Emile Durkheim, Claude Lévi-Strauss, and Michel Foucault. I begin during the Enlightenment with Rousseau, who, chiefly through the figure of the "civilized savage" and his conception of the state of nature, established the epistemological and thematic foundations for an inter-cultural diagnosis of Western modernity. Chapter 2 turns to Marx, whose unparalleled demystification of commodity fetishism in the mid-nineteenth century brought together his critique of political economy and his interest in noncapitalist forms of socioeconomic organization. During the late nineteenth and early twentieth centuries, Weber and Durkheim developed comprehensively cross-cultural outlooks aimed at shedding light on the major transformations sweeping across the Western world. Weber accordingly created a thoroughly compara-tive sociology of world religions, which closely studied Asian forms of moral and economic life conduct in relation to those prevalent in the North Atlantic region. Durkheim contested the emerging bound-aries between sociological and anthropological objects of study by directing much of his research toward "primitive" settings. The last two chapters of the book consider the transformations of the ethno-logical imagination in the latter half of the twentieth century, dur-ing which period it has come to occupy pride of place in the French intellectual landscape. Rather than being restricted to a taxonomic exercise solely relevant to "primitive" societies, Lévi-Strauss's struc-tural analysis of mythological systems can therefore be understood as containing a radical interrogation of some of the founding myths of modernity. Finally, I contend that Foucault's writings represent some of the most interesting recent attempts to develop an anthropology of home, namely a critical estrangement of Western modernity's defining institutional characteristics and processes through historical and inter-cultural juxtaposition.

Hence, the following chapters draw attention to the pivotal roles that conceptions of the non-Western and the nonmodern other play within each of the six theorists' work, in order to demonstrate the extent to which their assessments of the modern condition draw upon the ethnological imagination. I thereby hope to gain novel insights about their thought, as well as a better understanding of the ways in which their encounters with instances of cultural alterity fuel their diagnoses of what ails Western modernity or makes it flourish as a sociohistorical constellation. Its distinctive features—the emergence of the individual and the transformations of subjectivity, the control of nature by culture, the idea of history as teleological progress, the rise and conquest of rationalism, and new modes of socioeconomic domination and exclusion—are virtually commonplace by now, yet few people appreciate that such a theoretical understanding would have been impossible without a cultural outside to the modern West.

Additionally, I argue that the ethnological imagination represents an important yet hitherto neglected stream of critical social theory. Indeed, the encounter with radically different ways of being in the world and modes of social organization combats the omnipresent tendency toward one-dimensionality, the contraction of the field of sociohistorical possibilities leading to a widespread belief that the existing social order in the North Atlantic is necessary, natural, eternal, or universal. Yet the cross-cultural expansion of the horizons of what is possible cannot but put the here and now's *doxa* into doubt, the apparently self-evident character of modern society being confronted with the interrogation of its very raison d'être and the processes of its self-instituting. Accordingly, the ethnological imagination is underpinned by a critical hermeneutics composed of three principal analytical moments and normative ideals: an outward turn or moment of openness; an "in-betweenness" or moment of mediation; and an inward turn or moment of reflexivity. Critique of the familiar and the proximate can thus be fruitfully achieved through comparison and contrast with non-Western sociocultural universes.

Having described what the book strives to accomplish, I should now specify what it does not set out to do. In the first instance, the argument is not explicitly comparative in design. Although drawing attention to similarities and differences, as well as lines of anticipation and continuity among our cast of six theorists on certain points, I do not systematically put their diagnoses of modernity or of the non-Western world side by side. My intent is of a different order: to trace the existence of intercultural strands in the writings of some of the leading figures of Euro-American social theory and to demonstrate how their contributions generate a critical hermeneutics of the modern West's structures, habits, and creeds. At the same time, the book is not exegetical in character. Hence, I have not attempted to cover the full panoply of themes raised by Rousseau, Marx, Weber, Durkheim, Lévi-Strauss, or Foucault, or to pursue an immanent or transcendent critique of the body of their work. This treatment will invariably prove unsatisfactory to specialists of each of the six figures, yet the overall narrative about the ethnological imagination and the tack of honing in on cultural alterity to provide a different appreciation of their thinking should be kept in mind.

At another level, the book does not ponder in a sustained manner the historical and political context within which cross-cultural theorizing has been created in the modern age. The succeeding periods of European "discovery," invasion, and colonization of much of the world, as well as that of post–World War II formal decolonization accompanied by North Atlantic global dominance, is obviously of great significance, but it has been described elsewhere with much brilliance.[1] Furthermore, I fully recognize that colonialism and imperialism have made possible and been sustained by flawed, even highly objectionable, conceptions of non-Western peoples. Exoticizing, ethnocentric, and culturally chauvinistic tendencies are certainly present in many of the writings examined here, but to dismiss them out of hand would be to fall prey to two common fallacies: first, to engage in the crudest form of presentism, which unreflexively hoists contemporary criteria and expectations to assess the past; and second, to perpetuate the marginalization of the substantial tradition of ethnological self-critique of Western modernity found in these very same writings. For my purposes, then, the interesting question is not whether Euro-American representations of the non-Western world correspond to "actually existing" societies in Asia, the Americas, Africa, or Oceania, but rather how such mythical images have enabled a critical hermeneutics of the modern West. As such, the terms "savage," "primitive," and "Oriental" reflect the six theorists' use of them, though the "scare quotes" are meant to point to their dubious status.[2] I employ the designations "Western" and "non-Western" for heuristic purposes, as well as for convenience's sake. As I explain in the conclusion, one of the ethnological imagination's challenges today is to incorporate a vision of internally differentiated and multiple modernities, so as to envisage each sociocultural constellation as a "field of tensions" (Arnason 1990) structured by a range of dynamics and a plurality of spheres of life.

Before plunging into the thick of the argument, I should mention that the title of this book deliberately echoes the titles of two works that have been integral to my intellectual apprenticeship. C. Wright Mills's *Sociological Imagination* (1959) encouraged me, as a rather green undergraduate, to turn toward sociology at a time when other disciplinary paths beckoned, while Martin Jay's *Dialectical Imagination* (1996 [1973]) introduced me to the rich tradition of critical theory, from which I have drawn ever since. Without presuming to pay tribute to these books, the pages that follow bear witness to a considerable debt.

Acknowledgments

All books are the products of intellectual journeys, though the metaphor of travel is probably more literally apt here than in most other cases. This work's ideas gestated, took flight, and sometimes—I must ruefully admit—crash-landed on three continents, and the peripatetic character of the argument is indebted to a great number of people in different places. First, I would like to thank Peter Beilharz, the principal supervisor of the dissertation out of which this book emerged at La Trobe University in Melbourne, Australia; he has overseen the project in its many incarnations. He ably poked and prodded me to go further than I would have otherwise been able to do, all the while keeping the bigger picture in sight as well as demonstrating outstanding intellectual and personal generosity. Johann Arnason's erudition came to play in his rigorous critiques of several chapters, and Joel Kahn brought an anthropologist's trained eye to the task. Still at La Trobe, the intellectual support of Trevor Hogan, Lorraine Mortimer, and Chris Eipper was invaluable, as was that of a *Gemeinschaft* of fellow travelers: Charles Ambrose, Li-Ju Chen, Chris Dew, Chris Houston, Kyong-Ju Kim, Ray Madden, Wendy Mee, Anne-Maree Sawyer, Karl Smith, and Nick Smith.

The book would likely not have seen the light of day without Craig Calhoun. I am grateful for his enthusiasm and unflagging support, his perceptive comments on earlier drafts of the manuscript, and his agile guidance of a novice author through the process of academic publishing. Zygmunt Bauman and John Lechte provided detailed feedback and encouragement, while Jeffrey Alexander's and Arvind Rajagopal's external reports on behalf of the University of Minnesota Press were extremely helpful in prompting me to refine and reframe the argument. I thank the following people, with whom parts of the project were discussed: Marshall Berman, Sam Binkley, Nindy Brar, Marcel Fournier, Martin Fuchs, Ratiba Hadj-Moussa, Axel Honneth, Dick Howard, Martin Jay, Minna Lahti, Antje Linkenbach, Edgar Morin, Paul Rabinow, Rayna Rapp, David Roberts, John Rundell, Ikuko Sato, Patrick Savidan, Brian Singer, Ken Thompson, Michel Wieviorka, and Joel Whitebook. Thanks are also due the participants of the various conferences at which many of the ideas proposed in the following pages were first aired. While it would be tempting to distribute the responsibility for any errors and shortcomings in the book among those named above, I must carry that burden alone.

It has been a pleasure to work with Carrie Mullen and all the staff at the University of Minnesota Press. Karen Nachipo of IDP Education Australia administered the Commonwealth Fellowship I held while at La Trobe, and Wallace Clement offered institutional support at Carleton University during a crucial stage of writing. A Postdoctoral Fellowship from the Social Sciences and Humanities Research Council of Canada gave me time to rework the manuscript, thanks to the support of George Fallis and Robert Drummond, successive deans of the Faculty of Arts at York University. My colleagues and graduate students at York University have made the protracted revising of the manuscript enjoyable in an environment where social theory, interdisciplinarity, and political activism make for a heady brew that is all too rare in North American academia today. Patti Phillips was tremendously patient and skillful in whipping the final manuscript into shape, correcting the text, chasing the odd reference gone astray, and attempting to rein in my apparently incorrigible yet fatal attraction to mixed metaphors. Finally, I must thank my mother and stepfather, Christiane Benoît and André Dolbec, who have supported me through thick and thin. I would like to dedicate this book to my mother, who has been a constant source of inspiration.

Introduction

Western Social Theory and the Ethnological Imagination

The Theoretical Impasse

As we enter the twenty-first century, Western social theory finds itself at an impasse. For the most part born out of a fairly circumscribed sociohistorical environment and awkwardly carrying the traces of its Euro-American roots, it appears ill equipped to confront the serious challenge posed by what is undeniably one of the defining phenomena of our age: cultural pluralism in a globalizing world. If diversity has always been a feature of social life, the recent acceleration and intensification of transnational flows of all sorts have brought it to the forefront of contemporary academic and public discussion. Coupled with multiculturalism and immigration, the resurgence of ethnic and religious conflicts in various regions of the globe has led to a massive burgeoning of theoretically informed work in the human sciences devoted to the analysis of the various facets of cultural difference in the past decade or so.[1] Indeed, no topic has arguably provoked more heated debate or earnest reflection within theoretical circles in recent memory. And yet what still remains to be accomplished is a recasting of the very ways in which Western social theory is conventionally viewed and practiced in light of the reality of cultural pluralism. The task, in other words, consists of cultivating more cosmopolitan, cross-culturally based modes of theorizing that are capable of taking into account the multiplicity of forms of social organization and ways of being human in the world today—a task particularly urgent and salient for critical theory as it seeks to reinvigorate its radical questioning of the established social order. Hence, both the gravity of the impasse and the magnitude of the challenge appear clearly on the horizon.

The widespread recognition of globalization's significance is but the most recent moment during which the complex and fraught relationship between modern Western thinking and cultural difference has been exposed.[2] Already in the sixteenth century, Montaigne's (1948a, 1578–80) cannibals became a prominent leitmotif with which to ridicule his society and his epoch's self-understandings and representations of other cultures, an effect that Montesquieu's (1973 [1721]) Persians also brilliantly accomplished two hundred years later. Boasian and Durkheimian currents of cultural anthropology undermined evolutionary models and racialist taxonomies of humankind in the early part of the twentiety century, thereby putting into doubt attributions of inferiority to peoples deemed "savage" or "primitive." Closer to our own era, the rise to theoretical prominence of the question of cultural pluralism has been closely connected to the lasting impact of very concrete and meaningful historical developments, most notably the wave of decolonization and the subsequent gaining of political independence by Third World countries following the end of the Second World War, as well as the continuing struggles of indigenous groups, peoples of color, and immigrants in the Euro-American world. These developments have themselves inspired a host of intellectual currents that converge in their questioning of the authority and adequacy of Western systems of knowledge vis-à-vis other cultural realities: Third World feminism, which has criticized the universalistic pretensions of the predominant Western feminist construct of "woman";[3] postcolonialism, with its examination of the operations of colonial discourses and the ties binding North Atlantic literary and philosophical works to empire;[4] critical anthropology, which has rejected the discipline's earlier hierarchical ascriptions of developmental backwardness to indigenous societies;[5] and finally, French poststructuralism, whose varied permutations share a recurrent concern with figures of alterity.[6]

The crux of the issue, then, can be summed up by the idea of a tension between specificity and generality: on the one hand, the intrinsic spatial and temporal situatedness of theoretical endeavors formed in particular contexts, and on the other, the drive to display modern Western social theory's transhistorical and transcultural applicability. Indeed, contemporary theorists inherit an intellectual legacy shaped in the cauldron of the varied, complex, and sometimes contradictory processes of sociohistorical transformation for which "Western modernity" has come to stand as shorthand. As is widely recognized today, the classics' oeuvre can therefore largely be understood as a series of attempts to make sense and offer ambivalent assessments of the sweeping changes that followed in the wake of the French and Industrial "dual revolutions" (Hobsbawm 1977), in addition to what Nietzsche (1954) famously termed the "death of god." The concepts of alienation and exploitation (Marx), rationalization (Weber), and anomie (Durkheim), to name but the most obvious, all strove to encapsulate the problematic consequences and experiences stemming from the modern age's rapid transformation of conditions of life in Europe.

Social theory's historical and cultural specificity can be further demonstrated by examining two of its notable characteristics. In the first instance, until recently, it has taken the nation-state as its unstated unit of analysis, the terms "society" and "culture" implicitly referring to what have been perceived to be discrete, self-contained, and relatively homogenous entities bounded by national borders. Accordingly, theoretical reflection has for the most part operated with an unproblematized assumption of neat correspondence between nation, territory, society, and culture.[7] Second, as is the case for the human sciences more generally, many of the foundations of social theory were laid during the age of European empire. Political rule over, and economic appropriation of non-Western territories, resources, and peoples formed the historical background against which Western thinkers came to grips with other societies. This frequently fostered a denigration of such colonized societies, which were widely perceived as inferior and backward vis-à-vis their Euro-American counterparts. Another by-product of colonialism was ethnocentrism, whereby sociohistorical constellations outside of the North Atlantic region were ignored because they were deemed inconsequential or derivative. Many theories of modernity have thus drawn upon a very narrow range of national experiences (e.g., England in the economic realm, France in the political domain), which are presumed to be universally valid or, at the very least, to be eventually replicated in other parts of the world. Found to be always already lacking, the latter are fated to follow the developmental path originally traced by their allegedly more advanced counterparts. Hence, ethnocentric tendencies have been reinforced by the amalgamation of historicism (namely, teleological versions of the philosophy of history) and implicit evolutionism.

Vain attempts to resolve this tension between Western social theory's general and specific character have merely produced a series of additional dead ends, which, in the first section of this introduction, I regroup into two sets of misguided binaries—traditionalism versus postmodernism and false universalism versus radical particularism. Despite their ubiquity, such dichotomies do not entirely define the terms under which responses to cultural diversity can be framed. On the contrary, as the second section of this introduction suggests, an altogether different direction can be followed by rereading the history of Western social theory in a manner that foregrounds its unrelenting preoccupation with cross-cultural matters; among many others, Rousseau, Marx, Weber, Durkheim, Lévi-Strauss, and Foucault are particularly illustrative of this tendency to devise anthropologies of modernity that critically interpret Western societies by juxtaposing them against the non-Western world. In fact, I would argue that the significance of this interculturally inspired theoretical current amply justifies designating it by its own distinctive label: the ethnological imagination. As we will consider in the third part of the introduction, practitioners of this ethnological imagination have developed a critical and cross-cultural hermeneutics of Euro-American modernity whereby engagement with other societies has been essential to the project of self-understanding and self-critique of their own times and places. By engaging with other sociocultural universes, a number of Western social theorists have gained an appreciation for the human condition's remarkable diversity. The resulting comparative contextualization of the modern West has compelled both its decentering and the established social order's radical interrogation, since the latter becomes repositioned as one sociohistorical configuration among others, rather than the necessary culmination of human development. Furthermore, the corresponding sense of distance acquired vis-à-vis Western modernity estranges it, thus allowing its habitual and familiar aspects to be questioned as rather peculiar and localized expressions of humankind's modes of organizing social life. Learning about others is not simply an act of cosmopolitan open-mindedness, but an integral part of learning about ourselves and even viewing ourselves as other. As much as anything else, taking the challenge of cultural difference seriously should act as a remedy against one-dimensional thinking. The ethnological imagination's rediscovery, then, marks a contribution to critical modes of theorizing.

The Pitfalls of Polarization

Given the aforementioned complexity of the question of cultural difference in the human sciences, most responses to it have proven unconvincing. While striving to steer clear of the impasse between specificity and generality, these responses have merely exacerbated it by leaving social theorists bogged down or lurching between two sets of misleadingly polarized options: traditionalism versus postmodernism, and false universalism versus radical particularism.[8] Let us explore each of these positions in turn.

Traditionalism versus Postmodernism

The challenge of cultural pluralism has spawned a first dualism of note, that between traditionalist and postmodernist stances toward the legacy of Euro-American social theory. For traditionalists, who frequently employ historicist modes of inquiry, scholarship should aim to restore the original meaning of canonical works and rediscover their authors' intentions by reconstructing their intellectual and sociohistorical environments. Traditionalism attempts to shelter itself from what it construes as the here and now's passing fancies and fads, manifestations of a flagrant presentism that imposes the inappropriate "foreignness" of contemporary concerns onto thinkers living in other times and places.[9] If useful in reminding us of the need to bear in mind past worldviews and standards whenever we engage in the act of passing judgment on the writings of a particular epoch, traditionalism nevertheless treats classics as static components of a dead canon that is frozen in time and thereby resolutely turned away from the present. Such a position disregards the fact that the very constitution of any disciplinary canon, as well as the traditions of interpretation that grow around it, are shifting sociohistorical constructs transformed in response to lines of inquiry and discovery that appear in different eras and societies.[10] Consequently, as I contend throughout this book, the widespread neglect of classical social theorists' cross-cultural sensibilities has less to do with the content of their own writings than with the traditionalists' unexamined reproduction of past interpretive biases; conventional readings of the social-theoretic canon have consistently underappreciated its engagement with the issue of cultural difference, thereby paradoxically eroding a proper appreciation of its richness.

Traditionalism finds its antithesis in what can be termed postmodernism, which is used here as shorthand to describe a theoretical stream claiming to break with what it understands to be the modern tradition of engagement with cultural difference.[11] Postmodernists believe that being irreversibly tainted by the sexism, racism, and ethnocentrism pervasive during the period of European colonialism, and more generally by an apparently rigid Toryism, the classical edifice of the human sciences should largely be dismissed.[12] Some have even gone so far as to portray this edifice in toto as the handmaiden of (neo) imperialism, and its contributors as apologists for, active participants in, or collaborationists in the project of subjugating non-Western peoples.[13] Understood in this way, postmodernism comes dangerously close to advocating a theoretical tabula rasa, idealizing noncanonical forms of thought that celebrate radical alterity for its own sake and the proliferation of any and all cultural differences across the field of the social. To subvert the modern West's global stranglehold over knowledge, postmodernists strive to foster discursive spaces where the supposedly unfiltered and unrepressed voices of different subjects can be heard.

Postmodernism ambiguously slips between two sets of claims regarding Western social theory's relationship to colonialism. The more tempered and defensible version of the argument demands that the history of North Atlantic colonial and imperial hegemony be incorporated into any reading of classical theorists' work. However, its stronger claim suffers from a blatant reductionism that equates these writings with the will to dominate non-Western societies; the canon is simplistically converted into an ideological instrument of Euro-American power. Yet as will be explained below, this argument ignores the existence of a major theoretical current employing representations of other sociohistorical settings to effect a self-critique of the modern West—including the latter's racism, ethnocentrism, and colonial-cum-imperialist projects.[14] In addition, the task of listening to and including the experiences of those who have been historically marginalized from mainstream discourses is important, but it should not serve to smuggle in a form of essentializing nativism that would innately privilege or monologically embrace other voices. In and of itself, advocating difference for difference's sake will not do, since it favors a subject's sociocultural position over an assessment of the content of his or her speech. Whether accorded to Western or non-Western stances, wholesale adulation leaves untouched what must be earnestly undertaken today: the cultivation of interculturally dialogical and critical forms of social theory.

False Universalism versus Radical Particularism

Quite apart from the traditionalism/postmodernism binary, Western social theorists' responses to the issue of cultural pluralism are frequently caught between falsely universalistic and radically particularistic positions.[15] I have already alluded to the human sciences' tendency, from the Enlightenment on, to universalize specific Euro-American historical and cultural experiences. Frequently revealing metaphysical leanings, this tendency has been anchored in the belief that human reason could discover an a priori, objective, and general set of principles, or yet again, naturalistic laws of motion of the socio-historical dimensions of existence. Models created by extrapolating certain features from particular times and places have been applied to all societies and historical periods, for they are assumed to capture the essence of humankind's common trajectory. Historicism and evolutionism have traditionally represented two of the most prominent instances of false universalism, although under our current post-metaphysical condition, claims about the modern West personifying the most advanced stage of human development are favored over the construction of abstract sociohistorical laws. According to this logic, the North Atlantic's institutional configuration and sociocultural characteristics will and/or should be emulated by all other societies. Three well-known examples come to mind: Habermas's (1979, 1984) social-evolutionary schema of human rationality; analyses of global-ization viewing the latter as a process of homogenizing modernization and Westernization because of "time-space distantiation" (Giddens 1990) or "time-space compression" (Harvey 1989); and Fukuyama's (1992) neomodernization theory, a pseudo-Hegelian convergence the-sis about the "end of History" in a post–cold war new world order defined by the triumph of capitalism and liberal democracy.

Why speak of false universalism in these cases? Because, under the guise of universality, they display an unabashed ethnocentrism that implicitly denies its own cultural specificity. In reality, what occurs is the universalization of local phenomena and normative preferences, which are indiscriminately generalized to all parts of the world in a manner that is prior to and devoid of any engagement with non-Western societies or consideration of the meanings, values, and norms held by their members. In effect, the cross-cultural labor of looking beyond one's immediate and familiar surroundings to grapple with the substantial differences and similarities between peoples is nowhere to be found. In its neoconservative variant à la Fukuyama, false universalism is particularly pernicious in that it overtly disparages any recognition of domestic or global cultural pluralism—something perceived as akin to a betrayal of North Atlantic civilization itself. Therefore, ethnocentrism is metamorphosed into a virtue that reasserts an unwavering commitment to and defense of a supposed core set of Western values and institutions in the face of their imminent dissolution amidst a sea of diversity. Behind this kind of hectoring and boisterously assertive provincialism lurks a sense of unabashed cultural superiority and, as a result, the conviction that "others" are teleologically becoming more like "us" or, at the very least, that they should be doing so. Needless to say, intercultural and cosmopolitan modes of critique of the established social order in the Euro-American region become both impossible and undesirable from this point of view.

At the opposite end of the spectrum from false universalism lies radical particularism, a reaction to cultural difference that falls prey to a logic of overcompensation in trying to offset its counterpart. Instead of proposing a totalizing Universal History or Great Map of Humanity, radical particularists celebrate the fragmentation and sense of alterity stemming from the cultivation of distinct, localized, and partial micronarratives originating from various subject-positions. Two significant developments in the human sciences are aptly incorporated: acknowledgment of the historical and sociocultural situatedness of all knowledges, which always already reflect a view from somewhere (Haraway 1991); and phenomenologically inspired "thick descriptions" of the meanings of everyday symbols, beliefs, and practices in local settings (Geertz 1973, 1983). However, radical particularism misinterprets and overextends such fruitful insights by employing them to generate an essentialized and nativist parochialism.[16] It fetishizes or ontologizes alterity for its own sake, encouraging the proliferation of monologues of difference sealed off from one another. Only firsthand experience in and of a sociocultural setting, or of a kind of subjectivity, would entitle one to speak about and analyze it. Moreover, only local knowledges are admissible and any gesture to move from the particular to the more general is identified with totalization (Lyotard 1984, 1985; Seidman 1991b). This means, de facto, that we must withdraw and restrict ourselves to the proximate and the commonplace.

And if so restricted, authors are unable to assess the comparative merits and flaws of their own societies or those of others; absolute relativism would quickly follow suit. For some, such as Rorty (1991a, 1991b, 1991c), it is hardly worth being troubled by the specters of provincialism and cultural arbitrariness. In fact, a self-satisfied and quasi-narcissistic admission of the inexorable character of ethnocentrism and absolute relativism is in order, for "we" "rich North American postmodern bourgeois liberals" (Rorty 1991a) cannot but remain ensconced in our own lifeworlds—and indeed, "we" should do so without regret or need for justification beyond acknowledgment of such a predicament. There is something deeply disturbing about the complacency with which this kind of postmodern pragmatist argument warrants a blissful and willing ignorance of non-Western realities, for as Geertz (2000, 74) indicates, "an easy surrender to the comforts of merely being ourselves, cultivating deafness and maximizing gratitude for not having been born a Vandal or an Ik, will be fatal to both." In this respect, particularistic ethnocentrism is no better than its universalist mirror image.[17]

I should add that, more often than not, radical particularists cling to an assumption of necessary and a priori incommensurability between cultures, the cultures' radical alterity believed to make them exist outside of any possible interpretive horizons. All acts of translation are thus condemned to failure, or said to manifest an assimilationist logic exercising a homogenizing representational violence (Lyotard 1984, 1985, 1988; Winch 1970). Huntington's (1993, 1996) scenario of the "clash of civilizations" constitutes a new twist on such arguments, since it divides the world into discrete, ontologically irreconcilable, and thereby intrinsically hostile civilizational-cum-religious geopolitical blocs. Non-Western societies (and notably "Islamic" ones) allegedly foster ways of thinking and acting that are totally at odds with those in the modern West; "they" are completely different from, and thus incompatible with, "us." Hence, radical particularism promotes an absolutist understanding of cultural otherness, according to which sociocultural horizons are static and self-enclosed realities, instead of dynamic processes continuously being created and recreated by encounters with other ways of acting and thinking. In fact, contrary to what such authors imply, societies and civilizations are complex and internally diverse amalgams best located along a continuum of likeness and divergence—not a simplistic identity/difference binary. Cross-cultural comparison consists less of discovering sui generis forms of alterity or sameness than in dialogically studying the interaction of multiple practices, beliefs, and values at different levels of analysis (local, national, regional, and global).

Regardless of the camp within which they can be placed, most social-theoretic responses to the challenge of cultural pluralism have ironically reproduced, if not amplified, the cross-cultural impasse described above. They have supported rigid stances demanding either an uncompromising defense of traditionalist versions of the canon or else the complete dismantling of the legacy of modern Euro-American social theory. For its part, the problem of ethnocentrism has been unsatisfactorily addressed by falsely universalizing Western viewpoints and experiences, or yet again by radically particularizing knowledge in ways that turn away from the rest of the world. Echoing what Elias (1987a) has identified as a "retreat of sociologists into the present," I would go so far as to claim that a grave paradox has taken shape: a potential retreat of Euro-American social theorists to their own settings is taking place at the very moment when, in the shadows of globalization, cross-cultural reflection is most urgently needed.

Excavating the Ethnological Imagination

Up to this point, I have suggested that Western social theory finds itself in an unenviable situation with respect to the issue of cultural difference today, yet it is equally true that this impasse is neither intractable nor inevitable. One of the ways to overcome it is to rediscover the history of a substantial, albeit hitherto neglected, strand of cross-cultural thinking that has been integral to the project of understanding and critique of Western modernity since the latter's inception. Accordingly, the following pages propose to follow this strand in a manner that requires rereading part of the social-theoretic legacy in order to foreground how its analyses of the modern West have been made possible by way of constructs of non-Western realities.

In line with arguments in other fields of knowledge, I am claiming that repeated encounters and juxtapositions with a series of cultural alter egos have been indispensable to Western modernity's theoretical constitution; alterity does not live at the peripheries or within the interstices of our understandings of it, but at its center.[18] Though hardly providing ready-made solutions to the problems noted in the previous section, greater recognition of the ethnological imagination can unearth alternatives to the culs-de-sac promoted by traditionalism, postmodernism, false universalism, and radical particularism.

Aside from providing the basis for an adequate response to the challenge of cultural pluralism, the rediscovery of the ethnological imagination can assist us in developing a cross-cultural mode of critique of Western modernity—a source of critical theory that has so far been undervalued in comparison to its philosophical and historical counterparts. Indeed, social theorists have frequently employed philosophical critique, and done so in two familiar ways: immanently, by demonstrating that the operation of certain defining contradictions at the core of modern society will intrinsically lead to the latter's self-inflicted downfall (Marxist or ecological theories of capitalism, for instance); and transcendentally, by pointing out the gap between what is and what ought to be, the existing reality of modern society falling short of specific normative ideals (e.g., universal liberty, equality, and solidarity in feminist or antiracist discourses). No less widely used is historicizing critique, which juxtaposes the present to other eras to cultivate an effect of "detachment" (Elias 1987b) vis-à-vis the here and now. Importantly, since past and future states of existence are treated as strange, distant, and jarring, rather than as familiar and comfortable, the present can appear as neither necessary nor eternal; it is understood to be the ever-changing outcome of collective human action. Outstanding examples of this kind of temporal estrangement include Elias's (1994a) developmental approach to the study of civilizing processes,[19] Le Goff's (1980) "historical anthropology" examining the European Middle Ages as other to (rather than the ancestor of) modernity, Foucault's (1965, 1977, 1978) genealogical analyses of rationalities and practices, Taylor's (1989) investigation of the intellectual sources of modern identity, and various utopian scenarios that question the established form of social organization by contrast with the perfection of other social orders (communism, sexual freedom, gender equality, and so forth).

Because of their marked preference for philosophical and historical types of critique, Western social theorists have for the most part been blind to the spirit of radical interrogation engendered by cross-cultural encounter. Without denying the fact that the human sciences have created and perpetuated what are, by contemporary standards, flawed and objectionable assumptions about the non-Western world, several thinkers have nevertheless used representations of other societies to question the legitimacy and necessity of their own times and places. I will detail later how the ethnological imagination operates to produce a critical hermeneutics of Western modernity, but for the time being it is sufficient to mention that the confrontation with instances of cultural alterity has often broadened certain thinkers' sociocultural horizons and correspondingly cultivated a sense of far-reaching estrangement toward familiar and proximate beliefs, practices, and institutions. The self-evident, doxic quality of habitualized and naturalized patterns of thought and action is thus broken (Bourdieu 1977), while the processes of their self-institution are exposed in a manner underlining their socially and historically constructed character. If geographically remote societies have personified cultural difference, engagement with them has also persuaded many social theorists to consider their domestic surroundings as other.[20]

In the wake of Mills's (1959) and Jay's (1996 [1973]) studies, I have decided to designate this intellectual constellation "the ethnological imagination." "Ethnological" is intended in the broad and etymologically literal sense of the comparative study of societies aiming to produce critical interpretations of the modern West, rather than the more restricted disciplinary meaning it has acquired since the late nineteenth century (that is, the study of non-Western "races" or peoples).[21] Merleau-Ponty (1960, 150) wonderfully captures this generalized sensibility: "Ethnology is not a specialty defined by a particular object, 'primitive' societies; it is a way of thinking, one which imposes itself when the object is 'other,' and demands that we transform ourselves. Thus we become the ethnologists of our own society if we distance ourselves from it."[22] As for the term "imagination," it highlights the mythical character of constructs of otherness found in cross-cultural reflection (e.g., the state of nature, the "primitive" condition, the "Orient"). Such constructs are myths not solely in being opposed to the truthful or the observable—namely what is relegated to the realms of fantasy, fiction, or falsehood because not accurately reflecting reality. They are so in a more interpretive register, representing related sets of beliefs and values created to rhetorically explain what Euro-American societies have become in relation to their pasts and their futures.[23] Cumulatively, the ethnological imagination has produced what Dumont (1986, 8) calls an "anthropology of modernity," a critical examination of this sociohistorical formation from a distance and through a comparative perspective acquired by way of encounters with widely differing ways of being in the world.

A Portrait of the Field

This cross-cultural sensibility is hardly recent, being always already present in the human sciences and running through some of the modern age's towering intellectual figures.[24] It was already found in Montaigne's magisterial *Essays,* with its justly celebrated and previously mentioned remarks about the moral relativism of cannibalism: "[E]ach man calls barbarism whatever is not his own practice" (1948a, 152). Montaigne's merit also stems from his ability to grasp the destabilizing effects of the so-called discovery of the New World upon European civilization's self-conception:

> Our world has just discovered another world (and who will guarantee us that it is the last of its brothers, since the daemons, the Sybils, and we ourselves have up to now been ignorant of this one?) no less great, full and well-limbed than itself, yet so new and so infantile that it is still being taught its A B C. . . . If we are right to infer the end of our world, and that poet is right about the youth of his own age, this other world will only be coming into the light when ours is leaving it. The universe will fall into paralysis; one member will be crippled, the other in full vigor. (1948b, 693)[25]

A century or so after the intellectual Renaissance to which Montaigne vitally contributed, the idea of the state of nature had become a staple of social contract theory. Through it, a host of thinkers could explain, legitimate, or undermine the various core institutions of a new social order in Europe (e.g., the state, civil society, and private property). And so, regardless of whether one found Hobbes's (1962 [1651]) evocation of a "war of all against all" or Locke's (1924 [1690]) rather benign portrayal of humankind's "primeval" condition more convincing, the state of nature became a convention through which debate and discussion about the merits and flaws of the transition to modernity and the roots of capitalism had to be conducted (Macpherson 1962).

During the Enlightenment, representations of non-Western peoples came to be of exceptional importance for the major debates of the day: the place of religion within the emerging social order, the contributions of the arts and sciences to humankind, the role of reason and instinct, and the course of history, as well as the relationship between nature and culture.[26] Montesquieu's *Persian Letters* (1973 [1721]) dissected European rituals and beliefs, which appeared barbaric from the perspective of his two Persian travelers in Paris and Venice. As for his *Spirit of Laws* (1952 [1748]), its vast historical and geographical references make it stand as a pioneering masterpiece of comparative political sociology. Voltaire's *Essay on the Customs and the Spirit of Nations* (1963a, 1963b [1756]) was itself a universal history of civilization, while his *Philosophical Dictionary* (1956 [1764]) expressed a marked appreciation for Chinese and Indian societies. Diderot, the chief architect of the *Encyclopédie* with d'Alembert, wrote a *Supplement to Bougainville's Voyage* (1972 [1796]), where he enlisted the fictional assistance of Tahitians to expose Europe's excessive artifices. And Rousseau's tireless evocations of the state of nature to criticize Parisian social life, to which I will return in the next chapter, were the stuff of great intellectual controversy. In Germany, Herder (1966 [1784]) was defending notions of cultural particularism and pluralism against the universalizing ideal of civilization springing forth from France. His plea to analyze and cultivate all portions of the human garden was, as Kant (1991c, 213–14) observed, to set the comparative agenda in motion.

> [I]t would be a valuable present to the world, if any one, who has sufficient abilities, would collect such scattered delineations of the varieties of our species as are authentic, and thus lay the foundations of a perspicuous *natural philosophy and physiognomy of man.* Art could not easily be employed in a more philosophical pursuit: and an anthropologic map of the Earth, similar to the zoological one sketched by Zimmermann, in which nothing should be noticed except the real varieties of man, but these in all their appearances and relations, would crown a philanthropic work. (1966, 161–62)

Even Kant's (1991c) warnings against the wildly speculative and Romantic character of images of the state of nature—apparently so contrary to the rationalist spirit of the *Aufklärung*—could not temper the appeal of the non-Western world for European thinkers struggling to make sense of the modern condition.

Cross-culturally inflected social theory continued unabated in the nineteenth century, as Hegel's towering philosophy of history (1975 [1840]) illustrates. The teleological narrative of the universal spirit's *(Weltgeist)* final personification in the Germanic state was premised on its contrast to a childlike and stagnant "Oriental world." In the middle of that same century, the advent of social evolutionism reshaped dominant understandings of indigenous cultures, now projected backward in time as direct "racial" ancestors of North Atlantic peoples. Accordingly, Spencer's (1969) evolutionary theory of society became tremendously influential, in part because it was steeped in a conception of "primitive races" drawn from the Victorian inventors of scientific anthropology (such as Tylor [1974a, 1974b] and Morgan [1964]). On the other side of the Channel, Durkheim, Mauss (1969a, 1969b, 1969c, 1988), and Lévy-Bruhl (1923, 1965, 1966, 1975, 1983) led a French school of sociology and anthropology that applied intercultural research to rather opposite ends, that is to say, to undermine evolutionism and propose instead comparative understandings of civilization and modernity.[27]

Over the course of the twentieth century, the ethnological imagination took flight in numerous directions. Nietzsche and Freud, two of the great critics of Western modernity imbued by a fin de siècle spirit, are cases in point. The first revived images of the primeval, rampaging, and predatory "blond beast" to provoke a rejection of civilized life's domesticating tendencies (Nietzsche 1954, 1996). For his part, Freud (1990, 1994) put anthropological material to use as evidence for his psychoanalytical model of the human unconscious, which, as White (1978, 153–54) has put it, introduced a revolutionary vision of the self: "[I]nstead of the relatively comforting thought that the Wild Man may exist *out there* and can be contained by some kind of physical action, it is now thought . . . that the Wild Man is lurking within every man, is clamoring for release within us all, and will be denied only at the cost of life itself." Despite the fact that its comparativist orientation was not always explicit, sociology nevertheless sustained its ties to anthropology by way of various methodological innovations. Simmel's (1950) quasi-ethnographic "sociological impressionism" (Frisby 1981) was later transformed by Park (1950, 1952) and the Chicago School to study various aspects of the city, that great American "social laboratory." And from Garfinkel's (1967) ethnomethodology to Dorothy Smith's (1987, 1990) "institutional ethnography," techniques created in and through the study of cultural difference have continued to stimulate sociological analysis of everyday habits and customs.

During the second half of the twentieth century, France became the ethnological imagination's privileged *patrie,* in large part due to the determining weight of postwar decolonization (especially the trauma of the Algerian War) and the continuing influence of the Durkheimian tradition of blurring the divide between sociological and anthropological inquiry. In fact, both structuralism and poststructuralism, two movements whose influence is difficult to overstate, are scarcely understandable without reference to the impact of cross-cultural thinking within French intellectual circles. Derrida's (1976, 1978b) celebrated deconstruction of the logocentrism of Western thought, for one, aspires to underline the latter's ethnocentric character. Clastres (1977) has developed a political anthropology that inverts the conventional myth of the modern state by demonstrating that "primitive" societies are deliberately organized against the statist concentration of power, Dumont (1977, 1986, 1994) has pursued a comparative recasting of the genesis and specificities of Western ideas and values, while Jullien (1989, 1995, 1999; Jullien and Marchaisse 2000) has put forth a philosophical Sinology that uses China as a civilizational outside for rethinking the Euro-American world. Not to be forgotten is Bourdieu, whose virtuosity, his ability to extract novel and telling insights about the institutions and ritual modes of action of French social life, is attributable in no small measure to an intercultural viewpoint, first acquired during his early fieldwork in Algeria.[28]

This concise overview of the history of the ethnological imagination may be useful, yet what is required to demonstrate how it actually functions is a sustained discussion of the writings of a few of its central contributors. Thus, for the purposes of this book, I have singled out six representative figures: Rousseau, Marx, Weber, Durkheim, Lévi-Strauss, and Foucault. A number of considerations influenced this selection, such as historical impact, contemporary relevance, and the degree and kind of cross-cultural reflection. The choice of these exemplars does not satisfy all of these criteria equally, but strikes a reasonable compromise between competing requirements. As such, then, the reasons for and the implications of such a strategy should be pondered.

By assembling an intellectual constellation out of the six theorists' work, I am presenting a roughly chronological narrative of the ethnological imagination's "life and times." Each of the authors also serves as a compass point in the theoretical landscape, connecting intercultural thought to critiques of Western modernity: Rousseau and the Enlightenment debates about the state of nature; Marx and the quest for noncapitalist modes of production in the midst of European industrialization; Weber and Durkheim during the high modern heyday of universalist and comparativist social science; Lévi-Strauss and the distinct sense of unease with Euro-American hegemony in the middle of the past century; Foucault and the late-twentieth-century search for nonexoticizing modes of critique of Western societies. Nonetheless, this selection does not purport to be an exercise in the history of ideas that would systematically retrace all the central moments and individuals responsible for the ethnological imagination's development—just the kind of exercise prefigured in our abbreviated examination above. From a historicist perspective, it becomes clear that other theorists, forgotten today yet prominent in their time (say, Spencer, Lévy-Bruhl, or Sorokin), could be as equally valid as the six I have chosen. Yet this kind of retrieval of intellectual figures from the sands of time falls beyond the scope and objectives of my project. Despite the fact that the following chapters strive to respect the historicist proscription against a fallacious presentism imposing current standards of evaluation onto work from earlier epochs, the overall thrust of the argument is unabashedly intended as an intervention into the present. If it is careful to contextualize our six representatives' oeuvre within their own times and places, the unearthing and extension of the ethnological imagination represent a means for facing up to the challenge of cultural difference, as well as for reviving critical social theory today.

Conversely, this book should not be taken as an exercise in theoretical system-building that would, for instance, strive to forge a cumulative synthesis of the views of Rousseau, Marx, Weber, Durkheim, Lévi-Strauss, and Foucault into a single, generalized model of cross-cultural analysis. And though a three-part scheme of analysis of the ethnological imagination's critical hermeneutics of Western modernity is proposed in the next section, I am more interested in exploring how specific social theorists have put their intercultural sensibility to use than in building an abstract "how to" guide for comparative research. The choice of exemplars is motivated by a few additional and intersecting sets of considerations. First, despite the fact that an ethnological branch of thinking has persisted within both classical and contemporary Western social theory, its presence has not always been of the same kind or level of intensity. Therefore, I have tried to strike a certain balance between theorists whose writings overtly accord the ethnological imagination center stage (Rousseau, Weber, and Lévi-Strauss) and those for whom it exists in the background of their body of work (Marx, Durkheim, and Foucault). For the first set of authors, the task consists of explaining how their analyses of non-Western realities are pursued not only for their own sake, but in order to stimulate critical interpretations of the modern condition in the West. The reverse demonstration must be attempted in the case of the second trio, namely to uncover how their prominent diagnoses of Western modernity are tied to certain visions of the non-Western world. Regardless of this distinction, the crux of the matter is to reveal the considerable extent to which cross-cultural reflection has shaped the theoretical venture of making sense of and putting into question the here and now.

The selection of six theorists restricts itself to those seeking out the greatest possible geographical distance and sociocultural alterity between the settings they juxtapose. Other criteria could have been selected, such as the establishment of contrasts between relatively closer or more proximate Western societies (America and France for Tocqueville or Baudrillard, England and France for Voltaire, France and Germany for Herder and Hegel, and so forth),[29] or the recognition of figures of otherness within Euro-American societies themselves (such as women for Beauvoir or Smith, the stranger for Simmel, the marginal man for Park, and African Americans for Du Bois). Though such considerations are undoubtedly insightful, I would argue that encounters with non-Western and nonmodern beliefs, values, and practices have stimulated a distinctive, and ultimately stronger, effect of decentering and estrangement of Western social theorists' lifeworlds; in other words, the ethnological imagination has tended to foster a more drastic interrogation of the North Atlantic and of the very project of modernity. Relatedly, Clastres (1977, 17) has written about a "heliocentric" or "Copernican revolution" in the human sciences whereby Western modernity begins to be made to revolve around other sociohistorical constellations. Dumont nicely captures the implications of this inversion:

> Most often, what has been attempted up until now in terms of
> comparison is centered on the modern case: why did such and such
> of the other great civilizations not develop the science of nature,
> or technology, or capitalism, that is found in ours? The question
> has to be reversed: how and why did this unique development that
> we call modern occur? The central comparative task consists in ac-
> counting for the modern type on the basis of the traditional type.
> (1977, 15–16)[30]

Modern Western societies are exceptions that need to be explained and
problematized, rather than taken for granted, their strangeness becoming most glaring when juxtaposed to distant places and peoples believed to embody radical difference.

Despite all these provisos, other figures could have been included in our constellation: Montesquieu and Herder in addition to
Rousseau; Freud and Mauss as well as Durkheim; Bourdieu and
Dumont as much as Foucault, for instance. The six thinkers selected
here are certainly not the only ones to have contributed to the ethnological imagination, nor should the importance of those excluded for
reasons of space and the limits of this author's capacities be belittled.
Taken individually and as a whole, however, our six exemplars form
an intellectual cluster of sufficient range and depth to lend credence
to my claims about the vitality and diversity of cross-culturally attuned forms of theorizing. This book, then, is not intended to stand
as the definitive or last word on the ethnological imagination. On the
contrary, it is an invitation to further cultivate this strand of thinking
with an awareness of the latter's fertile legacy. That the cast of characters explored in the following pages could be supplemented is only
to be welcomed.

At this point, something should be said about the particular merits of our six thinkers' contributions to the ethnological imagination.
Rousseau is indisputably a founder of modern cross-cultural thinking, for his participation in the Enlightenment controversies about
the state of nature fuel his virulent attacks on Paris's rapidly changing
social life. These concerns also pervade his stance of civilized savagery, with which he challenges European societies' vision of history,
of the relationship between the natural and cultural realms, and new
forms of subjectivity. In Rousseau's stead is Marx, whose critiques
of political economy and modern capitalism draw upon notions
of a noncapitalist "natural man," as well as non-Western and non-
commodified social formations; the concept of commodity fetishism

is a lynchpin in this respect. Moreover, the cross-cultural tenor of Marx's writings stands at the juncture of Enlightenment naturalism, Hegelian philosophies of history, and the evolutionary tide that swept through the Anglo-American human sciences during the Victorian era.

Following Rousseau's and Marx's laying of the foundations of the ethnological imagination, Weber and Durkheim established its comparativist credentials on more solid ground. Indeed, Weber's sociology of world religions stands as a monument of intercultural research, not least because it inaugurates a move away from social evolutionism and racialism toward more cultural and interpretive accounts of non-Western realities. Weber's understanding of the manner in which Western modernity's defining dynamics (e.g., rationalization, capitalism, bureaucratization) have led to the cultivation of novel styles of life depends on contrasting analyses of Asian beliefs and practices. By contrast, Durkheim's brand of cross-cultural theorizing is nourished by the overlapping of sociological and anthropological forms of knowledge. His representations of "primitive'" sociocultural settings enable diagnoses of modern Euro-American societies' peculiarities: the faith in scientific rationalism, the sweep of industrialism, the expansion of individuation, and the pervasive crisis of morality within society.

The writings of Lévi-Strauss and Foucault are strongly indicative of the changing incarnations of the ethnological imagination in the second half of the twentieth century. Lévi-Strauss's elaboration of the structuralist enterprise is noteworthy in that it provided sociocultural anthropology with its theoretical *lettres de noblesse* and, as a result, further drew intercultural research into the mainstream of the human sciences. His complex investigations of "primitive" mythological systems are of interest less for their conceptual sophistication than for their evocation of alternative worldviews that fundamentally put into question many of the modern West's constitutive myths about rationality, history, and culture. And if Lévi-Strauss is animated by a search for redemption from the sins of colonialism, Foucault speaks to the possibilities of inverting the ethnological point of view in order to estrange Western modernity. In the wake of exoticism's death, he has sought to carve out an outside position from which to historically (and occasionally cross-culturally) defamiliarize and radically question processes of exclusion, rationalization, and subjectivation prevailing in the North Atlantic.

Collectively, the work of Rousseau, Marx, Weber, Durkheim, Lévi-Strauss, and Foucault demarcates an intellectual field emblematic of the ethnological imagination's numerous forms and possibilities. In consistently searching to engage with non-Western and nonmodern ways of thinking and acting, our six theorists have developed cross-cultural modes of interpretation and critique of the social order established in their own times and places. And although their writings do not in and of themselves perfectly or permanently resolve the current impasse with respect to cultural difference, they remain considerably more suggestive of a way out than does either traditionalism or postmodernism.

Recasting the Traditionalist/Postmodernist Binary

The strategy of cross-cultural reinterpretation of Euro-American social theory proposed above exposes the serious limitations of both traditionalist and postmodernist stances. Because it reproduces certain biases about the self-referential and discrete character of Western societies, traditionalism indirectly supports the mistaken yet commonly accepted notion that theories of modernity have been created without reference to sociocultural universes existing beyond the North Atlantic. To add to their woes, traditionalists take for granted the disciplinary split between sociology and anthropology, a divide that, in fact, needs to be historicized as having gradually taken root from the late nineteenth century onward with the institutionalization and professionalization of each field. Moreover, this intellectual division of labor is highly dubious, since it was originally based on a rather tenuous geographical-cum-civilizational distinction: the "advanced" North Atlantic world was to become the principal object of sociological analysis, with "backward" non-Western, and nonmodern peoples forming the bulk of anthropological investigations.[31] Apart from the unconvincing sociocultural hierarchy that it betrays, this position effectively erases or marginalizes Western social theory's intercultural thrust.

Traditionalism leaves us with rather selective and partial renditions of the work of classical theorists. Writings and facets of their thought concentrating on the dynamics of Euro-American modernity have become canonized, while those dealing with different sociocultural realities are relegated to other subfields or disciplines (e.g., the sociology of religion and cultural anthropology). To take the two most glaring examples: Durkheim's *Division of Labor in Society* (1984 [1893]) and *Suicide* (1952 [1897]) are widely read as core theoretical texts, although the magisterial *Elementary Forms of Religious Life* (1995 [1912]) still fails to enjoy a similar status; and Weber's essay on the Protestant ethic (1930b [1904–5]) is often discussed in isolation from or with complete ignorance of his major studies of Confucianism, Taoism, Hinduism, and Buddhism (1951 [1915], 1958 [1916]).[32] Even influential and systematic reconstructions of social theory that are far from the spirit of traditionalism—such as Parsons's (1937a, 1937b) *Structure of Social Action* and Habermas's (1984, 1987b) *Theory of Communicative Action*—adopt this narrow reading of the classics. Furthermore, traditionalists' sociocultural selectivity is carried over into contemporary theoretical endeavors. For instance, as will be explained in chapter 5, Lévi-Strauss's disciplinary identification as an anthropologist obscures his standing as a social theorist who has elaborated a substantial critique of Western modernity. From a different perspective, I will argue in chapter 6 that the impact of cultural anthropology upon Foucault's analyses of modern society has been drastically underestimated in the English-speaking world.[33]

Overall, then, traditionalism impoverishes the work of social theorists, rendering it a pale reflection of the initially lively cross-cultural sensibility that animates their inquiries about the modern condition in the West. This is no minor matter, since as I have already contended, proper consideration of this intercultural orientation is a prerequisite for fully appreciating the ongoing project of critically interpreting Western modernity. Contra the traditionalist notion of social theory's cultural self-referentiality, several authors' viewpoints are created out of the entwinement of different sociohistorical constellations; representations of non-Western societies are essential for understanding and questioning their own. Conventional perceptions of the history of the human sciences must thus be reassessed.

I hasten to add that pointing out traditionalism's failures should not be mistaken for a ringing endorsement of the postmodern quest for a complete rupture with the canon of Western social theory. As has already been suggested, this strategy suffers from a kind of reductionism and political overdeterminism that subsumes all Euro-American frameworks of understanding and representing non-Western peoples to the project of imperial expansionism and domination. There is no doubt that Western human-scientific knowledge about other societies has often portrayed the latter in denigrating and stigmatizing terms that undervalued or demeaned their sociocultural achievements and institutional arrangements. Further, that such attributions of inferiority and developmental backwardness or stagnation legitimized—and in some cases, paved the way for—colonialism's political, economic, and sociocultural technologies of ruling is undeniable, as is the fact that modern Western thinkers have lived in a period of global North Atlantic hegemony. Nevertheless, the assertion that this political context entirely determines the intentions or effects of all such authors' writings is belied by a close reading of them. Over the course of the modern era, an unstable dialectic between inferiority and superiority (or, to put it differently, scorn and veneration) has produced ambiguous, shifting textual and visual representations of non-Western peoples; the constructs of the noble and ignoble savage are the most telling illustration of this point (Smith 1989). Pejorative and condescending ideas about unfamiliar cultures have certainly pervaded theoretical circles, but opposite conceptions have also been rife. In several instances, distant and "exotic" societies have been celebrated to expose the failings and inadequacies of modern social life in the West, or treated as alternative civilizations sustaining different forms of economic and sociopolitical organization. When Euro-American modernity is compared to a multiplicity of ways of life existing around the world, ambivalent assessments of it most commonly stream forth.

Whether they are positively or negatively oriented, the tropes employed to represent non-Western peoples should be recognized, in the vast majority of cases, as fictional discursive constructs that are created and projected onto actually existing societies without much correspondence to them. Accordingly, the "savage," the "primitive," and the "Oriental" are signifiers without referents, the meaning and images they evoke having little to do with how inhabitants of those worlds understand themselves or how their sociocultural institutions function—something that postcolonialism and critical anthropology have convincingly established.[34] Yet it does not necessarily follow, as postmodernism would claim, that recognition of fictions about cultural difference must lead to the wholesale dismissal of the systems of thought that invented them. A more promising line of inquiry, I believe, involves inverting modern Euro-American worldviews in order to treat their depictions of other societies as myths that reveal more about the societies and periods from which they have originated than those they allegedly describe. Hence, the following pages turn the mirror onto Western thinkers, to investigate the roles that such myths about the non-Western world have played in the creation of theories of modernity. Reiterating what has already been mentioned, these imaginary representations have acted as alter egos to the modern West, horizons of meaning and existence outside of the latter through which understanding and critique could emerge. Indeed, without them, the possibilities for critical interpretations of the modern condition in the North Atlantic would have been considerably diminished.

Toward a Critical Hermeneutics of Western Modernity

I would like to devote the rest of this chapter to strengthening the ethnological imagination's theoretical backbone, a task that will simultaneously enable us to move past the second binary within which Western social theory has become ensnared—that between false universalism and radical particularism. As has already been mentioned, the most compelling way to understand the project binding our cluster of six thinkers to one another is through the lens of a critical hermeneutics of Western modernity. And while a detailed consideration of the philosophical underpinnings of such an approach is well outside the scope of this book, a succinct discussion of it is nevertheless warranted here.

Critical hermeneutics can be understood as an attempt to articulate the activities of interpretation and critique, by way of a reconciliation of the hermeneutical and critical theory traditions with which they have been respectively affiliated. In part, it has been stimulated by and represents a response to the influential yet polarized Gadamer-Habermas debate of a few decades ago, according to which a fundamental opposition between two seemingly incompatible paradigms existed: on the one hand, the Gadamerian position asserted the primacy of the Romantic concern for the recovery of tradition and the respect of interpretive authority in order to hermeneutically arrive at understanding; on the other hand, the Habermasian stance reoriented critical theory in an Enlightenment direction by stressing how and why the prospects for human emancipation are dependent on an ideological unmasking of the sources, mechanisms, and pathological effects of social power (including techniques of discursive coercion, manipulation, distortion, and legitimation).[35] However, in the footsteps of many other commentators—including, it should be pointed out, Habermas's own more recent rapprochement to Gadamer's argument—I would argue that hermeneutical and critical perspectives intersect with one another. Taylor (1985b, 131) puts it thus: "Understanding is inseparable from criticism, but this in turn is inseparable from self-criticism."[36] In fact, the juncture of the two yields a potent theoretical framework for the analysis of social life.

Since it is attuned to the quest for meaning, critical hermeneutics is particularly well suited to our purposes. It elevates the act of interpretation to a pivotal position within the human sciences; these, in turn, are not taken to constitute positivist or monologically driven enterprises, but humanistic and historico-cultural disciplines devoted to the discovery of sense-giving and sense-making knowledge (that is to say, the decoding and clarification of existing sociocultural systems of signification, as well as the possible creation of new significations). Understanding is constructed intersubjectively and dialogically, through processes of exchange between the author's intentions or the subject's experiential self-understandings and the interpreter of a text or action. Two of Gadamer's ideas are especially appropriate for analyzing the ethnological imagination's functioning: the problem of distance, according to which the interpreter is indubitably alienated from the sense of belonging to, and originary meaning of, an artifact; and the concept of "fusion of horizons," which enables the overcoming of such alienating distantiation.[37]

Nevertheless, the kind of critical hermeneutics advocated here leaves aside the Gadamerian insistence on the rehabilitation of tradition and authority, which stand as the privileged loci of understanding. By contrast, I prefer to adopt critical theory's stance of putting into question the "naturalness" or necessity of the established social order by demonstrating how the here and now has been sociohistorically constructed in and through relations of power. Hence, aside from grasping an author's intentions or an actor's self-definition, critique seeks to identify the structural sources and consequences of domination that systematically distort experiential understandings of the existing mode of social organization while simultaneously obstructing the potential for collective and individual self-realization. As has already been discussed, ethnological modes of critique realize this effectively to the extent that they contrast and contextualize immediate and familiar lifeworlds in relation to a range of different modes of putting the world into form. Encounters with and reflection on utterly other ways of life and normative principles trigger self-questioning of a society's raison d'être.[38]

Whereas the hermeneutical tradition strives to achieve proximity to its object of analysis to facilitate understanding and critical theory conversely works to enhance distance to nurture critique, critical hermeneutics reframes the issue in terms of a dual movement away from and closer to the existing social order. Indeed, "involvement" and "detachment" (Elias 1987b) occur concurrently in a cross-cultural situation. At first, the ethnological imagination detaches itself from Western modernity, which is decentered by being comparatively situated in relation to non-Western and nonmodern societies. Yet the resulting process of the transformation and widening of the socio-cultural outlooks of cross-culturally sensitive thinkers foreshadows a renewed sense of involved return to their own societies, one that provides a clearer and more critical grasp of their distinctively problematic features. Put differently, intercultural comparison stimulates detachment and involvement in tandem, thereby enabling the simultaneous pursuit of self-understanding and self-critique of the modern Euro-American world.

More concretely, how have our six representatives of the ethnological imagination enacted a critical hermeneutics of Western modernity? Like many other authors, they have sought detachment or distancing from their own epochs and societies by way of historicizing forms of critique: the contrast between "savagery" and civilization (Rousseau), precapitalist and capitalist modes of production (Marx), traditional and industrial society (Durkheim), or yet again Weber's historical sociology of forms of conduct of life and Foucault's Nietzschean genealogies of systems of thought and practice. All of these devices undermine the present's eternal, natural, or necessary appearance, for when confronted with past ages' invention of different yet internally coherent possibilities for organizing social life, its socially constructed character bursts forth. The here and now can be perceived as the shifting outcome of struggles between social groups and, in a genealogical vein, of the narrowing down of the field of historical prospects. Be that as it may, what makes our six exemplars stand out from other social theorists is less this widely practiced historicization of the present than the cultivation of cross-cultural critique, the development of a "view from afar" and a *technique de dépaysement* (Lévi-Strauss 1985a; 1968c, 117) by virtue of looking elsewhere for variations of the human condition.

I would go so far as to argue that our six protagonists' sense of critical detachment from what is close at hand has been more readily sustained by geographical and sociocultural difference than by its historical counterpart. This is not because previous epochs of North Atlantic history inherently possess greater kinship with the modern West than do other societies, but rather because such similarity and temporal continuity is conventionally taken to be self-evident. Hence, a Western lineage stretching from Greco-Roman antiquity to the European Middle Ages, frequently related to a shared Judeo-Christian heritage, is widely believed to provide civilizational unity in a manner that is not extended to Africa, Asia, or the Arab world. A pervasive belief in Western modernity's ancient and medieval ancestry makes it difficult to replicate in historical terms the powerful effect of estrangement that the ethnological imagination provokes. In fact, the latter has inspired novel types of historiographical research, which treat the past as an alien territory whose otherness in relation to the present should not be tamed (e.g., Foucault's genealogies and Le Goff's anthropological history).

From detachment follows ethnologically minded social theorists' reinvolvement in their own times and places. Comparison with other sociohistorical realities broadens their interpretive perspectives and sharpens their critical skills, since the existing social order can be contextualized and its specificity discovered.[39] And as we will see in the following chapters, some of the most famous and telling diagnoses of modern societies in the West are thereby made possible: Rousseau's analysis of the corrupting effects of the arts and sciences, Marx's study of the difference between capitalism's exploitative essence and its fetishistic appearance, Weber's writings on the dialectic of rationalization, Foucault's claims about the normalizing intentions of humanist reforms, and so forth. At their core, these arguments problematize the universality, necessity, and second nature or habitualized character of Euro-American norms, beliefs, and practices. Instead of being legitimized by appealing to preordained principles, inherited customs, or self-evident truths, commonplace ways of thinking and acting are reexamined as processes involved in the "self-instituting of society" (Castoriadis 1987, 1997a)—namely, the multiplicity of kinds of collective human action through which social life is perpetually created and institutionalized. In other words, cross-cultural involvement pushes us to recognize that other ways of life would have been possible in North Atlantic societies, and thus confronts us with a troubling yet vital set of questions: why should these societies' current paths of development have been adopted over others, and what have been the pathologies, as well as the benefits, engendered by such paths?

Returning to Merleau-Ponty's (1960, 150) previously cited statement about the generalized character of ethnology, I would now like to propose an elaboration of our constellation of thinkers' cross-culturally grounded critical hermeneutics of Western modernity. Three components of the ethnological imagination can be distinguished for heuristic purposes: an outward turn or moment of openness toward cultural alterity; an "in-betweenness" or moment of comparative detachment and mediation; and an inward turn or moment of reflexive involvement within one's surroundings. Figuratively moving between two or more sociocultural lifeworlds, Rousseau, Marx, Weber, Durkheim, Lévi-Strauss, and Foucault have all adopted this three-pronged strategy of critical interpretation, which, it should be added, averts the misleading dichotomy between false universalism and radical particularism.

Openness and the Outward Turn

The ethnological imagination is initially sparked by a basic curiosity about and interest in other ways of life and systems of thought, which have prompted modern Western thinkers to look beyond the confines of their own societies in two related manners: figuratively, by creating mythical representations of nonmodern and non-Western societies (the state of nature, the "Orient," and so forth); and literally, by leaving their own surroundings to study distant and utterly different settings (e.g., the convention of fieldwork in anthropology).[40] Quite apart from the lure of the "exotic," what drives this outward turn is an appreciation of the significance of cross-cultural juxtaposition for grasping Euro-American modernity's self-identity. The latter is created and transformed over time, being bound up and contrasted to other sociocultural universes through a series of complex and asymmetrical relations of exchange, borrowing, appropriation, and domination. Thus, for our six figures, the search for and the attempt to make sense of instances of cultural alterity must replace the temptation to remain provincially ensconced; investigations of different cultural realities become integral to the double task of interpretation and critique of the modern West, rather than adjunct to them.

A willingness to remain open to the provocation of cultural difference must sustain this refusal to be comforted or content with familiarity and proximity. Openness, then, demands that we plunge into the lifeworlds of other societies to grasp their self-definitions and understandings of personhood, as well as the reasons for organizing collective life in certain ways. And this process of intercultural interpretation often results in a powerful effect of cultural estrangement and disorientation, according to which a realization of the incredible diversity of ways of being human shakes our self-certainties about the world and forces us to reexamine it.[41] In some cases, the ethnologically minded social theorist acquires a sense of sheer wonder or astonishment about an apparently extraordinary, uncanny, or outrageous reality—human beings actually do and believe *that*. Rather than xenophobically recoiling in horror or retreating to the safety of the ordinary at the sight of such seemingly strange ways of acting or thinking, the ethnological imagination seeks to grasp their meanings on their own terms, without readily assimilating them to practices and outlooks in the modern West. The ethnocentrism of falsely universalized models cannot account for the particularities of various societies' different, yet internally coherent, cultural systems; "they" are not merely a variation or other version of "us." Hence, openness also entails welcoming Clastres's (1977) aforementioned "heliocentric revolution," to which Derrida (1978b, 282) has also given voice: "[O]ne can assume that ethnology could have been born as a science only at the moment when a decentering had come about: at the moment when European culture—and, in consequence, the history of metaphysics and of its concepts—had been dislocated, driven from its locus, and forced to stop considering itself as the culture of reference." The realization that things are done and viewed differently elsewhere leads cross-cultural social theory to embrace this decentering and to remain incessantly attuned to it.

Mediation and In-Betweenness

Openness to non-Western societies' alterity is but an initial, albeit vital, step in the process of intercultural theorizing that our six representatives practice. The outward turn, for its part, is built around a moment of mediation during which domestic sociohistorical worlds are directly compared with and contrasted to beliefs, norms, and forms of action found in distant societies. For if it acknowledges the existence of cultural alterity, the ethnological imagination resists radical particularism's fondness for single case studies and local micronarratives isolated from more general, comparative social analysis.

Even more questionable is radical particularists' frequent slippage into assumptions about the inexorableness of cross-cultural incommensurability, societies from across the globe being necessarily and mutually unintelligible because they are trapped into static and self-enclosed horizons existing outside of any possible common frameworks of understanding.[42] Accepting such an idea, of course, is tantamount to abandoning the key task of mediation between different societies. On the contrary, the ethnological imagination sustains a dynamic process of "in-betweenness," an endeavor to analytically connect divergent sociohistorical constellations in a manner that recognizes their similarities and differences. "In-betweenness" shuns the attribution of pure and unmediated otherness, or just as problematically, of perfect identity, to unfamiliar cultural processes and ideas; "they" are neither the total negation of "us," nor exactly the same as "us." Instead, it works to create an interpretive space of simultaneous distance and proximity resulting from what Taylor (1985b, 125) has called "perspicuous contrast" and Gadamer's (1994) celebrated notion of "fusion of horizons." This space is not formed out of the melding together or seamless overlap of different sociocultural universes, but of an attempt to move between them, whereby dialogical encounter enables better mutual interpretive capacities for developing and, through juxtaposition, for discovering points of intersection and divergence.[43]

Mediation of this kind involves a gradual widening and deepening of the cross-cultural thinker's perspective on the human condition. Hence, theoretical projects can only be enriched by cultivating an ethnological sensibility, that is, an appreciation of humankind's incredible and endlessly varied mosaic of identity and difference, of intimacy and remoteness. Elias has made this point strongly:

> One may investigate how particular human societies differ from one another. One may also investigate how all human societies resemble one another. Strictly speaking, these two research preoccupations are inseparable. Anyone seeking a clear picture of the similarities in all societies—the universal features of human society—must be able to draw on a great wealth of knowledge, available in his own society, about the variations possible in human societies. (1978, 104)[44]

The broadening of horizons achieved through cross-cultural comparison seeks to embrace—and not resolve—the dialectical tension between sameness and otherness, since this tension is integral to the process of "in-betweenness" and the capacity to critically engage with an array of ways of life. Side-by-side with a range of modes of social organization, Western modernity is situated as one possible configuration among others. Doxic modes of conduct and thinking in Euro-American societies can be critically studied because they are put into play as objects of comparative analysis. Rather than serving as reference points against which the non-Western world is assessed, they are particularized and, by being put into question, relativized. As Bartra (1994, 208) points out, "The European wild man reminds us that we might have been something else." Accordingly, one-dimensionality stands on shaky ground.

Reflexivity and the Inward Turn

For social theorists inspired by the ethnological imagination, the principles of openness toward sociocultural alterity and of intercultural mediation prepare the terrain for a final moment of the critical hermeneutics of Western modernity: that of reflexivity toward one's surroundings, which the Tocquevillian idea of "turning the mirror on ourselves" (Dumont 1977, 23) and the notion of a "reversal of the ethnological perspective" (Fuchs 1993) forcefully evoke. The outward immersion in other worlds and cross-cultural "in-betweenness" nurture an estrangement from the familiar and the proximate, for the return home is undertaken with an expanded and self-critical vantage point. To that extent, one can indeed never go back home, something Bourdieu understands well:

> The sociologist who chooses to study his own world in its nearest and most familiar aspects should not, as the ethnologist would, domesticate the exotic, but, if I may venture the expression, exoticize the domestic, through a break with his initial relation of intimacy with modes of life and thought which remain opaque to him because they are too familiar. In fact the movement toward the originary, and the ordinary, world should be the culmination of a movement towards alien and extraordinary worlds. (1988, xi–xii)

This movement between different lifeworlds cannot and should not be equated with some sort of naïve quest to exit from one's original sociocultural horizons, to "go native" by purportedly negating or overcoming processes of socialization stemming from a particular time and place. Rather, it suggests that exposure to radically different ways of life in the world can beneficially alter and enlarge our horizons through self-distantiation and exteriorization. Euro-American modernity can thus be put in perspective cross-culturally, without compromising previously established relations of involvement with it. "Exoticizing the domestic" does not imply absolute alienation or remoteness from it, which would only hamper interpretation, but a putting into doubt of its second-nature standing.[45] In the same vein, I would claim that cross-cultural social theorists are neither unreflexive insiders who take everything for granted, nor complete outsiders who are unfamiliar with everything. Like the many figures of alterity within the modern West (e.g., women, Jews, people of color, homosexuals, madpersons), they combine features of both positions to become partial outsiders inside their own societies.[46]

As a key component of the inward turn, the stance of the outsider inside brings the ethnological imagination back full circle. In the case of our set of six authors, it compels them to contemplate the historical and cultural specificities of modern Euro-American societies, and thereby to particularize—I would even say to "peculiarize"—some of its defining structural and behavioral characteristics. Comparative contextualization of the North Atlantic region establishes a rupture with its *doxa,* in light of the fact that habitual or inherited customs and creeds are stripped of the veneer of "self-evidentness," common sense, or normality that they would have gained through acculturation and dehistorization. As a result, a fresh and critical eye can be cast onto Western modernity, whose cross-cultural strangeness becomes too striking to ignore; uncanniness *(Unheimlichkeit)* is revealed where the obvious, the banal, and the natural were believed to silently reign. Social theorists can reinsert apparently commonplace institutional arrangements and practices, as well as deeply held value orientations, into the sociohistorical domain, subjecting them to scrutiny because they are taken to be outcomes of human action and struggles between groups at specific epochs and in given locations.[47]

Cross-cultural perspectivism resists the falsely universalistic slide into epistemological and normative absolutism and the radically particularistic attraction toward a myopic brand of complete relativism in equal measure. Comparatively situating modern Western societies within the universe of possible modes of social organization makes one acutely aware that things are thought and done differently elsewhere, without believing that theories about Euro-American modernity are necessarily applicable everywhere, that "our" way of life is superior to all others in every possible respect, or, on the contrary, that "we" can only truly understand and assess the familiar and the proximate, that all patterns of thought and action are beyond exogenous criticism and thus equally valid. Instead of simplistically condemning or idealizing the North Atlantic as a whole, comparative analysis can identify and evaluate the relative merits and flaws of its different facets and spheres of social action in relation to what takes place in other parts of the world. What emerges, then, is a much more nuanced and ultimately revealing portrait than either false universalism or radical particularism can offer: an interculturally inspired, critical hermeneutics of the modern West.

Conclusion

Throughout this chapter, I have contended that, in our global age, cultural pluralism presents Western social theorists—and notably those of a critical persuasion—with an immense yet fascinating challenge. The current impasse is an opportunity to reassess the social-theoretic legacy in a manner that underscores its intercultural sensibilities much more extensively and explicitly than has hitherto been done, at the same time that it nurtures a cross-culturally grounded critical hermeneutics of Western modernity. If it is to be undertaken at all, however, such a response must resist the lure of the polarized reactions that the question of cultural alterity conventionally spawns. Neither the traditionalist reestablishment of an unrevised version of the canon that altogether ignores comparative matters, nor the postmodern advocacy of a clean break with the canon, which uses certain undeniable flaws in the classics to dispense with them altogether, is convincing. As an alternative to these dead ends, the following pages propose a reading of the history of Euro-American social theory that excavates an ethnological imagination running through six of its pivotal figures: Rousseau, Marx, Weber, Durkheim, Lévi-Strauss, and Foucault. A detailed examination of their writings makes it apparent that the constitution and self-definition of Western modernity are inextricably bound up with representations of other societies, myths that have been created as much with an eye to provoke a self-critique of the North Atlantic as to legitimate its superiority.

Similarly, I have claimed that the choice between, on the one hand, an unapologetic false universalization of models or diagnoses exclusively derived from Western experiences, and on the other, a radical particularization of all knowledge that provincially precludes comparison while supporting a parochial satisfaction with what one already knows and what is culturally close at hand, is unsustainable. The three moments and adjoining normative principles of the ethnological imagination's critical hermeneutics of the modern West generate a more promising lead: an outward turn prompted by an openness to alterity, an "in-betweenness" supported by an effort at comparative juxtaposition and mediation, as well as an inward turn providing critical reflexivity. From this dialogical movement of detachment and reinvolvement emerges a cross-cultural perspectivism that is capable of situating Euro-American modernity in time and space, as one possible sociohistorical configuration among others. A few generations ago, Lévi-Strauss's *Tristes Tropiques* stretched back four centuries to Montaigne, reminding its vast audience of the need to venture beyond the West's geographical and cultural boundaries:

> I was about to relive the experience of the early travelers and, through it, that crucial moment in modern thought when, thanks to the great voyages of discovery, a human community which believed itself to be complete and in its final form suddenly learned, as if through the effect of a counter-revelation, that it was not alone, that it was part of a greater whole, and that, in order to achieve self-knowledge, it must first of all contemplate its unrecognizable image in this mirror, of which a fragment, forgotten by the centuries, was now about to cast, for me alone, its first and last reflection. (1978a, 326)

That crucial moment represents, as Lévi-Strauss was himself eager to note, the precursor of European colonial expansion and the destruction of countless indigenous peoples around the world. Yet it also triggered a radical self-questioning of the modern project by some of the North Atlantic region's leading intellectual figures—a disposition that critical social theory can rediscover. For to encounter a variety of utterly different ways of thinking and acting remains essential for appreciating and interrogating the peculiarity of modern Western societies, and thus for gaining a better understanding of them. Indeed, what is striking, from a comparative perspective, is the vast range of forms of collective and individual existence that the human condition encompasses. Above all else, an ethnological sensibility allows us to dispute the unproblematized, self-evident, and one-dimensional status of the established social order, of that which is taken to be commonplace and proximate. Among our protagonists, no one personified this incipient realization more than Rousseau, whose use of the device of the state of nature and whose development of a stance of civilized savagery set the ethnological imagination ablaze.

One

On Civilized Savagery: Rousseau and the Birth of the Ethnological Imagination

Among the dazzling constellation of figures to have participated in the French Enlightenment, that still unparalleled intellectual epoch, one stands out above all others: Jean-Jacques Rousseau. Much like it did for his contemporaries, his body of work continues to fascinate and provoke us today, no doubt because of its uncanny ability to go to the very heart of the modern condition. Indeed, his writings provide what is widely regarded as the most insightful and devastating critique of Western modernity in its still nascent phase, made even more remarkable by the fact that the institutional features and patterns of interaction characterizing modern society were only just visible on the horizon.[1] However, despite the wide acclaim and controversy sparked by Rousseau's oeuvre, what has barely been noticed—except, significantly, by certain social anthropologists (Lévi-Strauss 1977b, Diamond 1974)—is the vigorous ethnological sensibility animating his prescient and penetrating analysis of bourgeois culture. His interrogation of some of the latter's key practices and beliefs, his capacity to estrange and denaturalize them in order to culturally and historically situate the processes of their formation, are frequently performed through the evocation of other, mythical sociocultural universes. In fact, I would contend that this is one of the keys to understanding Rousseau's enduring appeal and contemporary resonance. To this extent, Rousseau is not only the "founding father" of anthropology in its modern, disciplinary sense (Lévi-Strauss 1977b), but more significantly for this book, the pivotal figure among the ethnological imagination's eighteenth-century progenitors and the source of inspiration for much of its subsequent development. Either by direct filiation or thematic congruence, his stance of civilized savagery and analysis of social life can be connected to Marx's denaturalization of capitalism and attack on private property, Weber's study of the conduct of life, Durkheim's preoccupation with forces of moralization, Lévi-Strauss's vision of anthropology as a self-critique of Western modernity, and Foucault's position of outsider inside modern society. Though they have taken varying paths, all of them have tried to answer what Taylor (1989, 265) calls the "Rousseauian challenge which still reverberates through our culture."

That debate about Rousseau's life and work has not abated since the Enlightenment hardly needs to be reiterated. During his lifetime, he developed a tortuous relationship with the French philosophes, while later in Germany intellectual giants such as Kant, Hölderlin, Schiller, and Goethe celebrated him. Even the most perfunctory examination of Rousseau's legacy makes it obvious that, more so than for any other representative of the ethnological imagination, no interpretive consensus exists: assessments of his work span the gamut from libertarianism to totalitarianism, passing through Romanticism, modernism, evolutionism, primitivism, liberalism, conservatism, and socialism. Rather than striving to resolve these disputes, my aim in this chapter is more circumscribed and modest, namely to demonstrate how Rousseau's vision of eighteenth-century European bourgeois society is facilitated, and even made possible, by his ethnological vantage point. In other words, the following pages are not an exegetical exercise, but an exploration of the manner in which Rousseau's conjuring up of imaginary cultural universes nourishes his critical hermeneutics of the burgeoning moments of Western modernity.[2] I will therefore begin by explaining the stance of civilized savagery that he adopts, then consider his use of such a perspective to put into question the modern West's emerging peculiarities in the realms of history and subjectivity, as well as his urging humankind to transcend the existing social order to become autonomous.

The Ethnological Imagination Takes Flight

As I have indicated in the introduction, Rousseau was clearly not the first modern Western thinker to cross-culturally estrange his society and epoch. Such a genealogical honor would have to be granted in the sixteenth century to Montaigne, whose *Essays*—and notably among these, the celebrated "Of Cannibals" (Montaigne 1948a [1578–80])—have had a lasting impact. The idea of a state of nature (and an accompanying social contract) was a convention of seventeenth- and eighteenth-century political thought, of which Hobbes (1962 [1651]) and Locke (1924 [1690]) are the best-known representatives (Cassirer 1951, 256–58). And yet it was during the Enlightenment that mythical figures of cultural alterity, such as the "wild man," the "noble savage," and the "Oriental gentleman," took on a vital role as vehicles of self-critique of the established social order in Europe. Montesquieu's *Persian Letters* (1973 [1721]) and Diderot's *Supplement to Bougainville's Voyage* (1972 [1796]), as well as Voltaire's *L'Ingénu* (1954 [1767]) and sections of his *Philosophical Dictionary* (1956 [1764]), all bear witness to the prominence of tropes of cultural difference for the philosophes.[3] In their midst stood Rousseau, the most eloquent spokesperson for the ethnological imagination as it was being born into the world.

Why should Rousseau be granted such a prominent place? In the first instance, his writings contain one of the earliest and strongest denunciations of ethnocentrism, the false universalization of one's culture and society. For Rousseau, considering what is close at hand and similar as the only possible way of life, or refusing to look beyond it, can only result in a partial, myopic understanding of humankind. The *Discourse on the Origins of Inequality* is explicit about this point:

> In the two or three centuries since the inhabitants of Europe have been flooding into other parts of the world, endlessly publishing new collections of voyages and travel, I am persuaded that we have come to know no other men except Europeans; moreover it appears from the ridiculous prejudices, which have not died out even among men of letters, that every author produces under the pompous name of the study of man nothing much more than a study of the men of his own country. . . . The entire world is covered with peoples of whom we know only the names, and yet we amuse ourselves judging the human race! (1984, 159–60)[4]

Not only does Rousseau employ this argument to mock the narrowness of his fellow European thinkers, and thus undermine their claims to universal knowledge, but he uses it as a springboard to prompt them to broaden their cultural horizons. In this can be recognized the rallying cry of what was eventually to become the program of academic anthropology, the scientific description and analysis of the world's diverse cultures.[5]

Rousseau advocates in favor of an ethnologically oriented outward turn, a search for encounters with other peoples so as to properly take stock of the incredible variety among human societies. In this way, he believes, expanding the scope and range of what is conceivable can assist us in gaining a deeper grasp of what it means to be human. "When one wishes to study men, one must look nearby; but to study man one must learn to look far away" (1995b, 394).[6] The study of other cultures is also directed at self-understanding; through a cross-cultural lens, the characteristics of European society come into view more crisply and their self-evident character rapidly dissipates. Intercultural juxtaposition of this kind enables Rousseau to gain a certain distance from taken-for-granted ways of acting and thinking, which are comparatively relativized and situated back into the sociohistorical domain. Instead of being shielded from assessment through attribution to extra-social forces (God, nature, and so forth), the processes of modernity's formation can properly be viewed as the consequences of human action; they thus become amenable to critical questioning and change, which can anthropocentrically be guided by reason.[7] His creation of a sense of estrangement from his epoch and place is realized by way of three media: autobiography, fiction (particularly through the characters of Émile and St. Preux), and the notion of the state of nature. These can be discussed one by one.

Principally composed of the *Confessions* (1953), the *Dialogues* (1959), and the *Rêveries of the Solitary Walker* (1972, 1979), Rousseau's autobiographical texts form an integral part of his body of work. The distinction between private experience and public thought is particularly blurred in his case, for he explicitly envisaged his life as the application and extension of his social philosophy—and the latter as the formalization of the former. Hence, he mobilized his Genevan identity to establish and maintain a position of relative detachment vis-à-vis Parisian milieux, deliberately cultivating and regularly reminding his readers of his foreign status in order to move more easily between and amidst the different spheres and layers of the French capital. Paris could be dissected with the quasi-anthropological vantage point of an observer who is considered, and considers himself, neither the perennial insider nor the pure outsider; as a proud son of Geneva, Rousseau became a self-styled rustic stranger living in the most sophisticated outpost of European civilization.[8]

At the same time, this perspective of outsider inside was pushed even further by Rousseau's nomadic existence and self-imposed exile from Paris. Especially toward the end of his life, Rousseau tried to follow his own advice by escaping from the corrupting grasp of civilization and retreating to the countryside, which he deemed much more congenial to realizing his ideal of the natural man. Authenticity, that is to say, remaining true to one's inner voice, could best be achieved through a life of pastoral solitude. Nevertheless, his withdrawal from society was and never could be complete, for he deliberately maintained ties with Parisian intellectual and social circles while being profoundly shaped by his immersion in them. He strove to become a civilized savage, familiar with and influenced by bourgeois society, yet he also chose to remain estranged from it. "Everything external is henceforth foreign to me. I no longer have any neighbours, fellow-men or brothers in this world. *I live here as in some strange planet on to which I have fallen from the one I knew*" (1979, 31–32).[9] Located in-between worlds, Rousseau could feel free to observe prerevolutionary Europe from a distance, and fell much of what passed for common sense and convention.

Émile and St. Preux, two of Rousseau's most important fictional characters, personify this ethnological standpoint of civilized savagery. Émile's tutor, who was in fact one of Rousseau's alter egos, claimed to derive his pedagogical legitimacy and philosophical wisdom from his own hermit-like existence. Though never fully integrated into society, Émile himself could not, however, be a complete recluse. His education was to teach him to become an "amiable foreigner" (Berman 1970, 184) who, only after being completely trained outside of civilization, could enter into it yet remain detached from its whims. Rousseau (1974, 167) is adamant about this distinction: "There is all the difference in the world between a natural man living in a state of nature, and a natural man living in society. Emile is no savage to be banished to the desert, he is a savage who has to live in the town." In addition to ensuring the preservation of the subject's authentic self, the perspective of a civilized savage affords a different relationship with one's surroundings. Émile can witness, and thereby come to understand, the trappings of social life without being overwhelmed by them or relying on public opinion for guidance. He is not a player, but a critical, autonomous observer of the modern condition and human destiny.[10]

In the second part of his great novel, *Julie, or The New Heloïse*

(1964a), there are further indications of Rousseau's ethnological mindset. St. Preux, the novel's protagonist and another of Rousseau's fictional selves, is also portrayed as a civilized savage. As the story unfolds, he travels to Paris and provides us, through his letters, with what amounts to a series of reports from the field in which the mores of different Parisian social groups are dissected with precision. Nothing is spared from his ethnographic gaze: the habits and ways of thinking of both the rising bourgeoisie and the still-dominant aristocracy of prerevolutionary France, sexual and gender relations among individuals, widespread doctrines and cultural conventions, leisure and artistic pursuits, philosophy, even dress, behavior codes, and physical appearance. Parisians are represented as inhabitants of an exotic land, out of which initially sprung deep difference and strangeness. St. Preux's outlook is supported by his being an outsider from the Valais (in the Swiss countryside), entering a foreign world while constantly and critically comparing it to other sociocultural realities. The prejudices, foibles, and falsehoods of civilization can best be discovered by simultaneously participating in courtly or bourgeois social rituals and contextualizing them vis-à-vis alternative ways of being and thinking.[11] Hence, St. Preux's struggle consists in discovering and maintaining an intermediary position where he is neither completely assimilated nor utterly excluded from early modern society.[12]

The state of nature constitutes the third and best-known device through which Rousseau's ethnological imagination is made visible.[13] Whether he considers the state of nature to be an actual sociohistorical condition, or yet again an entirely fictional construct, there is no doubt that it features prominently as a trope of cultural and historical alterity to be juxtaposed to early modern Europe. By blending empirical observation (from travelers' tales and missionaries' reports) with his own personal observation and figments of his fertile imagination, Rousseau holds a mirror up to the established social order of his time in order to radically put it into question. The significance of this interpretive move is grasped more fully when compared to the doctrines of Hobbes and Locke, two of his most famous predecessors. Albeit in different ways and drawing differing conclusions, both of them employ the state of nature as a speculative tool to naturalize private property and thereby support the ethos of "possessive individualism" (Macpherson 1962). The birth of the state and the development of civil society are declared essential to the protection of the "natural" right of ownership. Regardless of whether it is represented as a bestial condition of individualized warfare (Hobbes 1962, 143) or a peaceful period during which possessions could be accumulated (Locke 1924, 119–20), the state of nature serves to effectively legitimate the need for a social contract to formalize and regulate social relations between individuals and among social classes; it is the foundation of private property.

By contrast, most famously in the *Discourse on the Origins of Inequality* (1973b [1755]), Rousseau turns this logic on its head by representing our natural condition as one where generalized equality and abundance prevail; everything belongs to all, and therefore nothing belongs to anyone. Pace *homo economicus,* it never occurs to the "savage" to parcel off a piece of land and call it his own, to the exclusion of others.[14] Because he is self-reliant, dependence on others, rooted in exchange through the creation of the market, cannot take root. Isolation and independence militate against the formation of social sources of domination. Consequently, in Rousseau's hands, the state of nature becomes a means through which to denounce the devastating socioeconomic consequences of the bourgeois ethos and the political institutions that sustain it. Far from being natural, private property is nothing more than a social convention that inscribes a momentous historical rupture modifying humanity's destiny forever by entrenching the power of the strong over the weak and the latter's dependence on the former. Simultaneously, an increasing division of labor and a specialization of economic roles take place, each person thereby being compelled to rely on others for his or her own survival.[15]

Staging an encounter between a budding modern Europe and the state of nature, Rousseau aims to dispute the former's sense of inherent superiority, as well as comparatively decentering it by underlining its historical and cultural specificity. For him, the state of nature is not a viable alternative to be emulated in the eighteenth century, but a vehicle of perspicuous contrast: "For it is by no means a light undertaking to distinguish properly between what is original and what is artificial in the actual nature of man, or to form a true idea of a state which no longer exists, perhaps never did exist, and probably never will exist; and of which it is, nevertheless, necessary to have true ideas, *in order to form a proper judgment of our present state*" (Rousseau 1973b, 44).[16] Critical examination of the here and now's assumptions, opinions, and habitualized practices can accordingly be undertaken, for when juxtaposed to another lifeworld, they cannot be presumed to be normal, eternal, or universal. Rather, they appear to be socially and historically contingent, and thus open to rational contestation.

A Spectator at Modernity's Birth

Having discussed Rousseau's cultivation of a vantage point of civilized savagery and his trope of the state of nature, I would now like to demonstrate the extent to which this sort of cross-cultural juxtaposition is indispensable to his critical portrait of modern Europe's dawn—a portrait so revealing that it captures the essence of Western modernity's self-understanding to this day. Indeed, by direct contrast to the state of nature, Rousseau is able to presciently detect some of the distinctive features of modern society, to the extent that his "ethnologization" of the latter has inspired numerous projects of interpretation and critique of Euro-American social life. Accordingly, I will focus on how Rousseau's ethnological imagination interrogates the creed of unilinear progress and historicity, in addition to their effects on forms of subjectivity fostered by bourgeois culture.

The Paradoxes of History

It should be mentioned from the outset that, contrary to what has been commonly believed since the Enlightenment, Rousseau's myth of the state of nature does not represent a manifestation of primitivism celebrating the figure of the noble savage while condemning civilization in toto, nor is it intended to be an ideal to which European society should return.[17] Conversely, it does not function as the first stage in humanity's evolutionary-cum-hierarchical sequence, or yet again as a crude means of legitimizing modern Europe's civilizational superiority. Instead, Rousseau conceives of the state of nature as an imaginary device through which to stage an encounter with cultural alterity, and thus to cross-culturally estrange his surroundings and put into question the established social order's apparent inevitability and its self-evident ways of thinking and acting. Put differently, his goal is to comparatively pinpoint what has been forgotten or lost, as well as what has been conserved or gained, in the process of modernity's emergence, always with an eye toward breaking away from any restrictive conception of what is humanly possible.

The first tenet Rousseau seeks to puncture is the Enlightenment creed of necessary human progress, which, as formulated in works such as Voltaire's *Essay on the Manners and the Spirit of Nations* (1963a, 1963b [1756]), Condorcet's *Sketch for a Historical Picture of the Progress of the Human Mind* (1955 [1795]), and Kant's "Idea for a Universal History with a Cosmopolitan Purpose" (1991a [1784]), posits a rather reductionist and unidimensional view of history not unlike that of their primitivist foes. For him, then, the Enlightenment has been as much a process of blinding as one of illumination, for the war waged against ignorance and superstition has been accompanied by an alienation from the law of nature. Europe's self-proclaimed civilizational greatness should be viewed with skepticism. His own vision of history is multidimensional in that it locates a tragic paradox at the core of human existence: perfectibility is our accursed fate, whereby the inevitable blossoming of innate individual capacities and the development of social institutions have led to a disequilibrium between nature and culture, resulting in our moral decrepitude as a species, yet they also hold the key to our eventual attainment of virtue and happiness through the use of reason.[18]

Nowhere is Rousseau's ambivalence toward early bourgeois society more striking than in his assessment of the arts and sciences, taken by many to be the crowning glory of European civilization since the much-vaunted Renaissance. At one level, he believes that they undeniably mark an advancement over the state of nature, a rather brutish and unrefined condition where our minds and souls lie dormant. And yet this primeval situation is one of harmony with nature, of earnest simplicity and spontaneous beauty. Before eating from the tree of knowledge, human beings inhabit a realm of blissful ignorance sheltered from the cultural vices introduced by modern social life.[19] Eighteenth-century bourgeois culture, Rousseau observes, has meritoriously cultivated artistic and scientific endeavors, but it has done so in a manner that perverts humankind's intrinsic goodness and potential virtue by estranging us from the voice of nature and substituting the latter by artifice. Superficial refinement, pompousness, and luxury are valued above all else, fanning the flames of vanity, jealousy, and most worrying of all, moral decay. Moreover, rather than acting as media for original thinking, self-expression, and creativity, the Parisian arts and sciences have become excessively rationalized and formalized. They are products of abstract rules and precise calculations, no longer communicating our intimate emotions, conscience, or inner thoughts, let alone the vital human qualities of spontaneity and passion.[20] Rousseau even goes so far as to accuse early modern scientific and artistic pursuits of acting as ideological props legitimating the established social order:

> So long as government and law provide for the security and well-being of men in their common life, the arts, literature, and the sciences, less despotic though perhaps more powerful, fling garlands of flowers over the chains which weigh them down. They stifle in men's breasts that sense of original liberty, for which they seem to have been born; cause them to love their own slavery, and so make of them what is called a civilized people. (1973a, 4–5)

According to this argument, the version of the arts and sciences prevalent in bourgeois society merely distracts and entertains individuals, preventing them from realizing that they are oppressed and identifying the institutional sources of such oppression. It is in this context that Rousseau's hostility to modern forms of theater, most virulently expressed in his *Letter to d'Alembert* (1995a), must be read: unlike Greek tragedy, modern forms are devoid of any moral or pedagogical lessons for the audience, simply representing vain and illusory means of escapism.[21]

If Rousseau's writings critically interrogate the credo of necessary progress, they do recognize that Western modernity is defined by a self-conscious historicity. In fact, many of them are devoted to reflecting on the sociocultural effects of this sense of historical flux, which Rousseau takes to be constitutive of the modern condition. This contrasts vividly with his image of the state of nature's nonhistoricity, its location outside of history. Albeit stagnant, the state of nature also allows individuals to escape from the tyranny of temporal change and thereby remain intimately in contact with their invariable inner voices. Perfectibility eventually thrusts humankind into history, where it incrementally succumbs to temporality without embracing it. Historical development is endured rather than made by human beings, nonmodern societies being primarily oriented toward the preservation of established institutions, mores, and beliefs that enable them to satisfy what are immediate and limited needs.[22] Modern society could not be more different: it ontologizes historical transformation, which is virtually valued for its own sake. Rousseau captures this sheer restlessness, the inability and unwillingness to remain content with what exists; the stability of tradition pales in comparison to the lure of the new and the unknown. All ways of life and systems of thought are caught up in this social whirlwind, which leaves the natural foundations of truth and virtue in ruins. While this ephemeral and innovative quality of modern life liberates humanity from the strictures of inherited modes of thought and action, Rousseau also contends that the moral vacuum is filled by the groundless fickleness of public opinion. The common good is constantly being redefined according to the tastes and moods of the day, with no regard for eternal truths. The public sphere is not an arena of informed debate among citizens, but a forum for the expression of the powerful's opinions, to which the masses are all too eager to acquiesce.[23]

The Masks of Modern Subjectivity

According to Rousseau, the corrupting influence of the existing versions of the arts and sciences and the social whirlwind that modernity has unleashed ultimately come to weigh on the shoulders of the individual. Modern society gives birth to a new and peculiar kind of personality, one that endangers the essence of our humanity. Rousseau encapsulates the latter, embodied in the natural "savage" of the state of nature and the civilized savage living on the margins of society, through the related notions of authenticity and liberty. We can and must be true to ourselves, that is, be able to externalize our inner beings in the world around us and let ourselves be guided exclusively by our interior voices; public presentation and identities should correspond to its private core. The natural "savage," being isolated and self-sufficient as well as purely driven by instinct and emotion, cannot help but obey his amoral inclinations, whereas the civilized savage deliberately strives for an authentic and free existence through the exercise of reason, virtue, and feeling within society.[24] Once civilization comes about, preserving one's true self and independence must very much be accomplished against society.

Much like his rendition of history, Rousseau's analysis of modern subjectivity is built on a remarkable paradox. On the one hand, he is himself one of the chief architects of what Taylor (1989, 1991, 1995) has termed "the expressivist turn," the ethos of authenticity, self-expression, and individual assertion that forms the culturally and historically specific cornerstones of Romanticism.[25] The celebrated opening passage of his *Confessions* encapsulates such ideals: "I know my own heart and understand my fellow man. But I am made unlike any one I have ever met; I will venture to say that I am like no one in the whole world. I may be no better, but at least I am different" (1953, 17). With these words, Rousseau lays claim to being one of the first modern Western thinkers to believe in the individual's uniqueness and the significance of her or his existence qua an individual. Bearing witness to the process of individuation, he notes that, by being true to their conscience, those living in European society can forge their own original personalities. Yet at the same time, the characteristically modern embrace of constant flux and the development of artistic and scientific pursuits militate against the realization of authenticity. The self becomes lost in the Sturm und Drang of social life, attempting to stay afloat by incessantly remaking his or her identity according to ever-changing popular trends. For the first time anywhere, individuals live in and for the moment, transforming themselves at an instant's notice as some masks are discarded and others are donned to impress or cater to public opinion. Rousseau never tires of reminding his readers of the comparative peculiarity of this new, transient form of personal identity, but also warns them about the perils of being drunk on glitter and artifice.[26] The heart and conscience are drowned out by the need to conform to the whims of public fashion, to say nothing of the vanity and self-love (amour propre) stemming from unceasing competition to win approval from one's peers. Individuals become estranged from their inner core, surface replacing depth as the main feature of modern life. In reality, the opacity and artifice of social relations is reflected in the self, for as Berman (1970, 71–72) points out, "[T]he problem . . . was not simply that men *appear* 'unlike themselves,' but that they actually '*are* unlike themselves.'" The true self may be lost behind masks, or indeed may be transformed into an empty shell to be filled by a superficial public opinion.

The Perils of Heteronomy, the Promises of Autonomy

Rousseau's importance for the ethnological imagination does not originate solely from his uncanny ability to recognize the comparative distinctiveness of early modern Europe's apprehension of history and types of subjectivity, but also, I would argue, from his denaturalization of ancien régime societies. In effect, he is able to demonstrate that the established social order is the outcome of human action and sociocultural convention, rather than divine will or the voice of nature. Removed from the extrasocial (and thus self-evident) domains of the inherited, the eternal, and the universal and firmly situated within the sociohistorical realm, early modern society becomes open to critical scrutiny because its ills cannot be deemed to exist everywhere else or since the beginning of time; they are, instead, the poisoned fruit of a particular place and time. Against the grating Panglossian optimism about living in "this best of all possible worlds" (Voltaire 1947, 144), Rousseau contends that the existing state of affairs is far from being the best possible, let alone the only possible. One can see how, read in this light, his writings strive to expand our horizons of possibilities for organizing social life and personal existence. Parisian rituals and creeds are tirelessly depicted as strange, historically and culturally localized products of a particular conjunction of socio-cultural dynamics, to which other lifeworlds (e.g., Geneva, Corsica, Rome) are juxtaposed in order to pluralize our grasp of ways to put the world into form.

Most significant among different sociohistorical constellations is the state of nature, a tabula rasa from which humanity, stripped of all culture, can be observed in its purest, most naked form, as well as a device for the radical historization and "ethnologization" of the burgeoning moments of Western modernity. In Rousseau's hands, the state of nature becomes a means for critiquing bourgeois society, not a device of legitimation, as it had previously been employed. It is in this context that Rousseau's assault on competing versions of the state of nature must be understood, since they effectively naturalize what he holds to be socially constructed, as well as historically and culturally specific, characteristics:

> The philosophers, who have inquired into the foundations of society, have all felt the necessity of going back to a state of nature; but not one of them has got there. . . . Every one of them, in short, constantly dwelling on wants, avidity, oppression, desires, and pride, has transferred to the state of nature ideas which were acquired in society; so that, in speaking of the savage, they described the social man. (Rousseau 1973b, 50)

Hobbes and Locke, for instance, erroneously project the premises of "possessive individualism" (Macpherson 1962) back onto humankind's origins, thereby failing to realize the sociohistorical contingency of such assumptions. Moreover, their views of human nature are derived from a false "deculturalization" and "dehistoricization" of what they observe around them; both the memorable Hobbesian scenario of generalized and perpetual warfare and Locke's more benign conception of the natural right to property and socioeconomic inequalities are merely reflections of the aristocratic and bourgeois worldviews of seventeenth-century England. Competition, diffidence, and glory, the three defining attributes of human nature for Hobbes (1962, 143), are the results of socialization. According to Rousseau, self-preservation and pity (that is, compassion for others) are the only truly natural instincts defining our common human essence—and acknowledging their existence does nothing to justify the established social order.[27]

Rousseau's rendition of the state of nature is directed toward pointing out human responsibility for the pathologies of early modern social life, the loss of liberty and authenticity that I have discussed above. "Man is born free; and everywhere he is in chains," declaim the first lines of *The Social Contract* (Rousseau 1973e, 181).[28] Above all else, what revolts Rousseau is the fact that the sources of the enslavement and opacity are socially created, through institutions and patterns of thought and conduct prized in the most visible instances of modernity (epitomized by Paris). Entering the modern age, humankind is poised to become autonomous, yet instead finds ways to invent sociocultural forms of heteronomy. Individuals develop their reason and moral sense to an extent that would have been impossible for the brutish and amoral natural "savage," but they build a social order that stifles such qualities. The result is a society that sustains the worst of both the natural and the cultural worlds. Nature is perverted because the call of conscience and the heart are no longer heard, whereas reason and virtue are overwhelmed by a misleading and superficial public opinion. From inequality to the rule of law, from the arts and sciences to the division of labor and private property, all trends and principles conspire to render subjects dependent on their fellow citizens and the body social as a whole.

For Rousseau, the juxtaposition between the mediocrity of what is and the potential of what ought to be functions to put the former into question. And so it is that he advocates a humanly created republican transcendence of the ancien régime, one founded on a new, genuinely democratic and egalitarian political covenant that would bind all citizens to one another. As Cassirer put it, in a rather Kantian vein:

> [I]t is futile to hope that this salvation will be accomplished through outside help. No God can grant it to us; man must become his own

savior and, in the ethical sense, his own creator. In its present form society has inflicted the deepest wounds on humanity; but society alone can and should heal these wounds. The burden of responsibility rests upon it from now on. (1954, 76)[29]

Rousseau's ethnological sensibility allows him to appreciate the comparative uniqueness of this republican ideal in which, for the first time anywhere, a humanly willed reconciliation of nature and culture would take place in a manner equally eschewing the intellectual and moral slumber of our primeval condition and the established sociocultural perversions of our instincts. The breathless historicity of European modernity's beginnings would be broken; human beings would escape from temporal metamorphosis not by returning to a "prehistorical" state of nature, but on the contrary, by deliberately entering into a posthistorical, eternal present where perfectibility has been realized and the vagaries of incessant flux have ended. History would no longer dictate a path of change for change's sake, as the arts and sciences would be organized around permanent truths, rather than fleeting fashions. Furthermore, Rousseau's vision of the citizen living in the republic corresponds to his model of the civilized savage. Much like their counterparts in the state of nature, republican citizens enjoy a condition of independence, equality, and transparency, albeit the progress of their intellectual faculties and moral maturity clears the way for the attainment of individual autonomy, that is to say, self-reliance on one's reason and conscience.[30] Collectively, this same principle takes shape in the creation of a society utterly different from those that have existed during previous ages and in other places, a society where sovereignty is found in the people themselves, who, by way of the general will, participate together in rationally deliberating and establishing the institutional arrangements under which they agree to be governed.[31] Beyond the state of nature and the dawn of bourgeois society, the republic awaits creation through conscious human intervention; it is another sociocultural universe from which to critically interpret the existing social order from a comparative distance.

Conclusion

During the Enlightenment, itself a turning point for the role played by cultural otherness in Euro-American intellectual debates, Rousseau personified the nascent ethnological imagination's critical spirit. Since then, his writings have laid much of the groundwork for the advancement of a cross-cultural stream within Western social theory over the last two centuries, constituting the most compelling and influential early endeavors to formulate an anthropology of modernity. Through his viewpoint of civilized savagery, his support for and practice of cross-cultural reflection, and his evocation of a sociohistorical alter ego in the form of the state of nature, he has presciently identified some of modern society's central predicaments: its historicist onto-logization of chronological flux; its valuing of artifice and surface over nature and depth; its corruption of authenticity and freedom; and its dialectic between the promise of autonomy and the reality of self-generated heteronomy. In this sense, his legacy consists of relent-lessly turning the comparative mirror onto ourselves, thereby demon-strating the extent to which self-critique draws upon the encounter with mythical representations of cultural and historical alterity. Rous-seau compels us to observe our own surroundings in a different light. Being denaturalized, the origins of our current modes of social organi-zation are deprived of their self-evident or habitual status; their his-torical and cultural peculiarity, as well as their socially constructed character, come to the fore once again.

There is thus good reason to view Rousseau as a key catalyst for the meeting between intercultural and critical thought, a meeting that eventually altered the Western human sciences in significant ways. Sub-sequent contributors to the ethnological imagination have periodi-cally revisited this original crossroads since its inception. Not least among them is Marx, who was no doubt inspired by his predecessor's ire toward the birth of private property and the bourgeois ethos. Both features were to become the institutional undergirding of modern capitalism, a system whose power Marx was to challenge through his own set of cross-cultural and historical juxtapositions.

Two

Disenchanting the Commodity: Marx and the Defetishization of Capitalism

Rousseau's devastating indictment of the roots of bourgeois culture echoed throughout many corners of Europe during the Enlightenment, finding one of its most receptive listeners in Marx nearly a century later—at a time when industrial capitalism was ascending to new heights, forever transforming the socioeconomic landscape of the Western world. In the spirit of his forerunner, Marx advocated "the *ruthless criticism of the existing order*" so as to arrive at "the self-clarification [critical philosophy] of the struggles and wishes of the age" (Marx 1974b, 207, 209), a formulation that has earned him an undisputed place among the founders of the project of a critical hermeneutics of the modern West. As many commentators have noted, this critique is undertaken both immanently and transcendentally. Whether Marx locates the locus of capitalism's internal contradiction in the incompatibility between modes of production and appropriation, as more traditionally oriented Marxism insists, or whether he does so in that the incompatibility is found within the domain of production itself—pointing to the overcoming of the industrial logic of both capitalist relations and forces of production (Postone 1993)— there is no doubt that immanent critique enables him to demonstrate the historical specificity of the capitalist system. At the same time, Marx's transcendent critique is equally significant, to the extent that a historicizing and "culturalizing" perspectival distance is achieved through his explorations of other epochs and societies. Of specific interest here is the role of the ethnological imagination in his thinking, a role whose importance should not be overstated, yet which warrants greater attention than has hitherto been devoted to it.

If a sustained engagement with the vast array of Marxist theory would take us well beyond the scope of this chapter, the argument presented here can be clarified by briefly situating it within the debates between Marxism's humanist and structuralist currents. On the one hand, I side with the former's claims about the profoundly historicist tenor of Marx's work, which sought to reveal capitalism's contingency by situating it as one mode of production among others over the span of human history (Gramsci 1971, Lukács 1971), rather than being aimed at producing an ahistorical, universal science of society. On the other hand, structural Marxism's antihumanist stance is persuasive to the extent that it contends that his later writings moved away from his earlier reliance on philosophical anthropology and an essentialist conception of human nature (a labor ontology) toward a more social-constructivist position insisting on the advance or hindering of freedom and equality by humanly created institutions and forms of practice (Althusser 1969, Althusser and Balibar 1970).[1] Hence, while the structuralist claim about an absolute epistemological break between the young and the mature Marx is unconvincing, and while it is not a matter of choosing between the two, Marx's analysis of capitalist modernity undeniably develops over time—and of most relevance to this chapter, in a manner whereby the ethnological imagination becomes increasingly visible. Yet apart from Marxist anthropology (Bloch 1983; Godelier 1977), neither humanist nor structural interpretations give the cross-cultural component of Marx's thinking its due. And even among Marxist anthropologists, the tendency has been to elaborate on and apply his concepts to non-Western contexts (e.g., through the notion of articulation of modes of production). As a result, the question of how Marx's comparative sensibility informs his understanding of Euro-American capitalism has remained relatively neglected in social theory circles.

I would argue that the theme of commodity fetishism serves as a useful device with which to tease out these issues, since it cogently links his critique of political economy and capitalist forms of modernity to his cross-cultural viewpoint. The chapter thus begins by tracing and assessing this theme's various manifestations in Marx's writings. It then considers how the idea of commodity fetishism underlines the functioning of his ethnological imagination, which is grounded in an interrogation of the comparative peculiarity of the capitalist cult of the commodity form. This is pursued through an analysis of Marx's defetishizing critique of political economy, which uncovers the dismal science's effort to naturalize capitalism. Finally, I will discuss the ways in which his cross-cultural concerns contribute to his identification of some of capitalist modernity's most striking features, namely its Prometheanism and paradoxical socioeconomic consequences.

The Development of Marx's Intercultural Sensibility

Although Marx's transcendent critique of capitalist modernity is predominantly historical in character—juxtaposing the established social order with a past of medieval craftwork or a teleologically imagined communist future—its ethnological component should not be forgotten. Accordingly, the cross-cultural thrust of his writings merits chronological reconstruction and assessment.

Preludes

Despite the fact that Marx consulted writings about non-Western peoples as early as 1842 (Carver 1975, 11), there is little evidence of this influence in his earlier writings. At that point, Marx's interest lay more in the direction of an immanent questioning of German philosophy (Hegel, Feuerbach) and French socialism (notably Proudhon). The *Paris Manuscripts* (Marx 1974f [1844]), for instance, retain a highly speculative tone regarding that which has existed or could exist outside of capitalist society.[2] It is with *The German Ideology* (Marx and Engels 1976 [1845–46]) that the beginnings of a more pronounced historicist and comparative perspective become visible, according to which capitalism is considered a fledgling mode of production slowly emerging from its feudal womb, without having yet established firm structures (particularly in Germany). By calling on pastoral images as well as the more urban figures of the craftsperson and the artist embodying medieval production, Marx is able to present capitalism as a historically novel set of beliefs and practices involving a host of previously unknown or weakly developed institutions: the rule of money, the factory system, private property, a rigid division of labor, and so forth.[3] Relatedly, far from representing an attempt to romanticize feudalism, his positing of the European Middle Ages as one of the historical alter egos of capitalist modernity is intended to estrange the new socioeconomic system and thereby undermine claims about its eternal, natural, or inevitable status (Marx 1976a, 174). And evocations of precapitalist property regimes (tribal, ancient, and feudal) and of so-called "primitive communism" in his early works are of a polemical and speculative nature.[4]

Marx's well-known articles on British colonialism in India, which were published in 1853 in the *New York Daily Tribune* (Marx 1968a, 1968b), should be read in a similar vein. They problematically borrow the concept of Oriental despotism (found in the writings of Montesquieu, Smith, Mill, and Hegel, among others) to describe the political and economic organization of Indian society. It is also here that the concept of the Asiatic mode of production finds its roots; according to this thesis, the state (often through the person of the despot) is the actual landowner, while the social structure is organized around a village system or clan.[5] Though not detailed in Marx's articles on India, the Asiatic mode of production subsequently reappears in his writings as counterfactual to capitalism, operating on the basis of the principles of the union of agriculture and manufacturing, a limited division of labor, and most important, communal or state ownership of property. The ethnocentric and Orientalist tone of such ideas cannot be ignored, for they smack of the false universalization of the modern West's civilizational and productivist biases. In essence, Marx characterizes India as a primordial and inherently inert society whose development is stifled by a combination of Asiatic and aborted capitalist modes of production, the whole being reinforced by the legacy of Oriental despotism.[6] Hence his qualified support for British colonialism there, something that could force the country out of its supposed socioeconomic stupor through the enforced introduction of capitalism's modernizing dynamics.[7]

The Ethnological Turn

Despite the fact that, as we will discuss below, Marx never entirely dispenses with such flawed understandings of the non-Western world, his cultural reference points are visibly broadened in the *Grundrisse* (1973 [1857–58]). There, in order to identify the defining traits of capitalist modernity, he contrasts it to the socioeconomic realities of ancient Greece and medieval Europe, yet also to phenomena found in

Asia and in North and South America. Marx's comparative palate, which includes various forms of "primitive" communism (Oriental, classical, Germanic, Slavonic, and so forth), serves to break with the self-evident character of capitalist institutional arrangements. For him, the creation of a social order structured by the antagonistic relationship between wage labor and capital, itself underpinned by the sacrosanct status of private property and an intensely rationalized mode of production, cannot be taken for granted or appear as inherently legitimate; it is historically and cross-culturally peculiar, demanding critical examination.[8] This line of inquiry is pursued in *Capital*, where Marx favors an immanent mode of critique of political economy that undermines capitalism through its own systemic requirements (e.g., valorization of capital, expansion of the forces of production, profit maximization), since the existence of a series of constitutive structural contradictions demonstrates its crisis-ridden nature and eventual overcoming.[9] This is not to say that *Capital* entirely dispenses with historicist and cross-cultural devices of analysis: Marx continues to draw on the comparison between European feudalism and its capitalist descendent to denaturalize the latter (notably in chapters 26 to 31 of the first volume), while he reflects on the noncapitalist features of the Asiatic mode of production—such as communal land ownership, a limited advance of productive forces, and the predominance of use value over exchange value—to estrange and circumscribe its Western counterpart both temporally and geographically.[10] However, there is no doubt that the *Grundrisse*'s comparative perspectivism takes a backseat to the scientific analysis of the inner workings of the capitalist mode of production. In the pursuit of this objective, Marx returns to his earlier productivist and ethnocentric tendencies, which are fully displayed in his famed remark about the fact that "[t]he country that is more developed industrially only shows, to the less developed one, the image of its own future" (1976b, 91).[11]

Though the significance of the writings produced during this period should not be exaggerated, the decade before Marx's death saw the most active deployment of his ethnological imagination. As Hobsbawm (1964, 49) declares, "It is certain that Marx's own historical interests after the publication of *Capital* (1867) were overwhelmingly concerned with this stage of social development [primitive communalism], for which Maurer, Morgan, and the ample Russian literature which he devoured from 1873 on, provided a far more solid base of study than had been available in 1857–8."[12] Consequently, the concept of the Asiatic mode of production is employed to characterize societies outside of its original geographical reference point at the same time that the North American aboriginal gens becomes, in Marx's mind, a more appropriate archetype of primeval production than the Indian village.[13] Yet it is in his *Ethnological Notebooks* (Marx 1972)—a series of posthumously edited annotations and commentaries compiled between 1880 and 1882 on the work of Morgan, Phear, Maine, and Lubbock, part of which Engels borrowed for his "Origin of the Family, Private Property and the State" (1969 [1884])[14]—that Marx's ethnological sensibility is most strongly felt. His overtures toward cultural anthropology are born out of its capacity to provide sociohistorical universes from which to radically interrogate modern capitalism in the West. Morgan's *Ancient Society* (1964 [1877]) and other pioneering anthropological works enable Marx to ground *The German Ideology*'s and the *Grundrisse*'s preoccupations with the origins of humankind in less speculative ways; the theory of primitive communism can thus receive empirical confirmation through Morgan's concept of the gens, the actual starting point of human history.

Marx's heightened comparative perspective is further evidenced in his discussions of the Russian question. Indeed, he connects the anthropological discovery of the gens to the fate of the Russian rural commune, believing that evidence of the former's existence reinforces the viability of the latter. Despite the fact that the capitalist mode of production is solidly entrenched in Western Europe, a path of development based on uninterrupted communal ownership of the land cannot be ruled out in the rest of the world (Krader 1972, 5–6). The shift vis-à-vis his earlier tendency to posit a unilinear process of socioeconomic evolution should be underscored, as should his reply to the characterization of the first volume of *Capital* as deterministic and falsely universalist:

> It is absolutely necessary for him [Mikhailovsky] to metamorphose my historical sketch of the genesis of capitalism in Western Europe into a historico-philosophical theory of general development, imposed by fate on all peoples, whatever the historical circumstances in which they are placed. . . . By studying each of the evolutions on its own, and then comparing them, one will easily discover the key to the phenomenon, but it will never be arrived at by employing the all-purpose formula of a general historico-philosophical

theory whose supreme virtue consists in being supra-historical.
(Marx 1989a, 200–201)

Put differently, Marx reinterprets his work's intention as that of
providing a historically and geographically specific analysis of the
birth and development of capitalism, rather than an abstract model
of humanity's ironclad destiny. His much discussed drafts of the 1881
letter written to Vera Zasulich (Marx 1989b) are also worth mention-
ing in this regard, since they draw on anthropological material to flag
the possibility of a distinctly Russian road to socialism. In addition to
noting Russia's specificities, he conceives of a path of sociohistorical
modernization diverging from the Western European model. Situating
the Russian commune within the context of other instances of noncapitalist formations studied in his previous works—e.g., the self-
sustaining Indian village communities and the 1870 Paris Commune
portrayed in *The Civil War in France* (Marx 1969e)—Marx defends
their viability as economic systems without, or organized against,
private property. Shedding the stagnant shell of the rural commune
while incorporating the superior elements of capitalist production,
Russia may be in a position to leapfrog to socialism.[15] Overall, then,
I would argue that Marx's late encounter with cultural anthropology
was fortuitous, for it prompted him to widen his horizons while cultivating a greater perspectivism toward his own stance; it becomes
less a matter of how or when the rest of the world would follow in
Western Europe's footsteps, and more of why this particular region
has adopted a socioeconomic order differing so widely from those
preceding and surrounding it.[16] If political economy acts to restrict
the range of social organizing structures that humanity can imagine,
history and ethnology work to widen it.

Contextualizing Marx's Ethnological Imagination

Before examining the substance of Marx's defetishizing critique of
political economy and his vision of capitalist society, I would like to
consider his cross-cultural perspective in relation to two key frameworks of representation of non-Western cultures, namely naturalism
and evolutionism. In the first instance, he jettisons the attachment to
naturalist critiques of the established social order, which had characterized modern European thought between the sixteenth and the eighteenth centuries. Pace Rousseau, to whose aims he is otherwise largely

sympathetic, Marx dispenses with the myth of the state of nature as a viable device through which to interrogate capitalist modernity. Deriding the way Enlightenment primitivism and utopian socialism idealized humankind's primeval condition, Marx refuses to contemplate the idea of a presocietal level of pristine intimacy with the natural world.[17] On the contrary, he shifts the radical questioning of modern society onto the terrain of the sociohistorical, thereby providing the ethnological imagination with a firmly intercultural foundation—that is to say, one that juxtaposes various forms of social organization, rather than the natural and the cultural. Here can be found the reason that Aristotle's (1981, 60) description of the human being as a *zoon politikon* rings true for Marx, though not in the restricted or literal sense of the phrase; it points to the indispensability of social life, which in turn connects us to our species-being.[18] Even his zero point of history, primitive communism, is an original state of culture in which social relations are always already present; productive forces necessarily mediate our interaction with our natural environment, which cannot be an unspoilt realm external to humankind. Instead, nature is the milieu enveloping our activity and existence; the direct means of human reproduction provided by raw materials and food; as well as the object of labor, modified and appropriated by human activity.[19]

If Marx rejects naturalism, his relationship to various strands of evolutionism, which became prevalent in the second half of the nineteenth century, is more complex.[20] By establishing a universal taxonomy of modes of production set in a fixed temporal sequence, some of Marx's writings do suggest a linear-cum-evolutionary scheme of history: primitive communism, the ancient mode of production, feudalism, capitalism, and socialism are the stages usually denoted, most concisely in the preface to *A Contribution to the Critique of Political Economy* (Marx 1969d; Melotti 1977, 8–9). Marx therefore occasionally falls prey to what Fabian (1983, 31) has termed the "denial of coevalness," the projection backward in time of noncapitalist and non-Western societies, whose temporal simultaneity with the modern West is denied in favor of a belief in their representing past stages of the latter's own path of development. This is visible in Marx's understanding of indigenous societies, which he believes to correspond relatively closely to humankind's original state of primitive communism, as well as in his Orientalist treatment of Asian societies (Thorner 1990, 437).

Nevertheless, it should be pointed out that Marx's interest in evolutionism principally stems from its anthropocentric and historicizing effects, rather than its sociobiological implications. First, evolutionary theory allows him to represent human history by referring to strictly immanent and materialist tendencies and forces, without resorting to metaphysical or transcendental conjuring tricks. Second, evolutionism supports his historicist conception of modern capitalism, which can be viewed as a passing phase in the development of humankind— a phase engendered by other forms of social organization and one that will, in turn, spawn different modes of production (i.e., communism). For both reasons, Marx's cross-cultural perspective owes as much to the universalism and developmentalism of Enlightenment-inspired historical schemas (Voltaire, Condorcet, Hegel, and so forth) as to Victorian evolutionary ideas. Several other considerations should temper any facile classification of Marx as an evolutionary thinker. With Bloch's (1983) valuable distinction between Marx's "historical" and "rhetorical" uses of anthropology in mind, we can see that the latter's primary intention is less to offer a general theory of human history than to put capitalist modernity into question; instead of serving to reconstruct the precise evolutionary sequence through which humankind has passed, anthropological material about non-Western societies serves to explore modes of production that exist outside of, and thus estrange, the capitalist social order. This explanation is given further credence by the fact that, whenever they appear in his writings, the unilinear and mechanistic versions of Marx's historical schema remain sketchy and undertheorized, heuristic and rhetorical tools rather than fully elaborated models of history.[21]

In certain passages, Marx even explicitly distances himself from evolutionism. He is aware, for instance, that applying the principles of biological evolution to the sociocultural domain constitutes yet another form of fetishism that merely substitutes natural forces for their divine counterparts to explain society's institution and transformation over time; human agency and the processes of self-instituting society are accordingly obscured. In addition, this would unreflectively naturalize the particular sociocultural habits and beliefs (competition, survival of the fittest, etc.) of bourgeois culture (Ball 1990, 337). Marx also occasionally objects to the "denial of coevalness" rampant in the writings of others, as the following remark from *The Poverty of Philosophy* indicates: "When, after that, Mr. Proudhon proceeds to give birth to these other phases, he treats them as if they were newborn babes. He forgets that they are of the same age as the first" (1976a, 166).

This brings us to the question of Marx's ethnocentrism, a matter that must be approached in a nuanced matter. On the one hand, as I have already claimed, some of his earlier writings falsely universalize a Western European developmental pattern to the rest of the world. As a result, a specific sequence of historical progress with a set number of stages of production is claimed to be valid for all societies. More fundamentally, Marx's analyses of non-Western settings reflect a modern Euro-American perspective regarding the organization of and articulation between different spheres of social life: the privileging of the so-called economic "base"—or more specifically, of the level of technique and productivity, as measured by the expansion of productive forces—as the measure of a society's overall civilizational development displays economistic and productivist orientations that cannot be assumed to be relevant in noncapitalist contexts. Moreover, Marx tends to take for granted the distinctiveness and demarcation of the economy vis-à-vis other social domains in his comparative investigations, whereas such a separation (and the possibility of thinking it as such) tends to only be constitutive of modern capitalism in the West.[22] Consequently, he fails to reflectively and cross-culturally position his own point of view, something that could be realized by acknowledging the possible existence of other norms and worldviews.

On the other hand, a more perspectivist interpretation of Marx's thought is also plausible. Although believing that noncapitalist societies are inherently limited by the self-reproductive stagnation of their forces of production, he does concede that they satisfy their own internal requirements within their self-posited economic, technological, and cultural horizons. By no means are they to be taken as morally inferior, for "the old view, in which the human being appears as the aim of production, regardless of his limited national, religious, political character, seems to be very lofty when contrasted to the modern world, where production appears as the aim of mankind and wealth as the aim of production" (Marx 1973, 487–88). Despite being flawed in its execution, his ethnological imagination should be valued for its willingness to envisage non-Western and nonmodern forms of social organization. Hence, if the intercultural content of his findings about the Asiatic mode of production, primitive communism, and the Russian question are questionable today, the pluralizing and critical intent behind them should not be dismissed out of hand. At least in his later work, Marx employs such notions to seriously put into doubt the necessity, "naturalness," and universality of capitalist modernity. His treatment of commodity fetishism nicely illustrates the play of this cross-cultural sensibility in his oeuvre.

The Cult of the Commodity and the Defetishizing of Political Economy

I would argue that the theme of commodity fetishism is a useful window from which to observe both the historicizing and the ethnological dimensions of Marx's critique of modern capitalism in the Western world.[23] Indeed, he convincingly points to the curious nature of capitalist society's cult of the commodity, a form of superstitious inversion whereby the products of human labor are fetishistically objectified by the subjects who create them. Hence, his project of historicist defetishization of bourgeois conceptions of the capitalist market is in part driven by his quest to undermine commodity fetishism's ideological supports. This quest is, in turn, closely related to his comparative orientation, since the juxtaposition of capitalist and noncapitalist social formations allows Marx to identify and question some of the modern West's distinguishing features and mystifying properties. However, before tackling these substantive issues, a brief recapitulation of the role of commodity fetishism in Marx's thought is in order.

Marx was exposed to the general phenomenon of fetishism through his early reading of de Brosses's eighteeenth-century anthropological essay, *Du culte des dieux fétiches*. In this work, fetishism is defined as the superstitious worship, or sacralization, of inanimate objects or animals by "savage" peoples who ascribe to them intrinsic powers over human existence.[24] Marx transposes this idea onto capitalist society, initially through his remarks about the way in which alienation fosters the illusory belief in the omnipotence and worship of money. For instance, the *Paris Manuscripts* explain: "The inversion and confusion of all human and natural qualities, the bringing together of impossibilities, the *divine* power of money lies in its *nature* as the estranged and alienated *species-essence* of man which alienates itself by selling itself. It is the alienated *capacity* of *mankind*" (1974f, 377).[25]

In his later work, and notably in the first volume of *Capital*, Marx discovers that the fetishism of money under capitalism is but a manifestation of the rule of exchange value over use value, which itself culminates in the much more noteworthy process of fetishization of the commodity—a product of human labor misleadingly appearing to possess the attributes of a living being (Marx 1976b, 163–65). Marx's eventual subsumption of the monetary cult under that of the commodity demonstrates a greater focus on the systemic specificities of the capitalist mode of production, yet it also underlines one of the distinctive qualities of his critique of political economy: its defetishizing effect. Capitalism's naturalization is accordingly contested by demonstrating how it is constructed sociohistorically. If, in the spirit of the Enlightenment, de Brosses disenchants "savage" superstitions, Marx reserves the same treatment for the commodity form in his later work. Finally, it should be mentioned that his preoccupation with capitalist forms of fetishism illustrates the extent to which his cross-cultural forays nourish his critical hermeneutics of Western modernity; his argument about the strangeness of commodity fetishism is arrived at through an often implicit, and sometimes explicit, contrast with societies where it is absent.[26] The uncanny character of the phenomenon of capitalist reification is arrived at through comparison with other manifestations of objectification in different times and places. In traditional societies, he observes a form of heteronomous "nature-idolatry" (Marx 1973, 410), which encourages humankind to find its raison d'être in forces lying outside the social domain.[27] However, the cult of the commodity is absent from these settings, "in which the human being appears as the aim of production" (Marx 1973, 487–88).

Marx's analysis of commodity fetishism is located at the crossroads of two aspects of his thought: the critique of political economy and the cross-cultural understanding of modern capitalism. Put differently, he suggests that the fetishization of the commodity form is not solely the reflection of capitalist relations of production; it is also made possible by the widespread acceptance of the worldview promoted by political economy. In essence, then, I would argue that Marx's self-defined aim is to challenge this worldview by treating it as nothing more than an ideological support of bourgeois culture, and thus as the economic manifestation of fetishism in the modern Euro-

American world. It is thus possible to recognize the two steps in his analysis, namely the weakening of political economy's philosophico-anthropological underpinnings (its conception of human nature) and the rejection of its naturalization of the capitalist social order.

Marx's assault on the pillars of capitalist modernity is grounded in his challenge to political economy's bourgeois vision of human nature, according to which the subject is a *homo economicus* by his or her very essence—a being whose monadic, selfish, and self-maximizing inclinations find their "natural" outlets in the market, which channels them in economically productive directions. In his early writings, Marx counters such ideas by offering a rival philosophical anthropology, a transhistorical and universalist labor ontology of Hegelian provenance (Hegel 1977). The activity of material production, understood in the expansive sense as consciously willed and collective praxis consisting of intercourse between humanity and nature aimed at the latter's transformation in order to satisfy the former's needs, represents our common species-being. For the young Marx, then, labor is what defines us as human beings across time and space; it is an intersubjective means of self-expression and self-actualization through which we collectively develop our capacities and needs (from the more elementary biological ones to "higher" spiritual and moral ones). Political economy's myth of a state of nature populated by proto-bourgeois and isolated "natural men" becomes untenable, since labor has always already consisted of a communal process taking place in and through a thick web of socioeconomic relations between individuals and classes.[28]

Yet in his later writings, Marx's critique of bourgeois notions of human nature shifts register, largely abandoning philosophical anthropology in favor of a social constructivist and historicist position. Instead of countering one understanding of human nature *(homo economicus)* with another (a labor ontology), he becomes preoccupied with demonstrating the historically and culturally specific character of the former conception. This is what he terms the "Robinsonades," political economists' ideological appropriations of Defoe's *Robinson Crusoe* (1972 [1719]) to advance a tale about our natural inclination to behave like a *homo economicus*.[29] In other words, Marx points out that political economy ontologizes and naturalizes its situated and contingent beliefs about our shared essence, either because of its failure to realize the historically and socially constructed character of such beliefs or its willingness to legitimize capitalism through essentializing means. Armed with historical and ethnological knowledge of other societies, Marx inverts the Robinsonades: the bourgeois ethos and capitalist culture are not extensions of our natural tendencies, but rather political economy's portrayal of the latter is a product of the former. To rephrase de Beauvoir (1949), one is not born, but becomes, a *homo economicus*. Far from being a preexisting figure waiting to be discovered, it is a social construct produced in specific circumstances as well as an ideological device reflecting the interests of dominant socioeconomic groups.

At one level, the Robinsonades retrospectively project back onto humankind's natural or original condition a set of cultural assumptions and a worldview created at a particular place and time (namely, during the transition from feudalism to capitalism that began in sixteenth-century Western Europe). The dissolution of communal feudal ties, combined with the accelerating development of productive forces and the spread and intensification of market relations, reshaped social relations to the point where it became possible to believe a fable about our natural inclination toward self-interest and an existence that was independent of social ties within civil society. The resulting naked self could interact directly with the market, all other communal relations being conceived as "obstacles" impeding his or her capacity to exercise free choice.[30] Yet at another level, Marx's thinking suggests that the creation of *homo economicus* is neither accidental nor innocent. By seeking to render self-evident its conception of human behavior, and by deliberately conflating analytical and normative dimensions of social reality (what is and what ought to be), political economy normalizes bourgeois ways of thinking and acting. The sociocultural soil within which capitalism could burgeon has been laid.

In addition to contesting political economy's philosophical anthropology, Marx draws on historical and cross-cultural comparisons to undercut that which follows from it: the naturalization of the capitalist model of social organization, which is falsely universalized and made to appear eternal. A passage in *The Poverty of Philosophy*, where the ideological character of the endeavor is underlined, nicely makes this point:

> Economists have a singular method of procedure. There are only two kinds of institutions for them, artificial and natural. The institutions of feudalism are artificial institutions, those of the bourgeoisie

are natural institutions. In this they resemble the theologians, who likewise establish two kinds of religion. Every religion which is not theirs is an invention of men, while their own is an emanation from God. (1976a, 174)[31]

Political economy thus effectively strives to justify the existing social order as the only possible one. Having its historically and culturally specific practices and beliefs removed from the sociohistorical realm, capitalist modernity's self-institution can be denied, or at least obscured; because believed to exist outside of time and space, the socially determined ways of thinking and acting that undergird capitalism appear as objective, given, or necessary. However, Marx points out, political economists have failed to provide criteria of legitimation that are immanent to capitalism itself, and thus they have failed to adequately justify the latter's existence on its own grounds. Such a failure is a constitutive aporia of the bourgeois worldview, which must appeal to supposedly extrasocial forces (e.g., nature, God). What occurs, then, is an ideological inversion of appearance and essence—as well as, it should be mentioned, the natural and the sociocultural. The capitalist mode of production's comparative exceptionalism and processes of creation are erroneously generalized and abstracted to such a degree that they appear to emanate from beyond. At the same time, Marx points out, political economists apply the opposite logic to all noncapitalist systems, which are represented as outcomes of human action whose validity is limited to their own period and location. Capitalism is elevated to the status of the metaphysical embodiment of eternal, universal, and infallible laws of nature, while alternatives in the past or elsewhere are particularized and deemed temporary. As a result, the here and now can become a one-dimensional or always existing reality. "Thus there has been history, but there is no longer any" (Marx 1976a, 174). The rhetorical might of political economy stems from its equating bourgeois culture and the capitalist economy with culture and economy *tout court*.

Marx proclaims the dismal science's founding principles (the "law" of supply and demand, the "invisible hand" of the market, and so forth) to be fetishistic devices that, in the last instance, must call on a series of assumptions and institutional arrangements to emerge out of capitalist modernity's very specific configuration in the Western world. Among others, *homo economicus,* the dominance of exchange value, commodity production, private property, and an advanced division of labor are not objective, transhistorical, or universal phenomena, but cultural and historical products of, or preconditions for, the development of capitalism.[32] In particular, Marx is scathing about the ideological roots of commodity fetishism, the contorted belief that effectively naturalizes the prevalence of exchange value over use value in capitalist economic relations. As he demonstrates in *Capital,* this prevalence is a historical outcome of social relations reflected in the formation of the market, rather than being intrinsic to the product of labor itself. Additionally, the market must be considered a sociohistorically instituted economic structure that abstractly mediates interactions between individuals in capitalist society, yet which, like all other systems of production and distribution, is indelibly cultural—that is, embedded in a dense web of customs and habits that subjects acquire over time.[33] Consequently, there is nothing necessary or even compelling about political economists' representations of capitalism.

The Comparative Dialectic of Capitalism

Having considered the defetishizing facet of Marx's critique of political economy, I would like to explore another aspect of his critical hermeneutics of Western modernity, an aspect filtered through the theme of commodity fetishism: his comparative analysis of capitalism's distinctiveness, which relies on knowledge of counterfactual cases offered by noncapitalist socioeconomic contexts to estrange the practices and creeds of bourgeois civilization. By exploring other ways of putting the world into form, of articulating forces and relations of production, Marx elaborates a cross-cultural and historical vantage point, exposing the fact that the capitalist social order is neither eternal nor universal. On the contrary, it is a socially and politically constituted entity, the peculiarities of which can best be captured dialectically and comparatively.

Noncapitalist societies in the past and elsewhere are valuable for Marx in that they offer instances of a relatively greater degree of economic anthropocentrism. Whether via the state (under the Asiatic mode of production) or the producers themselves (in the case of the primitive commune or European medieval craftwork), sociopolitical relations structure the sphere of economic production throughout most of humankind's history and across many of the world's regions. Producers have thereby been united, or at least organically connected, with the means as well as the objects of production, which retain their character as manifestations of the process of objectification of human subjectivity; besides being directed toward the qualitative satisfaction of human needs, the products of labor maintain their sensuousness, their concreteness as creations by specific subjects. In other words, and strictly in the economic domain, alienation and fetishization cannot be present in noncapitalist forms of production.[34] This represents a far cry from what occurs under capitalism, where social relations appear to be objectively generated by the commodity and are necessarily mediated through the market.

Yet Marx is neither a primitivist nor a Romantic who simplistically idealizes noncapitalist societies. On the contrary, he believes that such societies are heteronomous in various ways because of nature idolatry (primitive communism), religious superstition (European feudalism), or political despotism (Asiatic mode of production). Under these conditions, social life is wholly determined by traditional or inherited patterns of thought and action, since what is given forms the full extent of what is, as well as what ought to be. They are essentially static, "definite and limited human conglomerates" (Marx 1973, 83) directed toward maintaining already existing social relations and institutions. Consequently, according to Marx, humankind's creative and rational powers are hemmed in by the socioeconomic structure's imperative to self-reproduction, the satisfaction of pregiven needs, and the limitations that nature imposes. The becoming of noncapitalist societies is their being, for they reproduce established patterns of domination and subordination sustained with ideological devices (tradition, nature, God, and so forth).[35]

By contrast, the Promethean aspect of capitalism captures Marx's imagination. Its modernizing thrust of "creative destruction" (Schumpeter 1950, 83) overturns everything that it encounters, liberating humankind from the tyranny of the past and the shackles of tradition. Personified in the bourgeoisie, capitalism represents perpetual flux, the constant negation of being by becoming and the incessant quest for the new where the only factors preserved from one moment to the next are the desire and need for change itself. The capitalist ethos is explicitly dedicated to shattering past constraints on the development of productive forces, as well as the expansion of social capacities and needs. By aiming for "the annihilation of space by time" (Marx 1973, 524), it appears to foster a boundless universe of possibilities.

Perhaps, then, not solely creative destruction, but also destructive creation: the solidifying of all that is air, as well as the melting into air of all that is solid.[36] Accordingly, Marx foresees that capitalism clears the way for humankind's complete self-determination (in the form of communism) by dispensing with religious, natural, and traditional sources of heteronomy. These extrasocial types of fetishism or the metaphysical *"opium* of the people" (Marx 1974d, 244) are unmasked as outward projections of the human power of self-creation. In other words, because social interaction takes place in a purely instrumental and immanent manner unencumbered by tradition, religion, locality, or personal dependence—the proletariat sells its labor power, the bourgeoisie owns the means of production—capitalist society in the modern West opens the door to autonomy. For the first time anywhere, human beings may realize that society is self-instituted, that it is a fully sociohistorical construct founded on labor and praxis.[37]

At the same time, Marx claims that, in reality, capitalism actively forecloses this opening toward self-determination by substituting immanent forces of heteronomy for the extrasocial or transcendental ones found in noncapitalist societies. The comparative particularity of capitalist modernity originates in the fact that the commodity form fills the fetishistic void created through the gradual mastery of nature, rejection of theological systems, or overthrow of the despot. In an animistic fashion, the commodity is invested with intrinsic and quasi-magical powers over humankind; if religion completely inverts reality through human objectification in a god who becomes the subject and will of the world, capitalism metamorphoses the commodity into an animated being worshipped by those who have produced it. It is this mysterious process of the "personification of things," whereby exchange value rules supreme, that the first volume of *Capital* summarizes by way of the M-C-M' formula (Marx 1976b). More broadly, the market appears to take on a life of its own, becoming the head of a "religion of everyday life" analogous to noncapitalist superstitions: "It is an enchanted, topsy-turvy world, in which Monsieur le Capital et Madame la Terre do their ghost-walking as social characters and at the same time directly as mere things" (Marx 1967b, 830).[38] Adam Smith's image of the "invisible hand" perfectly captures this metaphysical prop. Seemingly of its own volition, moved by laws independent of, and even incomprehensible to, mere mortals, the commodity underpins the modern age's mystical attitude toward the market. Marx holds that, in the end, commodity fetishism prevents subjects from arriving at an accurate self-understanding, namely that the structures as well as the patterns of thought and action prevailing in capitalist society are socially constructed—and thus that they can, and ultimately must, be overthrown to arrive at a fully autonomous social order.

Beyond its obstruction of autonomy, capitalism actually institutes comparatively unprecedented forms of economic heteronomy. In Marx's early writings, greater attention is paid to the intersubjective and class-based dimension of domination, that of the bourgeoisie over the proletariat being facilitated by private property and begetting alienation in the process of production. While in no way discarding such an analysis, his later work focuses more on the structural aspects of capitalist domination, that is to say, the creation by human beings themselves of an apparently objective, abstract, and self-reproducing system of production holding sway over them. What strikes Marx as especially aberrant is the fact that this system is socially and historically constituted, yet stands above and against those who gave birth to it and contribute to its existence.[39] Simply put, unlike what occurs at other times and places, we generate the institutions that lead to our own alienation and exploitation; we have lost control of the "animated monster" (Marx 1973, 470) that we created, something that the phenomenon of fetishization of the commodity form perfectly captures. Capitalism reorients material production and labor from the objective of satisfying human needs to that of ensuring the economic system's own reproduction and continuous expansion. For the vast majority of those living in the modern Euro-American world, the mere possibility that human needs could be fortuitously met is eliminated. "The bourgeois order . . . has become a vampire that sucks out its blood and brains and throws them into the alchemistic cauldron of capital" (Marx 1969c, 481–82).[40]

In so doing, purposive-instrumental rationality *(Zweckrationalität)* is spread to the furthest reaches of capitalist society, establishing mastery of the natural world and human beings. Vividly contrasting with other ways of structuring production that integrate normative and qualitative criteria of organization (values, individual attributes, personal needs, and so forth), capitalism is thoroughly rationalized because it is purely driven by a quantifying, impersonal means-end logic enforcing the rule of things and abstractions (e.g., the commodity, time, money, profit) over people. A passage of the *Paris Manuscripts*, in which the rationalized character of capitalism is contrasted to the personalization of social relations in noncapitalist social settings, nicely makes this point: "[T]he medieval saying *nulle terre sans maître* [no land without its master] gives way to the modern saying *l'argent n'a pas de maître* [money knows no master]" (Marx 1974f, 319). Further, an ever-intensifying regime of specialization and mechanization is imposed on workers, transforming them into mere appendages of machinery. By way of cross-cultural and historical comparison, Marx recognizes the specificity of capitalism's instrumentalization of wage labor and, ultimately, its degradation of the human being into a means serving a system of production's functional requirements.[41] Its most abject feature consists in turning the potential for economic self-determination against itself, accordingly resulting in its very negation. Having formally liberated human beings from the bonds of religion, community, and tradition, capitalist modernity reinvents modes of domination. Reversing what takes place in other historical and cultural settings, social intercourse can exclusively be entered into through the exchange of commodities; the market becomes the only medium of social relations.

Conclusion

Nearly a century after Rousseau's evocation of the figure of the civilized savage put into question the emerging modern social order in the Western world, Marx inaugurated the ethnological imagination's shift from its naturalist origins to historicist and cross-cultural vistas. This shift is mirrored in the transformation of Marx's critique of capitalist modernity, which moves from an early reliance on philosophical anthropology to a later turn toward social constructivism—itself related to the expansion of his comparative horizons and encounter with social-anthropological material. In this respect, I have underlined the significance of the interculturally and historically derived theme of commodity fetishism as a point of engagement with Marx's body of work. His critique of bourgeois political economy can thus be interpreted as a defetishizing attempt to radically "culturalize" and historicize the ideological naturalization of *homo economicus* and the capitalist institutional order on which it is built.

I have also claimed that a comparative perspective plays a significant role in Marx's estrangement of modern Euro-American capitalism and his coming to grips with its dialectical character. When juxtaposed to modes of production, capitalist modernity's rupture with what exists in other places and ages becomes salient and its dual character strongly comes to the fore: it points toward the realization of humankind's complete autonomy, at the same time that it invents unprecedented types of domination that sustain a massively heterono-mous socioeconomic order. Marx captures this through his analysis of the cult of the commodity, a strange set of rituals and beliefs pecu-liar to capitalism. By undermining commodity fetishism, the kernel of the latter economic system's "self-evidentness" and normality can be put into doubt since it is tied to a specific place and time. In the late nineteenth and early twentieth centuries, Weber and Durkheim were to continue this social constructivist strand of interrogation of industrial capitalism's institutional and subjective features, while con-solidating the ethnological imagination's cross-cultural credentials. Yet they went much further than their predecessor, entrenching compara-tive research at the core of modern Western social theory in a man-ner that Marx only foreshadowed. Weber did so through civiliza-tional analyses of theologically inflected life conduct, while Durkheim blended sociological and anthropological insights to make sense of the modern condition. Either way, the cultivation of an ethnological sen-sibility became essential to the project of a critical hermeneutics of Western modernity.

Three

The View from the Magical Garden: Weber's Comparative Sociology of the Modern Ethos

In the previous two chapters, I have underscored the cross-cultural thrust of Rousseau's stance of civilized savagery and Marx's defetishizing critique of capitalist society to demonstrate why their writings should be reread as contributions to a flourishing ethnological sensibility during the eighteenth and nineteenth centuries, respectively. Yet in the early part of the twentieth century, one theorist surpassed all others in establishing the ethnological imagination's comparativist credentials: Max Weber. Indeed, Weber undertook one of the most ambitious, as well as historically and geographically comprehensive, projects ever undertaken in the human sciences. More than any other classical social theorist, he grasped the fact that knowledge about non-Western sociohistorical realities was integral to any adequate understanding of Western modernity.[1] Nelson (1991a [1974]) has convincingly shown that Weber's thoroughly comparative 1920 introduction to his *Collected Essays in the Sociology of Religion* (1930a) should be considered a "master clue" to his entire oeuvre.[2] More generally, over the years key commentaries have stressed the intercultural dimensions of Weber's thought, while civilizational analysis has sought to extend Weber's global framework of analysis.[3]

What remains puzzling, then, is the extent to which most contemporary social theorists continue to downplay the importance of

Weber's writings on Asian societies and religions for his diagnosis of the modern condition, or yet again how they readily assimilate such writings to evolutionary models of world history. In fact, one observes a convergence of "mainstream" sociology and critical theory on this issue. In *The Structure of Social Action,* Parsons, whose pivotal role as translator and interpreter of Weber for English-speaking audiences in the first half of the twentieth century need not be restated here, claimed that his distinguished forebear's comparative analyses of Asian socioreligious complexes were primarily intended as negative test cases of the Protestant ethic thesis—which was itself viewed as a theory of modernization (Parsons 1937b, 539–42, 563).[4] And despite being heavily Weberian in both tone and content, Habermas's own synthetic masterwork follows Parsons and Schluchter's (1981) earlier writings in electing to convert Weber's comparative study of rationalization processes into an evolutionary theory of reason's progress across civilizational stages (Habermas 1984, 155; 1987a, 313–16). Parsons's and Habermas's interpretations are symptomatic of social theory's ongoing failure to fully appreciate the implications of Weber's comparativism. There is no doubt that he is vitally interested in assessing modernity's impact on Euro-American societies, or more precisely, in coming to grips with what he is fond of calling the "cultural significance" of modern existence in relation to the conduct of life *(Lebensführung).* Taking his cue from Tolstoy (1934), Weber (1946b, 143, 152–53) asks, "What shall we do and how shall we live?"[5] However, I would claim that the significance of this question can only be appreciated once his acknowledgment of the specificity of the modern West's predicament vis-à-vis other periods and societies becomes clear.

Weber's comparative sociology should be recovered in order to explore one of the most fruitful paths toward a critical hermeneutics of the established social order in the modern West. This chapter therefore begins by analyzing the gradual development of his intercultural outlook, as well as considering how the form of cultural perspectivism found in his writings avoids the pitfalls of evolutionism and naturalism, as well as false universalism and absolute relativism. I will then foreground the ways in which his rendition of the ethnological imagination assists us in differently or more clearly understanding Weber's interpretation of Western modernity. The view from the "Oriental" magical garden provides another, richer vantage point for considering the cultural significance and comparative distinctiveness of the Protestant ethic, the particularities of Western rationalization, and the difficulties of cultivating an ethos adequate to life in a disenchanted universe.

The Constitution of Weber's Comparative Sociology

To respond to his own Tolstoyan query about the peculiar fate of the self in the modern age, Weber must face another challenge: how can the distinctiveness of Western modernity, its sheer novelty as a socio-historical constellation that humanity has never before experienced, be best conveyed? For Weber, this can only take place by putting into question the self-evident, normalized, or habitualized status of the institutional configurations and forms of subjectivity with which we are familiar. What is more, I would contend that this process of interrogation of the here and now is undertaken through a transcendent critique of it in historical and cross-cultural terms. Hence, Weber relies on both genealogical and ethnological modes of critical detachment from the immediacy and proximity of Euro-American societies by simultaneously drawing attention to both the temporal gap between past and present and the cultural gap between different civilizations. This is not to say that Weber's ethnological imagination burst forth fully formed from his mind. In fact, it was acquired by a progressive widening of his civilizational horizons and his capacity for intercultural analysis, something I would like to briefly consider here.

In his early essays, Weber clearly favors historiography as a mode of transcendent critique and interpretation of Western modernity, which is frequently juxtaposed to the European Middle Ages. For instance, to explain the significance of the upheavals affecting East Elbian rural workers, Weber contrasts the declining feudal-patriarchal economy and the aggressively expansive logic of industrial capitalism. The specificity of this process of peasant proletarianization is further emphasized by comparing the East Elbian region with Silesia and England, where agricultural production is organized along more modern lines. Thus, by historically situating, rather than taking this situation for granted, he is able to portray it as a socio-cultural watershed in the process of modernization.[6] A decade after his article on East Elba, the first edition of *The Protestant Ethic and the Spirit of Capitalism* (1930b [1904–5]) still finds Weber primarily drawing on history to identify the peculiar character of rational capitalism's spiritual underpinnings. At that point, the essay did not significantly venture outside of the West, with Weber preferring to use the European Middle Ages as a point of historical juxtaposition; accordingly, he positions the Reformation, one of the linchpins for comparison and contrast, at the center of his narrative.

By the time *The Agrarian Sociology of Ancient Civilizations* (1976 [1909]) appeared, Weber had greatly enlarged his scope of analysis to include Mesopotamia, Egypt, and Israel (in addition to Greek and Roman antiquity), all of which served to facilitate analysis of their similarities and differences vis-à-vis Western civilization.[7] Nevertheless, it is truly from 1915 onward that Weber's intercultural sensibility came into its own. Thus, his self-described project of a "universal history" (Weber 1930a, 13) took shape in the form of a comparative sociology of world religions that was designed to identify the modern West's core features. *The Protestant Ethic* must be read within this broader context, as one of the spokes of a wheel composed of published surveys of ancient Judaism, Confucianism, and Taoism, as well as Hinduism and Buddhism—not to mention unfinished analyses of Islam, early and Eastern Christianity, and Talmudic Judaism. For Weber, exploring these widely differing religious worldviews offers a clearer, more precise sketch of the uniqueness of rationally determined Protestant and post-Protestant modes of existence, as well as their concomitant institutional manifestations. Differences between the original and the revised edition of *The Protestant Ethic* are instructive in this regard. The final footnote in the latter version could not be more explicit about the newly acquired significance of cross-cultural comparison: "[I]n order to correct the isolation of this study and to place it in relation to the whole of cultural development, [I have] determined, first, to write down some comparative studies of the general historical relationship of religion and society" (1930b, 284n119).[8] Therefore, it is possible to see that Weber's later writings bind spatial and temporal axes of comparison to one another, for both of them become powerful interpretive devices through which to illuminate the modern West's distinctive predicament.

Having discussed the formation of Weber's cross-cultural perspective, I would now like to position it in relation to the two principal European traditions of understanding and representation of non-Western peoples in the late nineteenth and early twentieth centuries, namely naturalism and evolutionism. The first can be dealt with summarily, since references to the state of nature are nowhere to be found in Weber's writings; for him, the idea of a presocietal and precultural condition is both historically untenable and logically flawed. The sociocultural domain is the very grounds of our existence as human beings, for it constitutes the only worlds within which we live.[9] Weber's engagement with evolutionism warrants more attention for, if admitting the limitations of an overzealous cultural determinism, Weber questions the racialist grounding of evolutionary explanations of human behavior. In fact, his comparative sociology stands substantially apart from the biologically driven evolutionism of many of the leading Euro-American minds of the preceding generation, e.g., Spencer (1969 [1876–96], 1971, 1972) in sociology, as well as Tylor (1974a, 1974b [1871]), Morgan (1964 [1877]), and Frazer (1922 [1890]) in anthropology. Weber's inaugural "Freiburg Address" (1980 [1895], 448–49n4) already expresses strong reservations about hasty applications of the principles of evolution, and more specifically the Darwinian concept of natural selection, to the sociocultural realm. In the so-called "Author's Introduction" and other writings, Weber adopts an agnostic stance regarding the significance of hereditary and "racial" factors in social life, yet he is critical of the lack of evidence supporting such arguments while refusing to reduce sociology to a biologically determined science (Schnapper 1998, 84–85; Weber 1930a, 31).

Aside from objections to the racialist basis of evolutionary theory, other problems with evolutionism noted in Weber's writings should be mentioned. First, his explicit focus on the interpretive *(verstehen)* dimension of the human sciences clashes with the nomological drive of evolutionary theory; because it takes what is as given, the search for general (that is, universal and transhistorical) principles and concepts evacuates the pivotal, ever-recurring task of understanding the meaning of social action. According to Weber, the supposed "laws" of social evolution may be of some limited heuristic appeal, but since they cannot assist in making sense of a specific milieu's concrete symbols, beliefs, or practices, such "laws" remain of limited appeal and utility. The cultural significance of an event or phenomenon can only be understood if its comparative distinctiveness and specificity come to the fore. Lest this be conflated with a call for radical particularism, it should be remembered that Weber is equally critical of the tendency to isolate and to tear particular facets of reality from their sociocultural environment for the sake of analytical "clarity." Model-building and decontextualization may be the two facets of social evolutionism, though neither creates the grounds for understanding other cultures.[10] Furthermore, Weber points out that evolutionary theories frequently and implicitly legitimize the established mode of social organization by naturalizing it. Flattening the distinction between what is and what ought to be, social evolutionism normatively validates the here and now (as the highest stage of human existence) and makes it appear as necessary because seen to be the outcome of natural forces.[11] Even the Enlightenment notion of developmental progress is not spared Weber's ire. The teleological belief in intrinsic civilizational ascent over time is indicative of a naive optimism, for the modern West's dizzying institutional and technical advances have not necessarily been accompanied by cognitive, aesthetic, or moral betterment. Rationalization of social life can lead to the impoverishment of human existence, as well as the thinning of our ethical and cultural fabric.[12] For all these reasons, Weber believes, evolutionism cannot be a sound foundation for comparative research.

To come to grips with the ways in which Weber's comparative sociology distances itself from naturalism and evolutionism, I would like to explore how the ethnological imagination's three moments are given form in his writings. Given their relentlessly cross-cultural premise of necessary engagement with non-Western societies, these writings are undoubtedly some of the highest expressions of Western social theory's outward turn. The search for unfamiliar and distant sociohistorical realities is not merely an indication of openness to alterity, but more crucially for Weber, an analytical and methodological prerequisite for understanding the modern Western predicament. Recognizing cultural and historical difference is important to the extent that the presentist or universalist temptations to equate the past or another society with the modern West always threaten to lead comparative research astray. Other epochs and sociocultural universes are alternative paths of human development that, instead of signaling backwardness or simplicity, put Euro-American societies' existing social order into perspective.[13] Even Weber's principle of prima facie objectivity can be applied here: what is defended is not a positivist value-neutrality claiming an Archimedean view from nowhere, but a kind of normatively informed research striving to reflexively step back from the assumptions and prejudices of one's culture and age in order to analyze another lifeworld with an open mind.

In Weber's work can also be discovered the ethnological imagination's moment of "in-betweenness," the juxtaposition of and mediation between civilizations to identify points of convergence and divergence. Accordingly, such an exercise expands the modern West's known range of social institutions, as well as ways of life and forms of thinking. In turn, "in-betweenness" contributes to the cultivation of his brand of cultural perspectivism, which, while reserving the right to make value judgments about specific aspects of a society, steers away from hierarchical, universal, and absolute cross-civilizational models. A tart remark toward the end of the introduction to his *Collected Essays in the Sociology of Religion* illustrates this point: "[W]hoever wants a sermon should go to a conventicle. The question of the relative value of the cultures which are compared here will not receive a single word" (1930a, 29).[14] And if Weber warns against distorted interpretations of non-Western cultures caused by hasty evaluations of their supposed worth, his perspectivist position does not imply an absolute relativism; the effort to make sense of what is does not in any way entail agreement or a belief that it represents what ought to be. "'Understanding all,'" he writes, "does not mean 'pardoning all' nor does mere understanding of another's viewpoint as such lead, in principle, to its approval" (1949a, 14). This remains a lesson that, still today, cross-cultural social theory forgets at its peril. Finally, as will be elaborated upon in the following section, Weber's thought enacts the sense of critical reflexivity that constitutes the ethnological imagination's third moment. Knowledge of the vast array of possible modes of social action and thought promulgates renewed interrogation of the modern West's seemingly eternal, universal, or natural habits and creeds. From a comparative vantage point, the "self-evidentness" of such customs and beliefs is replaced by an awareness of their historical and cultural contingency.[15] Hence, Weber's cross-cultural and critical hermeneutics turns toward Western modernity, whose cultural ethos becomes strikingly peculiar and, as such, in need of explanation.

So far, this chapter has considered the development of Weber's comparative sociology, the manner in which it differs from central paradigms of intercultural interpretation during his lifetime, and the extent to which it embodies the ethnological imagination's three basic principles. We can now begin to analyze how Weber's ethnological sensibility informs his inquiries about the modern West's sociocultural and spiritual situation by highlighting three of its distinctive particularities: the Protestant ethic, whose secularization manifests itself in processes of rationalization, which are themselves made manifest in the bureaucratization of social life.

The Spiritual Roots of Socioeconomic Conduct

Weber's contribution to and use of the ethnological imagination are striking in light of his project of critically interpreting the cultural ethos defining the North Atlantic region. At one level, comparative research enables him to discover the *differentia specifica* of Western modernity, that is to say, its creation of a habitus and processes of institutionalizing rational capitalism. Yet in addition, juxtaposition to systems of socioeconomic organization existing in the past and in other societies, including nonrationalized forms of capitalism, puts into question the taken-for-granted character of the bourgeois worldview and associated practices; once their intercultural and historical singularity shines forth, they can be examined with renewed scrunity and insight. Accordingly, Weber's comparative sociology of world religions is less preoccupied with their strictly theological aspects than with their varied influence on the self's socioeconomic conduct. Spiritual doctrines are therefore viewed as techniques of "ethical rationalization of life conduct" (Weber 1946c, 270), ensembles of rituals and beliefs designed to connect the sacred and the profane into a meaningful totality for the individual believer.[16]

To appreciate the significance of cross-cultural thought for Weber's analysis of the specificities of the modern West, I would like to begin by underlining a key distinction between Asian and Western Protestant religions. Whereas the former's cosmocentrism supports a vision of its followers as vessels of the divine, receivers and carriers of immutable and transcendental forces, the latter's theocentrism encourages the faithful to perceive themselves as tools of God devoted to the transformation of the profane world on earth in accordance with the sacred kingdom beyond.[17] Weber thus argues that "Eastern" religious rituals foster two types of subjective engagement with the immanent: a rejection and a turning away from it, prompting flight from the world (in Hinduism and Buddhism); and an affirmation of the world, fostering adjustment to it (in Confucianism and to a lesser extent, Taoism). The first set of Asian religions favor gnosis as the proper route to enlightenment—namely, the severance of our ties to the profane realm through contemplation and mysticism.[18] The Confucian doctrine, for its part, insists on humankind's harmonious accommodation to the given order of the world in order to avoid disrupting its delicate balance.[19] Taken together, all four of these religious systems believe in the impersonal nature of the divine, the presence in the immanent of traces of the sacred or the traditional to be discovered in both animate and inanimate beings. The individual is a vessel carrying the sacred suffusing his or her surroundings, a perspective whose consequences are captured in an essential passage from *The Religion of China*:

> Not reaching beyond this world, the individual necessarily lacked an autonomous counterweight in confronting this world. Confucianism facilitated the taming of the masses as well as the dignified bearing of the gentleman, but the style of life thus achieved must necessarily be characterized by essentially negative traits. Such a way of life could not allow man an inward aspiration toward a "unified personality," a striving which we associate with the idea of personality. Life remained a series of occurrences. It did not become a whole placed methodically under a transcendental goal. The contrast between this socio-ethical position and the whole religious ethic of the Occident was unbridgeable. (Weber 1951, 235)

Preserved intact, the Asian magical garden cannot give rise to rational capitalism.

I would contend that it is only once we become familiar with Weber's conception of Asian religions that his argument about the cultural and historical novelty of Protestant Puritanism fully comes into its own. The theocentric notion of the individual as a tool of God constitutes a radical break with Asian cosmocentrism, for access to the divine is achieved by concrete involvement in the world rather than by escaping or devaluing it. Weber shows that ascetic Protestantism seeks to resolve the tension between a transcendental god and the ethically irrational immanent world through deliberate human intervention directed at reshaping the latter. Action in everyday life is proof of one's calling, a way to establish a personal bond with the divine that vividly contrasts with the "passivity" of contemplation and the search for revelation. In addition, human intervention in the Puritan's surroundings is vital for refashioning them in God's image; they become a stage upon which the believer must inscribe sacred designs. In a comparatively peculiar manner, this kind of active asceticism strives to realize nothing less than mastery of believers' inner and outer universes.[20]

Although Weber's widely known analysis of the Protestant ethic need not be revisited here in any great detail, a few remarks about its ethnological foundation should nevertheless be raised. Weber excels in denaturalizing and defamiliarizing Protestantism's active and inner-worldly type of asceticism by demonstrating how it breaks with theological tradition and humankind's philosophico-anthropological inclinations. Through historical and cross-cultural means, the meticulous, continuous, and calculated accumulation of wealth and pursuit of profit for the grace of God (and even more strangely, in a post-Protestant context, for its own sake) is thereby radically estranged:

> But it is just that which seems to the pre-capitalistic man so incomprehensible and mysterious, so unworthy and contemptible. That anyone should be able to make it the sole purpose of his life-work, to sink into the grave weighed down with a great material load of money and goods, seems to him explicable only as the product of a perverse instinct, the *auri sacra fames*. (Weber 1930b, 71–72)

Comparatively speaking, *homo economicus* is an odd creature indeed, one whose personality is culturally and historically specific rather than universal, eternal, or given. Weber argues that the Protestant ethic reverses the conventional suspicion of material wealth formalized in numerous religious prescriptions against the corrosive influence of riches, such as the vow of poverty, even mendicancy, undertaken by some Buddhist and Christian monastic orders. Other magical and theological doctrines have proved deeply resistant to the rationalization of economic life, most often leaving such matters to the grace of sacred powers. Because the divine and the economy, that most profane of realms, have generally been seen as incommensurable, an unresolved tension has existed between them. With ascetic Protestantism, Weber believes, this tension disappears: profit-making is not merely tolerated as a necessary evil segregated from the sacred, but embraced as the point of reconciliation of life on earth and in heaven—in other words, the earthly means by which one's worthiness to ascend to the beyond may be proven. Converging in the ideal of the vocation, the concepts of predestination and calling transform tangible economic activity into a gauge of religious salvation. Contrary to what occurs elsewhere and in the past, the bourgeois deed par excellence, that of immersing oneself in the day-to-day running of one's business, is no longer devalued as an uncultured, trivial, or idle practice shunned by the leading sectors of society. Instead, it becomes an indicator of theological distinction, a vehicle through which God's favor can be put on display for the believer's social circles.[21]

Weber claims that, in addition to its inversion of most religious teaching, Puritanism domesticates the philosophico-anthropological impulse toward hedonism by way of ascetic rationalism. Rather than being realized through immediate gratification or the quest for instantaneous pleasure, the good life is attained through the single-minded, self-denying, and disciplined pursuit of one's calling while bliss is perpetually delayed until admittance beyond the gates of heaven. Other religious creeds inculcate a belief in retribution, according to which conduct on earth determines the shape of the afterlife (for instance, the Buddhist conception of reincarnation or the Catholic belief in eternal judgment). The Protestant idea of predestination moves in the opposite direction, since inner-worldly action serves to prove one's worth and demonstrate one's chosen status. In Weber's understanding, then, Protestantism contains no safety valve to temporarily release the individual from the pressure of consistently enacting divinely decreed virtue (unlike, say, the Catholic rite of confession or Indian orgiastic practices). The Puritan ratchet tightens, its spiritual corset binding the believer's movements to the point where one, and only one, course of economic activity remains viable: hard work, accompanied by the rationalized saving and investing of capital to ensure its exponential growth.[22]

The originality of Weber's analysis, I would argue, stems from the manner in which the ethnological imagination is used to denote Puritanism's invention of mechanisms for regulating daily existence and capillary techniques for managing the human soul that revolutionize the modern subject's personality and worldview.[23] Most nonmodern and non-Western moral-cum-theological systems have formulated a series of prescriptions and prohibitions to be heeded in public, yet stop at the doorstep of the faithful's home or place of work; sacredness is concentrated in particular sites (e.g., temple, church, synagogue, monastery) as well as at specific times (such as religious festivals and holidays). Outside of these locales and periods, however, the general population's profane existence is hardly regulated, thereby leaving the self immersed in a vast space of personal volition and arbitrariness beyond religious intervention.[24] According to Weber, this means that rational capitalism could not take off in China, for example, because of the absence of a rationalized "Chinese ethos" (1951, 104) that would penetrate the everyday lives of the masses. Not so with what he terms the "tyranny of Puritanism" (1930b, 37), which strives to bring all facets of one's public and private existence under its aegis. At every step and every moment, behavior is subjected to the strict gaze of a divine force penetrating every fiber of the rich texture of mundane life. At first under a religious guise, though later discarding even that, ascetic rationalism colonizes the modern West's lifeworld to an extent impossible at any other time or place. In Weber's mind, the contrast with the Asian magical garden could not be greater.[25]

This magical garden is what allows him to realize the historical and cultural distinctiveness of the Puritan concept of moral self-regulation. Non-Western religions operate through a sovereign, top-down model of power, whereby authority rests with a centralized body or elite group (e.g., church, religious leadership, monastic order) acting as an intermediary between the sacred and the profane. The Reformation dispensed with such a split between the virtuosi and the masses by squarely shifting the emphasis onto an individualized ethic formed through the believer's direct relationship with the divine; at bottom, the Protestant views himself or herself as alone and naked in the face of God. Thus, according to Weber, ascetic Protestantism effectively displaces the locus of the sociocultural regulation of conduct from external institutions to the faithful's (and later the bourgeois's) own conscience. Ascriptive and prescriptive canons are incorporated into the self's constitution of his or her personality, which bears the weight of staving off the pleasures of the flesh; the temptations of evil, the dark abyss of sin, lurk around every corner of the soul's spiritual labyrinth. Only intense self-discipline honed into an all-enveloping, thoroughly rationalized, and uncompromisingly sober style of life can save the believer.[26] This represents the rich soil within which rational capitalism takes root.

And yet, in Weber's writings, the Reformation inauspiciously and

unintentionally unleashed the forces of what was to eventually become a self-referential, post-Protestant capitalist universe in which
the pursuit of profit is converted into an end in itself. Bourgeois
modes of conduct no longer require support from traditional or transcendental sources. In fact, capitalist practices and beliefs themselves
begin to feverishly colonize everyday life, thus inverting other societies' and epochs' subsumption of the profane to metaphysical devices
of legitimation. As "the cradle of modern economic man" (Weber
1930b, 174), ascetic Protestantism facilitates the birth of rational
capitalism, which itself fosters the rationalization of modern social
life in the Western world.[27]

Rationalization and Its Discontents

The ethnological imagination is, I would argue, essential to Weber's
identification of the dynamics of rationalization that distinguish
modern Euro-American societies from other sociohistorical formations. Indeed, it is principally through his comparative sociology
of civilizations that he is able to denote the unique and problematic plight of Western modernity, where purposive-instrumental rationality *(Zweckrationalität)* transcends its theological origins to advance to an extent and with an intensity witnessed nowhere else and
at no other time. Although weaned at the bosom of Protestantism,
rationalization turns against the latter by extracting the kernel of
formal rationality from the shell of religious faith. Once this shell is
discarded, what remains is the accelerating and unlimited spread of
rationalizing processes across the social field, as well as their burrow-
ing into society's deepest recesses. Of course, Weber acknowledges
that rationalized behavior has been present in non-Western settings,
but exclusively among elite groups (e.g., the Chinese literati and mandarins, the Indian Brahmans) as a marker of distinction vis-à-vis the
masses. By contrast, the modern West's innovation is to pave a path
for the massification or popularization of rationalization, a trickling
down from the rarefied air of the illuminati to the prosaic world of
the ordinary subject. Initially existing in specific social institutions
(the monastery, the state, the corporation, and so forth), rationalizing
forces gradually and relentlessly mold the conduct of each individual.

Another aspect of the modern West's comparative peculiarity
stems from the fact that its dynamics of rationalization combat any
countervailing practices and phenomena. Across various ages and

places, the application of purposive-instrumental rationality has been combined with, and thus tempered by, other modes of social action (value-rational or substantive, affectual and traditional). In these settings, the formalization of specific areas of social life must be justified by calling upon nonrationalized ways of acting and thinking; the use of instrumental logic to restructure institutions or train segments of the population necessarily depends on inherited, "irrational," or transcendental systems (e.g., tradition, magic, charisma, patriarchalism, and patrimonialism). Such systems function according to inherited codes of rights and responsibilities by which the master's power can be exercised in an essentially discretionary manner. The legitimacy of his position is based on blood and kinship ties rather than expertise or skill. Hence, the patriarchal or patrimonial ruler can, within certain bounds, let his subjective preferences, values, and emotions color his judgment. For Weber, this signifies that non-modern and non-Western modes of social organization are imbued with arbitrariness, an ad hoc character resisting complete formalization. The arbitrary nature of charismatic authority, which thrives on blind personal devotion or utter submission to a leader, is even more pronounced. Weber claims that charisma flaunts all conventions and rules, and that it is thereby immune to rationalization because of the bond of trust built up between the prophet and his or her followers.[28] Accordingly, he portrays Asia as a vast magical garden: the supernatural is completely integrated into Hinduism and Taoism, whereas Confucianism tolerates it among the general population. This magical garden is geared toward harmonious reconciliation with the past or the beyond, whether through worship of ancestral spirits dwelling at the surface of the visible world (as in animism), or yet again reverence for the inviolable routines of ancient codes (for instance, the Indian caste system). Asian societies provide their members with a preestablished and fully integrated worldview to make sense of the relationship between humankind and the cosmos. The precepts of the true, the beautiful, and the good are meshed together in a way that gives each individual a sense of the meaning of life while legitimizing the established social order.[29]

    According to Weber, North Atlantic processes of rationalization gradually stamp out the magical garden, resulting in a modern condition of demagification *(Entzauberung)* or disenchantment of the world—that is, loss of belief in the inherent meaning of the universe or of human existence itself. The gap with nonmodern societies is considerable, as he makes clear in a key passage from his "Intermediate Reflections" ("Religious Rejections of the World and Their Directions"):

> The peasant, like Abraham, could die "satiated with life." The feudal landlord and the warrior hero could do likewise. For both fulfilled a cycle of their existence beyond which they did not reach. Each in his own way could attain an inner-worldly perfection as a result of the naive unambiguity of the substance of his life. But the "cultivated" man who strives for self-perfection, in the sense of acquiring or creating "cultural values," cannot do this. He can become "weary of life" but he cannot become "satiated with life" in the sense of completing a cycle. . . . Hence the harnessing of man into this external and internal cosmos of culture can offer the less likelihood that an individual would absorb either culture as a whole or what in any sense is "essential" in culture. It thus becomes less and less likely that "culture" and the striving for culture can have any inner-worldly meaning for the individual. (1946e, 356)

From the moment the meaning of existence and that of the existing mode of social organization descend from the immutable realm of the transcendental to the transient plane of the immanent, they become exposed to radical and perpetual questioning. Since the rapid proliferation of postmetaphysical outlooks precludes any decisive appeal to the beyond or the customary, differentiated, competing, and even incommensurable value spheres clash with one another; truth, goodness, and beauty can no longer be equated with each other a priori, for the domains of logic, ethics, and aesthetics follow separate paths in a universe "robbed of gods" (Weber 1946c, 282). The suggestive analogy of polytheism lodged at the center of "Science as a Vocation" (Weber 1946b, 147–48) conveys this fragmentation and pluralization of worldview. No single, synthetic Weltanschauung can ever again quell the war between the gods and demons of life, the ever-recurring collision of normative systems in the modern West's maelstrom.[30]

Weber's writings suggest that, beyond the demagification of the world, the unbounded character of rationalization opens the door to the pathological prospect of its becoming the modern West's dominant, and perhaps even singular, sociocultural logic. Purposive-instrumental rationality thus tends toward self-referentiality and self-validation, since it becomes incapable of, or unwilling to, incorporate criteria deemed to function outside of its cognitive boundaries. Any action or thought that cannot be converted into a means for attaining a specific end is considered extraneous to the task at hand, or dismissed as an obstruction to the realization of such an outcome. This is embodied in the modern bureaucratic mindset, which aims to strip social reality of its qualitative dimension in order to reduce it to a series of easily manipulated, generic parameters that can then be operationalized to resolve practical problems.[31] In vivid contrast to the uncontested primacy of the interpersonal in traditional or charismatic social relations, modern Western bureaucracy is an institutionalized technique for the legitimization of sociopolitical domination built around the total depersonalization, "juridification," and apparent objectification of power. The individual does not answer to an embodied leader (e.g., master, prince, prophet), but obeys a system of abstract rules and regulations originating from either a rigid organizational structure or the letter of the law. At bottom, as Weber (1978a, 975) puts it, the bureaucratic machine operates "without regard for persons."[32]

For the first time anywhere, the dynamics of rationalization are free to operate for their own sake, without deriving final authority from some sort of greater good; in fact, they become their own greater good. Consequently, in Habermasian terms, rationalization should be viewed not only as the formalization and instrumentalization of modern society's economic and administrative subsystems, but as a powerful force of colonization of the lifeworld that attempts to subject previously nonrationalized modes of action and thought to its unwielding dominion. It "de-ethicalizes" individual and collective conduct, as exemplified in the bureaucratic outlook, which evacuates considerations of the good from the tasks of decision-making and execution, or yet again simply dilutes the good into a problem-solving concept—that is to say, what is technically efficient, precise, and predictable. Bureaucratization revolutionizes social life from without: it gets underway by transforming institutional structures, then strives to train the individual to become an obedient subject, a proverbial cog in the machine with little room left for the exercise of her or his conscience or reflexive judgment.[33] At this point, Weber believes, a process of irrational rationalization is inaugurated, for once formal rationality is pushed to unsuspected heights and is uncoupled from any steering mechanism, it begins to turn against humankind. Supposed to free humankind from the "Dark Ages" of superstition and ignorance, thinking is converted into a tool of domination for mastering the social and natural worlds. Underlying Weber's concern is the possible disappearance of a normative threshold that rationalization cannot cross, such as the Kantian categorical imperative. Now everything and, worst of all, everyone, can be instrumentalized. Hence the celebrated image of the "iron cage" (Weber 1930b, 181) or more accurately, of the "steel-hard casing" (Weber 2002, 123–24), which envelops modern subjects: upon their backs and within their souls, they bear the heavy burden of the lure of a superficial materialism coupled with the mechanizing formalization of social life.[34]

How can the self react to the rationalization of daily existence and this mode of social organization? The answer, I would contend, lies somewhere within Weber's ambivalent diagnosis of Western modernity—a diagnosis arrived at through a densely cross-cultural and historical vantage point. On the one hand, the potential for personal autonomy blossoms because society is stripped of the belief in extrasocial or transcendental factors in its instituting. As we will see below, the opportunities for self-cultivation *(Bildung)* and the development of forms of life conduct combining an ethic of conviction with one of responsibility have never been stronger or more numerous. On the other hand, heteronomous forces haunt Euro-American settings, both by way of the deplorable embrace of the bureaucratic specialist and through the seductive siren calls of charisma. Through comparative research, Weber demonstrates that the bureaucratization of Western society fosters a culturally and historically aberrant cult of specialization symbolized by the ascendancy of the *Fachmensch* over the *Kulturmensch*. In all other sociohistorical contexts, the reverse is true: cultivation of the self aims to create a complete personality, well versed in a host of spiritual, literary, and philosophical traditions. This is the case with the elite training regimes of the Indian Brahmans and the Chinese literati, yet even bureaucratic education is different in China, where the mandarins are perceived as a ruling intelligentsia, rather than a cohort of administrative experts:

> The Confucian aspirant to office, stemming from the old tradition, could hardly help viewing a specialized, professional training of European stamp as anything but a conditioning in the dirtiest Philistinism. . . . The fundamental assertion, "a cultured man is not a tool" meant that he was an end in himself and not just a means for a specified useful purpose. (Weber 1951, 160)

Western culture itself is founded on humanist ideals that are not readily compatible with functional specialization. The Schillerian and Goethian vision of the cultivated person, striving toward the fullness of subjectivity through *Bildung,* proves resistant to bureaucratic operationalization.[35]

By presenting specialization as a singular, even isolated, trend informed by the dynamics of capitalism and bureaucratization, Weber intends to estrange and problematize it. It is only recently and locally that expert knowledge bolstered by formal qualifications has become the measure of a person's merit. Without applied outcomes, erudition for its own sake is disregarded. Instead of general culture and breadth attempting to embrace the store of human creation, the exercise of a specific function and mastery of narrow, predetermined areas of expertise are the distinguishing traits of the bureaucratic personality (Weber 1946b, 134–35). This marks the sociocultural victory of the *Fachmenschen,* the "specialists without spirit" so derided by Nietzsche; the steel-hard casing weighs heavily on our shoulders.[36] In such a context, heteronomy proliferates anew, for if ancestral customs or heavenly decrees are no longer believed to dictate the shape of the social order, citizens have lost their ability to influence and their interest in the processes of the latter's self-instituting. The determination of the mode of social organization is left to machine-like sociopolitical structures populated by bureaucratic specialists. Most individuals blink like the Nietzschean last men, those personifications of cultural mediocrity who believe they have invented happiness. They may have stepped outside of the Asian magical garden, but they graze, herdlike, on the modern West's perfectly manicured lawns. Of course, Weber is not claiming that modernity can be unidimensionally understood as the unfolding of the juggernaut of rationalization, for nonrationalized, disruptive, and creative counterforces survive in Euro-American societies. Chief among them is charisma, the uncontrollable and unpredictable power of the bond between a leader and his followers—an intensely personal and deeply emotional affair.[37] And though he admits that the aura of charismatic prophets and demagogues shines brightly in a demagified universe, Weber clearly believes that this kind of flight from the modern predicament cannot be the path to follow. No deus ex machina will save us. In contrast to nonmodern and non-Western worlds satiated with the transcendental, the sacred, or the magical, we have feasted on the tree of knowledge; the here and now must be envisaged as the totality of our experience, for nothing can be found beyond or underneath it.

If other societies' self-understandings appear to be traditionally inherited or transcendentally given, one of the particularities of Western modernity, according to Weber, is its demand that individuals create meaning themselves by forging a personal ethos of everyday existence. In the age of bureaucratic specialization and rationalization, this ethos cannot be modeled upon that of the Chinese literati, Indian Brahman, or even the much-fabled "Renaissance Man," however appealing all of them may be. Instead, it must adapt the humanist ideal of self-cultivation to the modern West's realities, in order to arrive at a different sort of *Kulturmensch*: neither a small-minded specialist, nor an overwrought universal spirit, but a "cultivated specialist" (Schluchter 1996, 30). Finding one's secular calling, and then unflinchingly yet responsibly dedicating oneself to it, constitutes the only viable kind of life conduct in the modern world.[38] For Weber, cultivated specialization holds the key to "re-ethicalizing" a social life that has been colonized by purposive-instrumental rationality. Under normatively polytheistic conditions, then, the duty of each person consists of selecting which ethical system to follow, as well as enacting it in one's daily existence in civil society. The personality capable of confronting the tribulations of modernity must strive to reconcile demands that other societies and ages have held to be incommensurable, namely what Weber terms the "ethic of responsibility" and the "ethic of conviction." Great moral-cum-political ideals and beliefs must inspire us to pursue the good life and to realize the good society, but always with the sobering influence of the imperative to take responsibility for the effects of one's actions—including, of course, for their unintended consequences, which are constitutive of a kind of historical agnosticism that exists beyond rationalization.[39] In other words, Weber holds that the "re-ethicalization" of life conduct takes place *with* regard for persons and, as such, represents the very negation of the bureaucratic ethos. Maturity of character is attained by relentlessly facing the implications of a rationalized, demagified world without escaping into irrational or hyperrationalist illusions; neither the nonmodern religious leader nor the Western bureaucrat can teach us how to live. Only the harmonious blending of creative passion and stoic sobriety, of the devotion to one's vocation through a secular yet ethically bound asceticism, can guide us through the perils of Western modernity.[40] Having compared and contrasted the worldviews of different societies and periods, Weber is convinced that this novel way of life is as necessary as it is strange.

Conclusion

Throughout this chapter, I have argued that Weber's comparative sociology offers one of the richest instances of social theory's cross-culturally grounded critical hermeneutics of Western modernity and that, by virtue of this, it has vitally contributed to the elaboration of the ethnological imagination. In contradistinction to the naturalizing and evolutionary tendencies of late nineteenth- and early twentieth-century paradigms of representation of non-Western societies, Weber developed a cultural perspectivism that decouples intercultural analysis of different civilizations from hierarchical judgment of their overall worth. I have also claimed that his substantive inquiries into the history of Asian theological-cum-moral practices and beliefs significantly informed his grasp and questioning of modern Euro-American societies' distinctiveness. As such, his juxtaposition of cosmocentric and theocentric religious doctrines enables him to identify the specificity of the Protestant ethic's inner-worldly asceticism. In addition, for Weber, a secularized and post-transcendental version of this asceticism represents one of the forces driving the rationalization and demagification of modern Western social life—the consequences of which are made all the more salient by what he believes to be a holistic and nonrationalized "Oriental" magical garden. Even his critical examination of the so-called "iron cage" is premised on his cross-cultural viewpoint: beyond shallow materialism and soulless bureaucratic specialization, other possibilities for social organization and individual conduct (from the Confucian and Enlightenment *Kulturmensch* to the reethicalization of the public sphere stimulated by a new ethos of modern existence), have existed before and elsewhere, and indeed should be envisaged today.

Hence, Weber can be read in the lineage of the other figures discussed in these pages. After Rousseau and Marx's important initial steps, Weber consolidated the ethnological imagination's standing by placing comparative research at the very heart of the social-theoretical enterprise. Based on his writings, it is clear that few adequate studies of the modern condition in the Western world could dispense with civilizational investigations. Moreover, laying the foundations for future comparativism, he inflected a more "realist" and interpretive imperative to the process of engagement with, and representation of, cultural otherness. Despite being tinged by certain Orientalist pre-conceptions, his work reveals a prescient effort to open-mindedly come to terms with non-Western societies' self-understandings and to portray them in an analytical manner that is quite removed from the fantastic myths of alterity sustained during the early parts of the modern era. In this, he was close to Durkheim, his fellow founder of the discipline of sociology, who developed its anthropological aspects. And yet the reception of their work within their respective national intellectual environments could not have been more different. Weber's investigations of Asia have had relatively few repercussions in German theoretical circles, while Durkheim's anthropological sociology pushed forward a French tradition whose influence can be witnessed to this day.

Four

In the Shadow of the Other:
Durkheim's Anthropological Sociology

I have already suggested that Durkheim can usefully be regrouped with Weber, for the two set up the classical undergirding of comparative social theory while contributing to the cultivation of the ethnological imagination in their distinctive manners. Indeed, what is particularly interesting for my purposes is that two of the founders of sociology as a discipline viewed it as inextricably cross-cultural. If Weber investigated its civilizational aspects, Durkheim elected to explore its more strictly anthropological connections. And despite the increasingly rigid disciplinary barriers being erected during his lifetime, notably in the English-speaking world, Durkheim's writings remain remarkable in their artful blending of sociological and anthropological insights about various modes of social organization in the past and the present. In this, he was following the lead of his intellectual predecessors (Montaigne, Montesquieu, Rousseau), yet also remaining true to the inclinations of what has come to be known as the French school of sociology and anthropology. This school, which encompassed an exceptional group of researchers revolving around Durkheim and Mauss in the early decades of the twentieth century, pioneered a brand of anthropologically inflected social research that turned its attention to cultural practices outside of and completely different from those prevailing in modern Europe. Implicitly, and sometimes explicitly, the French school's studies of, inter alia, the gift economy, sacrifice, magic, and sacredness were intended to affect an intercultural critique of the defining processes and institutions of Western modernity (capitalism, rationalization, anomie, and so on)—processes and institutions that were being questioned like never before in the context of lingering fin de siècle anxieties and the collective disillusionment resulting from the Great War.[1]

Today, the writings of most members of the French school are better remembered in anthropological circles, no doubt due to the fact that their ostensible objects of study (namely, beliefs and rituals in "primitive" societies) are widely believed to lie outside the geographical and thematic scope of sociological inquiry. Yet Durkheim is the exception here, having been consecrated as a founder of sociology because the bulk of his work was focused on the modern condition in the West and because of his success in academically institutionalizing the discipline in France. I would contend, however, that this sociological canonization of Durkheim generally neglects to ponder the extent to which his insightfulness about Euro-American societies is made possible by his ethnological imagination, that is, by the crosscultural inflection of his critical hermeneutics of Western modernity. The latter claim may initially seem rather surprising, for critical is hardly an adjective that one readily associates with Durkheim; he is certainly not a radical critic of modern society in the vein of, say, Rousseau, Marx, or Foucault. His early conception of sociology as a problem-solving science, his modernism, corporatism, and moral sociocentrism—to say nothing of his interest in social order as well as in mechanisms of societal integration and the regulation of individual behavior—none of this is the stuff of critical theory. Nevertheless, his legacy is more complex than is often understood, particularly if the work of his later years is taken into account. There, his initial modernist faith in industrial society's capacity to resolve its sociocultural pathologies is counterbalanced by the recognition of such pathologies' potentially intractable character; anomie may be the fate of the modern Western individual, and moral malaise our collective predicament, brought about by the processes of modernization. Moreover, both Durkheim's ethnological sensibility and what can best be described as his corporatist-cum-guild socialism enable him to simultaneously identify these pathologies and situate them historically and culturally. Never naturalized or universalized, they are shown to emerge out of specific processes of modern society's self-instituting since the French and Industrial Revolutions.

Accordingly, to understand how Durkheim has created an anthropological sociology with certain critical inclinations, I am proposing to examine in greater detail his intercultural diagnosis of Western modernity. His thinking can be organized around four main axes, each designating what he believes to be a comparative particularity of the North Atlantic region: the emergence of scientific rationalism, the advent of industrialization, the process of individuation, and the moral crisis ensuing from the scale and speed of these three transformations. But before plunging into the substance of Durkheim's work, a preliminary step should be undertaken: a discussion of the making of his anthropologically informed sociology, and more broadly, of his contribution to Western social theory's ethnological imagination.

Sociology's "Anthropologization"

Though one of the richest elements of Durkheim's thought, the entwining of sociology and anthropology, and their respective subject matters (the modern and the "primitive," respectively), was not always already present in his writings. Rather, the ethnological imagination was born out of his gradual realization of the merits of cross-cultural research. In his earlier work, Durkheim was quick to consider ethnographic material as unsuitable to the nascent science of society. Because he believed that anthropological knowledge was overwhelmingly composed of haphazard and unreliable travelers' reports, it could only represent a supplement to the more established field of historiography; with its methodological rigor and empirical accuracy, it was history that would serve as a blueprint for sociology.[2] Over time, Durkheim was to revise this opinion so dramatically that *The Elementary Forms of Religious Life*, his last major work and magnum opus, defends ethnography against the scorn of traditional historians. Far from acting as the handmaiden of history, anthropology was given its *lettres de noblesse* by becoming one of his privileged sources of theoretical inspiration and empirical information about humanity's varied forms of social life. Without Spencer and Gillen's *Native Tribes of Central Australia* (1899), *The Elementary Forms* itself is scarcely conceivable. More generally, Durkheim's inquiries into "primitive" rituals and belief systems increasingly came to inform the conceptual and institutional frameworks with which he critically interpreted Western modernity, and vice versa. Two examples should suffice to make this point: the notion of collective consciousness, mostly present in nonmodern or non-Western societies, is applied to analyze social representations in the modern Euro-American world, while his overarching interest in morality in the latter context prompts him to examine more closely religious rituals and beliefs among indigenous peoples.[3]

How is Durkheim's ethnological imagination related to his era's principal modes of representation and analysis of "primitive" societies, naturalism and evolutionism? In a word, he clearly rejects the first while being more ambiguous about the second. His writings constantly debunk the myth of the state of nature, notably Rousseau's celebrated rendition of it. The idea of a presocial and self-sufficient subject cannot be logically or historically sustained; one of its many misleading consequences is the promotion of extreme individualism, since the self is believed to have chronological and normative precedence over what appears to be an artificially created society. Durkheim is equally critical of collectivist versions of the state of nature narrative, which he argues underpin much communist doctrine. Unlike his own brand of corporatist and guild socialism, communism is judged to be primitivist and exceedingly romantic, for it advocates an escape from capitalist society toward a fictionalized past, during which equality reigned supreme because social differentiation had not yet taken root. Durkheim suggests that the state of nature, if it had ever existed, would have been a quasi-bestial condition deprived of the basic sources of our humanity. It would have been both asocial and amoral, characterized by the absence of social integration of persons as well as the lack of social regulation of their instincts and desires.[4] Without moral ideals and constraints to curb his instinctual selfishness, "natural man" would either be living in a Hobbesian state of warfare of all against all, or a condition of perpetual dissatisfaction caused by his inability to satisfy insatiable wants.

To further undermine the lure of the state of nature, Durkheim (1960, 85) poses a rhetorical question: "Granting that society is not in nature, must we conclude that it is contrary to nature, that it is and can be only a corruption of human nature, the consequence of some sort of fall and degeneration; in short, that society as such is an evil that can be reduced but not eliminated?" The sociocentric character of his body of work is intended to provide an emphatically negative answer, one that defends society as a positive transcendence of nature and celebrates humankind's exclusive dwelling in the social. The socio-cultural environments created by human action must not strive to imitate the natural world (and even less a mythical state of nature), but to emancipate themselves from reliance upon it. Pace Rousseau, then, modern society must not draw upon or search for extrasocial forces. Instead, it must concentrate on the processes of its self-institution, organizing itself according to rational principles. Our "humanness," Durkheim asserts, is constituted through society, by participating in social life and responding to various institutions' regulative and integrative mechanisms. In other words, socialization, the acquisition of norms and customs through, inter alia, language, family, education, religion, and law, is the sine qua non of our existence as moral and social beings. Individuals are ontologically enmeshed in the historical and cultural fabric of their surroundings, for as Durkheim repeatedly declares, society is "what is best in us," the source and guardian of civilization.[5] Within industrial civilization, Durkheim believes, personality cannot be modeled on Rousseau's civilized savage; instead, it must embody the Enlightenment and republican ideal of autonomy; that is, of struggle toward rational self-mastery through the overcoming of egoistic drives and participation in the elaboration of collective values and rules to be respected by all.[6]

Though Durkheim may renounce the idea of the state of nature, he is much less clear about the standing of the other popular framework of cross-cultural analysis in the late nineteenth and early twentieth centuries, evolutionism. In fact, one can speak of an enduring, albeit progressively receding, tension between the latter and cultural perspectivism in his writings. On the one hand, he retains certain evolutionary assumptions inherited from his intellectual predecessors and contemporaries, such as Spencer's organicist claims about the increase of a given society's degree of differentiation, scale, and complexity over time. Durkheim's Latin thesis even criticizes Montesquieu (1952 [1748]) for failing to superimpose an evolutionary conception of progress onto his political taxonomy. *The Spirit of Laws'* tripartite classification of "species of government" (republican, monarchic, and despotic) stops short of suggesting a diachronic movement from simpler to more complex societies.[7] On the whole, Durkheim tends to suggest that "primitive" societies are structurally simpler than those of the modern West.

On the other hand, I would contend that Durkheim's writings identify three of evolutionism's major flaws: first it assumes (rather than demonstrates) a tenuous causal relationship between earlier and later stages of human progress; second, it conceives of the existence of a single, unilinear mode of social organization applicable to all cultures and in so doing, patently violates humanity's observable diversity; third, it contains a teleological view of history, according to which modernity is believed to be the final stage toward which every society is moving.[8] Hence, Durkheim expresses his reservations vis-à-vis Comte's (1975a, 1975b [1830–42]) theory of the three states of humankind (from theological to metaphysical, and finally to positive), in addition to partially distancing himself from Spencer.[9] Furthermore, he opposes the idea of constructing a universal, evolutionary "scale of civilization" (Tylor 1974a, 24) along which all sociohistorical constellations could be measured—something that exists not only in Spencer's writings and Darwin's *The Descent of Man* (1981 [1871]), but also in the works of the founders of Anglo-American academic anthropology: Tylor's *Primitive Culture* (1974a, 1974b [1871]), Morgan's *Ancient Society* (1964 [1877]), and Frazer's *Golden Bough* (1922 [1890]). In a lengthy footnote to *The Rules of Sociological Method,* Durkheim explicitly rejects the hierarchical classification of cultures according to their supposed degree of civilization. Such taxonomies are based on criteria too complex or variable to be of any lasting usefulness, to say nothing of the fact that they are unable to take into account the specificities of each society (Durkheim 1927, 109n1).

Durkheim's later work makes his fraught relationship to evolutionism still more apparent. While he believes "primitive" societies are analytically useful in that they allow us to study sociocultural institutions in their most basic and least differentiated forms, it does not follow that such societies can be considered earlier stages of human development. Comparative thinking is not an occasion to go back in time, but to extrapolate the functioning of social structures in more complex settings:

> There are no longer any "genuine primitives": I said this on the first page of my book *[The Elementary Forms of Religious Life].* There is no doubt that the Australians have a long history behind them, as have all known peoples. I chose them simply because I found among them a religion that surpassed in simplicity all others of which I knew and which it seemed to me could be explained with-

out it being necessary to refer to an antecedent religion. If another religion is found that is still more simple, then let us study it, but for the time being it is useless to speak about this. (Durkheim, quoted in Lukes 1985, 519)

Even Durkheim's attributes of simplicity and complexity should not hastily be translated to signify that he posits an evolutionary continuum across time and space. If he accepts the idea of intrasocietal evolution, Durkheim falls short of embracing it intersocietally; a particular society can evolve from simpler to more complex forms, yet its internal stages cannot be converted into universal historical categories, or unproblematically serve to build a uniform model of development that would make sense of other societal trajectories.[10]

Having discussed the originality of Durkheim's stance in relation to naturalism and evolutionism, I would like to consider in greater detail his mode of cross-cultural interpretation by using the framework of the ethnological imagination's three analytical moments detailed in the introduction (the outward turn, in-betweenness, and the inward turn). First of all, there is no doubt that many of Durkheim's writings, especially in his later period, demonstrate a willingness to engage with nonmodern and non-Western sociohistorical settings, thereby countering Western sociology's creeping ethnocentrism. For instance, his "Note on the Notion of Civilization," co-written with Mauss and first published in 1913, constitutes an innovative attempt to pluralize the concept of civilization while retaining its usefulness for metasocietal comparisons (Durkheim and Mauss 1969b; Rundell and Mennell 1998, 20–21). Durkheim remains open to, and even welcomes, the provocation of cultural alterity to the extent that his analyses study the effectiveness as well as the raisons d'être of other customs and belief systems in an immanent fashion. As such, he ran afoul of the dominant tendency within the human sciences in the early part of the twentieth century, namely that of condescendingly branding unfamiliar or distant worldviews and practices as altogether false, illusory, or superstitious. One need only think of Comte's (1974a, 22; 1974b, 244–45, 254–55) dismissal of humankind's so-called theological state as its childhood, or evolutionary anthropology's repudiation of "primitive" religions as inferior "cobwebs of the brain" condemned to extinction (Frazer 1922, 263).[11] Instead of disparaging other norms and modes of conduct, Durkheim is interested in making sense of what they signify for the actors themselves. Encounters with and interpretations of unknown realities are preferred to summary judgment of them.[12]

Durkheim's writings equally promote the ideas of "in-betweenness" and intercultural mediation, which are the basis of the ethnological imagination's second analytical moment, since they reveal constant struggles and warnings against falling prey to the principle of intrinsic incommensurability between societies. During his lifetime, the most prominent advocate of such a position was Lévy-Bruhl, according to whom a vast chasm and total incompatibility exist between the "primitive" system of thought (which is prelogical and mystical) and modern rationality. The twine shall never meet.[13] Durkheim certainly acknowledges the substantial divergences between these worldviews and the possibility of incommensurability, yet he attempts to uncover the universal building blocks that, when combined in different ways, give birth to societies. In addition to discovering some of the roots of structuralism, we should appreciate how he consequently clears the way for a lateral reorientation of the axis of cross-cultural thought and analytical movement between sociocultural universes.[14] By striving to explain the sociocultural universes of "primitive" peoples, Durkheim is contending that they represent internally valid alternatives to our modes of social organization, and therefore that the range of human possibilities is wider than hitherto believed. Agreeing with Montesquieu, he claims that the incredible diversity of systems of thought and action across time and space should be held as evidence of the existence of, and the imperative to recognize, a plurality of forms of social life. His form of cultural perspectivism demands that ideas and practices always be historically and culturally situated, at the same time that it leaves open the possibility of creating universal criteria through cross-cultural means; accordingly, the bind between false universalism and absolute relativism is avoided. The former trend is realized in the naturalization and consequent universalization of attributes existing in specific sociohistorical contexts (fin-de-siècle Europe, ancient Greece, and Rome, etc.). On this topic, a section of *The Evolution of Educational Thought* is worth quoting at some length:

> Far from being immutable, humanity is in fact involved in an interminable process of evolution, disintegration and reconstruction; far from being a unity, it is in fact infinite in its variety, with regard

to both time and place. . . . The view that there is one single moral system valid for all men at all times is no longer tenable. History teaches us that there are as many different moral systems as there are types of society; and this diversity is not the product of some mysterious blindness which has prevented men from seeing the true needs of their nature. It is, rather, simply an expression of the great diversity in the circumstances under which collective living takes place. As a result those sentiments which we would dearly like to believe are the most deeply rooted in man's congenital make-up have been wholly unknown to a host of societies. (1977, 324–25)

Hence, Durkheim denounces an ethnocentric double standard: denying the worth of non-Western societies while claiming that Western modernity serves as the sole embodiment of civilization. Each culture develops a moral system suited to its social structure. Yet the capacity to comparatively contextualize one's sociohistorical horizons within the vastness of the human universe does not imply that all such horizons are inherently equivalent to one another—nor, for that matter, that anything goes.[15]

For Durkheim, cross-cultural interpretation cannot proceed through the crude imposition of a given cognitive paradigm onto every society to be studied; one size does not fit all. The opposite reaction, that of wholeheartedly adopting the "native's" point of view, is equally erroneous in his opinion. Intercultural research must be premised on a fusion of horizons, whereby the dialogical comparison and contrast between different lifeworlds makes understanding possible. Historical and cultural gaps are never insurmountable. It is therefore not the credo of intrinsic incommensurability that advances our knowledge of the human condition, but the work of exploring the articulations of identity and difference present in each setting that form the rich tapestry of social existence. In this sense, nonmodern and non-Western societies hold a mirror up to the North Atlantic region, underscoring both its comparative peculiarities and similarities vis-à-vis the rest of the world.[16]

The ethnological imagination's third moment, the inward turn, is also visible in Durkheim's writings. An anthropologically cognizant sociology reverses its gaze to draw on its knowledge of "primitive" societies to study their modern Western counterparts. Historical and cross-cultural perspectivism can combat the naturalization, normalization, and habitualization of the here and now: "It is only because we have so become used to it that the moral order under which we live appears to us to be the only one possible; history demonstrates that it is essentially transitory in character" (Durkheim 1977, 329).[17] Although social institutions fulfill universal human requirements, their shape in particular settings depends on sociohistorical processes and conditions—it is not derived from God, nature, or even common sense. Instead of being taken for granted or believed to be necessary, existing institutional arrangements and ways of life in the Euro-American world can be relativized because they are considered to be socially and historically constructed. Moreover, comparative juxtaposition enables a critical assessment of Western modernity's accomplishments and pathologies to take place. It can be seen in a new light, as a complex blend of unprecedented progress and what Durkheim (1960, 86) terms, paraphrasing Rousseau, abject "monstrosity."

Now that I have teased out the various theoretical implications of Durkheim's ethnological imagination, the task of considering how he applies it to create one of Western social theory's richest anthropologies of modernity remains. Thus, the rest of this chapter will focus on four major phenomena that Durkheim holds to be characteristic of the modern West's historical and cross-cultural specificity: scientific rationalism, industrialism's cultural ethos, the cult of the individual, and finally the moral malaise fostered by the combined effect of the three other trends.

Scientific Rationalism and the Disenchanted Universe

In a fashion similar to that of other contributors to the ethnological imagination, Durkheim's cross-cultural perspective enables him to realize the distinctiveness of Western modernity's Cartesian-cum-scientific brand of rationalism vis-à-vis systems of thought prevailing at other times and in other places. Durkheim believes that social life in the Euro-American world has been radically transformed and permeated by the rationalist revolution, which inaugurated an unprecedented series of conceptual and cultural ruptures: of the mind from the body, heart, and soul; of the profane and the material from the sacred and the supernatural; of the social from the natural; of the subject from the object; and last but not least, of the individual from the community. These changes represent the Enlightenment's permanent legacy, which modern societies should embrace rather than seek refuge from in an age of pre-Cartesian innocence. Romantic antiscientism must thus be avoided at all costs, for it falsely idealizes the knowledges of other peoples and epochs. Processes of rationalization have spread across and seeped deep into the modern West's socio-cultural fabric, helping to overturn many inherited creeds and traditional beliefs. Science has unleashed the force of rational inquiry and self-interrogation—not because of the solitary pursuit of truth, but due to the influence of modern institutions and the intense intellectual energies released by the mass grouping of individuals in society.[18] Such a scenario is made possible through comparison with the utterly different modes of apprehending the world and forms of social organization present in non-Western societies. For Durkheim, these societies reflect a holism that does not distinguish between the categories described above (e.g., reason and emotions, sacred and profane); they invent and employ taxonomical systems that, because of their sheer otherness and intermeshing of various parts of the human experience, may at first appear arbitrary and internally contradictory, yet in fact reveal their own internal logic.[19]

According to Durkheim, the articulation of Cartesian rationalism and Comtian positivism, which characterizes earlier incarnations of his own method, can produce a remarkable level of logical clarity and abstract systematicity. Derived from Montesquieu's *Spirit of Laws* (1952 [1748]), what Durkheim terms social morphology displays a unique taxonomic power to order all observable facts into elaborate classifications organized around precise sets of criteria.[20] His groundbreaking study of suicide stands as one of the first applications of this kind of analysis in the human sciences. Quite apart from their capacity to order the world that surrounds us, modern scientific techniques facilitate cross-cultural interpretation. For the first time anywhere, human beings can strive to understand the internal dynamics that underpin foreign, seemingly strange beliefs and rituals. The social researcher is presented with the opportunity to compare and contrast civilizations across time and space in a manner and to an extent not possible in the past or elsewhere.

Nonetheless, the gradual development of Durkheim's thinking from positivism to a more hermeneutically sensitive theory of symbolism[21] indicates that he believes that modern science's taxonomic prowess must be tempered by another principle: earnest search for the immanent meaning of collective representations and types of social action that are utterly different from our own, rather than their routine dismissal and demystification as superstitious, irrational, or intrinsically false (as was done by the French philosophes and Anglo-American evolutionary anthropology). "Primitive" societies may develop symbolic frameworks, which, though outside the conventional parameters of Western thought, display high levels of complexity and logic.[22] Religion must similarly be viewed in its proper sociocultural context, since it is not designed to provide an accurate reflection of the natural world (a mirror of nature), but to put into form a society's collective consciousness and give meaning to a community's existence by generating and enacting a shared symbolic order (Durkheim 1995, 226–27, 419–21). And if his earlier work expresses a sense of unbridled optimism regarding scientific rationalism's capacity to meet the new challenges of the modern age, his later work adopts a considerably more qualified tone. The tension in his understanding of the relationship between science and religion is revealing; while he frequently contends that the latter is the ancestor of the former, he also suggests that they exist along a continuum rather than being on either side of an unbridgeable chasm.[23] Scientific and religious perspectives are alternative and contemporaneous ways of viewing the world. Science can only be a mechanism, a vehicle and a means for arriving at certain solutions or gaining a clearer understanding of the human condition. In Durkheim's hands, then, it is a reformer's tool, not an object of veneration.

Industrialization as a Cultural Logic

Scientific rationalism may well express, for Durkheim, the modern outlook's comparative specificity, but it is industrialization that engenders a series of culturally and historically peculiar changes in the fabric of Western social life. I would argue that the central problem that Durkheim ponders can be rendered in the following terms: with the rise to prominence of industrial society for the first time anywhere, how can bonds between individuals be maintained when traditional institutions, beliefs, and practices are weakened, if not entirely rejected? As is well known, his first major study finds an answer in the social division of labor, which fosters a kind of "organic solidarity" based on functional interdependence between actors performing specialized roles in modern society. Because it implicates each person in a dense network of rights and responsibilities toward others, the social division of labor resulting from industrialization is a morally binding and socially cohesive force that need not draw upon preexisting ties of kinship or locality (Durkheim 1956, 68, 117; 1984). What is significant here is that this diagnosis of Western modernity is only possible through juxtaposition with other sociohistorical environments (e.g., the ancient polis, the medieval European village, the "primitive" community), against which the outline of industrial society becomes clear; "mechanical solidarity" is attributed to societies at other times and in other places, where similarity and homogeneity ensure both social integration and regulation.[24] It should also be noted that, contrary to naturalism and evolutionism (with their notions of the amoral or immoral character of the "savage"), Durkheim's conception of mechanical solidarity posits the existence of morality in "primitive" societies, which, no less than their modern Western counterparts, are buttressed by a moral environment connected to a collective consciousness. Yet by doing this, and in accordance with his sociocentrism, Durkheim displaces the locus of morality from the self to society, or more specifically, from the subject's inner being to a sociohistorical setting's communal orientations to the world.[25]

Apart from his concern with industrialization's transformation of solidarity, Durkheim observes that it has engendered a cross-culturally and historically novel type of personality: the specialist, who strives to be fully integrated into society by becoming one of its organs. The Kantian categorical imperative is metamorphosed into a functionalist injunction: *"Equip yourself to fulfill usefully a specific function"* (Durkheim 1984, 4). Such pronouncements indicate a bold departure from the humanist vision of "Renaissance Man" (Heller 1978), the self as a work of art that should be cultivated through the utmost development of its various faculties (the *Kulturmensch*); dandyism, the movement striving toward the aestheticization of everyday life (Baudelaire 1976 [1863], 709–10), is treated as a form of dilettantism. At the same time, Durkheim is attempting to make the Romantic myth of the self-sufficient and isolated "natural man" obsolescent because ill-suited to industrial civilization. What becomes necessary is not the burgeoning of a well-rounded person or the preservation of individual independence, but the honing of particular skills complementing those of one's peers to form a dense web of social interdependence.[26]

However much Durkheim urges us to embrace the *Fachmensch*,

his position should not be mistaken for a full-fledged defense of industrial capitalism. In fact, his writings sustain a comparative critique of the rule of the market, whereby other modes of socioeconomic organization are evoked in order to underline the modern West's questionable exceptionalism. The economic sphere has gradually expanded, to the point of becoming unregulated by either the state or civic institutions. For Durkheim, this situation poses a serious problem, since in addition to becoming a self-referential domain (the fictional "free play" of market forces in Adam Smith's metaphor of the "invisible hand"), the capitalist economy has developed a logic that colonizes the rest of the social field. Such is not the case in "primitive" settings, where the realm of production and exchange is always already encased in a moral and social environment; since it does not exist as a distinct realm, the economy is subordinated to the common needs of the community. Nor is it the case under socialism, since the social division of labor would reintegrate economic activities into the fold of the social, and thus rearticulate their logic to serve the collective consciousness's moral imperatives. Thus, rather than being a reflection of the natural order of things, the principles of "possessive individualism" (Macpherson 1962)—including the idea of a presocietal and inalienable right to private property, as well as the innate drive toward self-maximizing economic behavior—are social and historical constructs created during the rise of modern capitalism in Western Europe.[27]

The Cult of the Individual

One of the most widely acknowledged aspects of Durkheim's thinking is his sociocentrism, which strongly manifests itself in his critique of the process of individuation and the resulting trend toward excessive individualism set off by industrialization. Nonetheless, I would contend that the importance of cross-cultural juxtaposition for his argument has not been sufficiently recognized. To hold that his sociocentric stance is solely derived from philosophical conviction (a latent organicism, and so forth) would, I believe, be mistaken, for it is equally grounded in comparative knowledge of other sociohistorical contexts. Whether in "primitive" societies, ancient Greece and Rome, or the European Middle Ages, individuals are indistinguishable from, and fully incorporated into, society. "In fact, if in lower societies so little place is allowed for the individual personality, it is not that it has been constricted or suppressed artificially, it is quite simply because at that moment in history *it did not exist*" (Durkheim 1984, 142). The emergence of the individual as a distinct entity, as well as of forms of subjectivity and institutions that invert the traditional ontological and moral relationship between individuality and collectivity, thus appear as radically new sociocultural developments only found in the modern West.[28]

This should not be taken to mean that Durkheim denounces individualism per se—quite the contrary, as we will see below—but rather that he questions the philosophical foundations of utilitarian and monistic understandings that inherently privilege the individual over the community (e.g., social contractarianism, economic liberalism, social Darwinism). Challenging a philosophical anthropology grounded in self-interest and self-sufficiency, he asserts the importance of altruistic and societal tendencies. As a type of social interaction, competition is balanced by cooperation and the search for solidarity. Concisely put, Durkheim's argument is that it is not the individual who creates society, but society that creates the individual while depending on him or her for its very existence.[29] The opposite view can only lead to excessive individualism and produce a series of pathologies specific to modern Euro-American societies: egoism (or inadequate social integration) originates from the modern subject's lack of participation in, and sense of belonging to, society; anomie (or inadequate social regulation) is caused by the relative weakness of the moral environment within which modern individuals live. Without external limitations on their conduct, and deprived of the minimal capacity for self-mastery afforded by a strong inner conscience, anomic selves proliferate. They either fall prey to their insatiable appetites and passions or are caught in an anarchic vortex of generalized warfare. Perpetually dissatisfied or insecure, they are unable to enjoy the here and now. Human beings cut off from traditional modes of life and ways of thinking are left to struggle in the world on their own. For Durkheim, a state of cultural atrophy could result from such a predicament, whereby social dissolution joins moral disorientation to sap the individual's vital forces. Cut adrift and nourished by what is at most an anemic collective consciousness, the anomic subject loses his or her capacity for creative action and reflection.[30]

Ethnological and historical juxtaposition is what permits the full extent of the pathological character of excessive individualism and the unbridled processes of individuation to come to light. Indeed, in Durkheim's portrayal of them, "primitive" societies are the very negation of their modern Western counterparts. Thoroughly collectivist, the former are marked by inadequate levels of individuation and are devoid of a distinctive sense of the person; the individual and the collective consciousness are more or less indistinguishable. Consequently, their ailments could not be more different from those plaguing Western modernity: altruistic suicide is the outcome of excessive social integration, while disproportionate regulation of the "savage" by his community fosters fatalism (which remains an underdeveloped concept in *Suicide*). Durkheim believes that, through different mechanisms (the temporary merging of the collective consciousness with that of groups and individuals, strict discipline and respect for traditions, and so forth), nonmodern and non-Western societies quell the sources of radical moral interrogation.[31] What is already given encompasses all that is possible, since the "primitive" does not search beyond what is inherited. By plunging us into this completely different cultural universe, Durkheim intends to interrogate the necessity, universality, and "naturalness" of the process of individuation as the sole measure of civilization and of its dislocating effects on the modern subject.

What, then, is to be done? Whereas *The Division of Social Labor* (1984 [1893])[32] contends that individualism is a weak basis for social solidarity and morality, Durkheim shifts his position by the time of his intervention into the Dreyfus Affair, arguing that "the cult of the individual" in which "man is a God to mankind" (Durkheim 1970f, 272) represents the principal and most valuable moral system in liberal democratic societies. Instead of combating individualism, modern Western settings should cultivate it in a manner that promotes social solidarity. They must embrace the common set of beliefs that unite citizens living in them, the liberal humanist ideal of protecting the sanctity of the individual qua human being against the violation of her or his inalienable rights. This shared attachment to human rights, this cross-culturally strange yet potentially fruitful cult of the individual, can act as the central dynamic of social integration within Western modernity. Binding us to each other, it is less the distinctive features of each person than his or her "humanness" (that is, his or her universal attributes as a member of the human species) that is prized and defended.[33] Since such principles constitute the soul of

Euro-American societies in the modern age, the latter can only be invigorated by an attachment to the former; the celebration of the individual is actually a celebration of society by its members, which counters modernity's atomizing trends. Hence, Durkheim puts a strong societal emphasis on Rousseau's and Kant's notions of autonomy: the crux of the matter moves from the exercise of personal judgment to reflexive deliberation about and adherence to collectively determined patterns of thought and action. According to Durkheim, what is in the interest of society is necessarily in the interest of its individual members.[34]

The Moral Malaise of Western Modernity

So far, I have claimed that Durkheim found adequate responses to Western modernity's corrosive influence on traditional sources of solidarity and morality within modern society itself. To the previously described division of labor and the cult of individualism should be added Durkheim's interest in certain republican institutions that would serve similar purposes of transmitting common values, customs, and norms of conduct: the state, notably through public education and the legal system, as well as professional associations (modeled on medieval guilds) operating within modern civil society.[35] But as his later work makes clear, the uninterrupted and rapid spread of scientific rationalism, industrialization, and individuation combine to bring about a moral malaise in the modern West. This is so, Durkheim believes, because transcendental divinities have faded away while immanent moral and solidaristic mechanisms have not yet become sufficiently effective in generating societal vibrancy; they may be formally attractive, yet they do not adequately feed the heart and soul of society. "In short, the former gods are growing old or dying, and others have not been born" (Durkheim 1995, 429).[36]

Such an assessment, however, directly draws from his cross-cultural analyses of religion among "primitive" peoples, on the basis of which its key functions of social integration and regulation are discovered. Durkheim is fascinated by the fact that religious rituals and beliefs inject vitality into human existence and conjure up a sense of community: they provide both the space and time for individuals to join together, reaffirming their commitment to shared values and rules mediated by a common symbolic order. "Primitive" religious ceremonies reinforce the existence of a sacred realm operating above, and informing the shape of, the profane world. Acknowledging and striving toward sacredness allows persons to surpass themselves, to move beyond their daily lives in the profane world and to uplift the mundane with transcendental significance. In addition, these same ceremonies are an unmatched source of social creativity, for they produce states of "collective effervescence"—that is to say, moments of communion and synthesis when collective consciousness is aroused to such an extent that individuals participating in them become spiritually fused together. If properly channeled, communal energies of this kind invigorate society; the latter thereby celebrates itself, through the intermediary of its members who recognize their belonging to it and agreement with its established practices and symbolically organized systems of thought.[37]

Having learned these lessons from other contexts, Durkheim strives to adapt them to address the moral atrophy plaguing Western modernity. "Primitive" religion cannot unproblematically serve as a blueprint for Euro-American societies, because it brings about and sustains heteronomy. Through their devotion to divine or natural forces, nonmodern peoples project their own collective powers onto an extrasocial plane; what is in fact created by immanent human action within society appears as something that exists beyond it. Put differently, when they engage in religious worship, the members of a "primitive" society are actually yet unknowingly celebrating it. Behind God lies society, the true object of their reverence and the hearth of morality. Despite this process of misrecognition, Euro-American societies must unearth and nurture their own collective rituals and creeds, in order to immerse social life in a republican sense of civic morality nourished by the sacred's creative forces (though not its actual content of unquestioned adherence to transcendental principles). Modern ceremonies would include large-scale popular events (such as the French Revolution, an example Durkheim often cites) and democratic assemblies, for they help us overcome anomie and egoism by stimulating societal intensity and the exaltation of its citizens.

Counteracting atomizing tendencies, bursts of collective energy and moments of collective effervescence heighten social creativity to the point where a society's self-instituting can be revived through intersubjective deliberation about, and the production of, norms and ideals by which individuals reflexively agree to be governed.[38] Under these conditions, an autonomous society, in which citizens recognize themselves as the sources of their own moral order, becomes possible. Once human beings come to terms with the reality of their dwelling alone on earth, yet doing so empowered by social institutions and moral conventions of their own making, the modern condition's malaise will dissipate. The sacralization of the individual, and through it, of society itself, gives birth to a vibrant republican morality. Citizens can become full participants in the construction of a social order that actively counters the centrifugal tendencies of modernization.

Conclusion

In this chapter, I initiated discussion of Durkheim's contribution to the ethnological imagination by pondering the place of anthropology within his vision of sociological research, the relationship of his anthropological sociology to competing paradigms of interpretation of non-Western and nonmodern societies, and the various dimensions of his cross-culturally driven analysis of Western modernity. I then turned my attention to the manner in which he employs this anthropological sociology to study Euro-American societies' distinguishing features and trends. The first of these is the unprecedented valuing of Cartesian rationalism and science at the expense of religious or mythical modes of understanding the world. Durkheim also describes how industrialization shifts the sources of solidarity from identity to functional differentiation, which itself gives birth to the specialist, as well as to a comparatively peculiar domination of the market over society. In turn, industrial society unleashes processes of individuation, which, if redirected toward a societal cult of the individual person, can become a force of solidarity. Finally, I considered how Durkheim's later writings identify a serious moral malaise at the modern West's core, a malaise that could be rectified by fostering an effervescent civic religion inspired by "primitive" rituals and beliefs suited to a secularized and republican ethos.

Situated in the French lineage of cross-cultural thinking running from Montaigne to Montesquieu and Rousseau, Durkheim has created an anthropological sociology that, with Weber's civilizational analysis, has established classical social theory's comparativist credentials. His influence on the subsequent development of the ethnological imagination is difficult to overstate, notably because of the way and the extent to which the school of thought he founded prospered through the work of its collaborators and the avenues of investigation of the social world they opened, as well as the later generation of scholars whom they trained. In the aftermath of the Second World War, one of the illustrious figures reclaiming Durkheim's heritage was none other than Lévi-Strauss, who discovered in his predecessor a kindred spirit who had laid the groundwork for a critical anthropology of the modern West.

Five

Mythologizing the Modern West: Lévi-Strauss's View from Afar

In the previous chapters, I have traced the ethnological imagination's presence in the work of some of the canonical figures of classical Western social theory. In their own ways, Rousseau, Marx, Weber, and Durkheim all engaged in a cross-cultural driven critical hermeneutics of the modern West, whereby the latter was estranged, situated, and put into question from a position of comparative distance. It is now time to investigate how this project has taken form among contemporary theorists. When surveying the ethnological imagination in the latter half of the twentieth century, what rapidly becomes apparent is the fact that its edifice, which had been supported by the dual intellectual pillars of Germany and France until then, has become a rather one-sided affair. A single column now stands, that of French thought, which (as was discussed in the introduction) has nurtured a constellation of major figures centrally preoccupied with cross-cultural matters (Derrida, Dumont, Bourdieu, Clastres, and so on).[1] Lévi-Strauss's body of work comes into its own within this context, acting as the bridge between such contemporary thinkers and the French intercultural tradition (Todorov 1993)—not least because it triggered reflection on the legacy of French colonialism. In other words, it provides a vital link between classical social theory's comparativism and more recent anthropologies of the modern condition.

Lévi-Strauss is the legitimate heir to the Enlightenment's universalistic project (the philosophes' "Great Map of Mankind") and the Durkheimian school's anthropological sociology,[2] while at the same time completing the inversion of the ethnological imagination's focus; non-Western societies, rather than the modern West per se, have been his principal object of study. The decentering of Western modernity has thus proceeded further than for any other theorist examined in this book, to the point where the "self-evidentness" of familiar customs and beliefs is shattered by being approached from the other's perspective. Furthermore, his vocation as a cultural anthropologist has pushed the ethnological imagination in the direction of a more open-minded ethos, one that requires careful, meticulous, and systematic study of non-Western and nonmodern ways of life and thought.

Nevertheless, Lévi-Strauss largely remains a forgotten figure within social theory, a neglect that can only partly be explained by his disciplinary attachment to social anthropology. More significant, I would argue, is his reputation as the "pope" or "father" of structuralism, an intellectual current widely held to have had its day in our poststructuralist times.[3] Yet neither his disciplinary allegiances nor his paternity of structuralism should obscure the substantial contributions he has made to the ethnological imagination. His analyses of indigenous societies always implicitly or explicitly contain a critical message, one that prompts us to reexamine our habitual, naturalized, and seemingly necessary forms of social order. By anthropologizing modern society, Lévi-Strauss has succeeded in portraying it as a strange sociohistorical constellation that uneasily exists within humanity's purview. I would go so far as to contend that his work represents, quite simply, one of the most acutely perceptive and devastating critiques of Western modernity ever mounted.[4]

This chapter begins by explaining why Lévi-Strauss's work has been instrumental for the cultivation of the ethnological imagination during the latter half of the twentieth century. It then discusses the uses to which he has put a reversed anthropological viewpoint, that is, the ways in which his intercultural approach has "mythologized" some of the defining yet taken-for-granted patterns of Euro-American societies. Reason, history, and culture—or more specifically, the modern West's troika of inherent cognitive superiority, linear and progressivist philosophy of history, and faith in the domination of culture over nature—have been put into myth by Lévi-Strauss. Relativizing these three features through cross-cultural contextualization, he pushes us to confront the following question: why have we chosen this mode of social organization over others, and would other possibilities not have been preferable? Any belief in manifest destiny or necessity, let alone any facile answer grounded in a sense of rational, historical, or cultural superiority, is soon deflated. The ensuing interrogation of our societies' fundamental orientations, of their ways of putting the world into form, is exactly the effect of critical distancing that Lévi-Strauss provokes.[5]

The Architecture of the Lévi-Straussian Perspective

The geographically remote and the culturally other have consistently spurred Lévi-Strauss's version of the ethnological imagination, a view from afar whose critical potential he has always sought to cultivate. This is visible in one of his earliest published articles, where his reading of the French sociological tradition attempts to belie the widespread belief in the latter's conservative origins. On the contrary, Lévi-Strauss argues:

> In France, from Montaigne on, social philosophy was nearly always linked to social criticism. The gathering of social data was to provide arguments against the social order. It is true that modern sociology was born for the purpose of rebuilding French society after the destruction wrought, first by the French Revolution, and later by the Prussian War. But behind Comte and Durkheim, there are Diderot, Rousseau and Montaigne. In France, sociology will remain the offspring of these first attempts at anthropological thinking. (1971, 505)[6]

In a similar vein, his appreciation of the Boasian and Durkheimian schools originates from their preference for synchronic and lateral comparisons between societies, instead of hierarchical schemes of evolution and normative cultural chauvinism.[7] Hence, Lévi-Strauss returns the ethnological imagination to a blurring of the boundaries between sociology and anthropology, his "technique de dépaysement" (Lévi-Strauss 1968c, 117) consisting of a cross-cultural mode of estrangement of the modern West, from which it could be interpreted and radically put into question.[8] Let us see how this unfolded.

Three Moments, Three Critiques

Lévi-Strauss's intercultural viewpoint is best understood through the framework of the ethnological imagination's three moments, as laid out in the introduction. The outward turn or moment of openness is always already present in his vision of social anthropology, which primarily concerns itself with cultures most distant and different from the Euro-American world. According to Lévi-Strauss, cultural diversity should be valued for its own sake and staunchly defended, for it is the guardian of diverging orientations and ways of organizing social life.[9] But instead of merely being content with the assertion of cultural pluralism, he has devoted considerable energy to understanding the Western quest for alterity. The elementary curiosity about other societies is, he suggests, partially grounded in the researcher's personal marginality—social anthropology being more often than not a refuge for outsiders, voices of dissent or difference inclined to look elsewhere for alternative ways of thinking and possibilities of existence.[10] He also suggests a considerably less benign rationale for Euro-American societies' desire to learn about other societies: a sense of guilt.[11] Experiencing horror toward and remorse for the evils perpetrated by our civilization—none worse than colonialism, tantamount to the original sin in Lévi-Strauss's mind—we search for morally equivalent forms of barbarism elsewhere.[12] It is a search that ultimately remains futile, for nothing can compare to signing the death warrants of many of the world's peoples; we must bear this burden in perpetuity.

For Lévi-Strauss, the outward turn is additionally prompted by the fact that, as I claimed in the introduction, the modern West must seek out alter egos for its self-constitution: ancient Greece during the Renaissance, India and China in the eighteenth and nineteenth centuries, and indigenous societies in the twentieth century.[13] These repeated encounters with cultural alterity must be grounded in a principle of open-mindedness, an "anthropological doubt" sustained by a readiness to put one's worldview into question: "This 'anthropological doubt' does not only consist of knowing that one knows nothing, but of resolutely exposing what one thought one knew—and one's very ignorance—to buffetings and denials directed at one's most cherished ideas and habits by other ideas and habits best able to rebut them" (Lévi-Strauss 1977a, 26).[14] Lévi-Strauss's own tireless confrontation with the most distant and unfamiliar sociocultural constellations revels in the disorientation it provokes which, in turn, leads to a profound sense of relativization: a multiplicity of ways of life, all containing their own internal logic, exists outside of Western modernity's apparently necessary creeds and practices.

In addition to this initial openness toward cultural difference,

Lévi-Strauss's writings contain the notions of "in-betweenness" and mediation forming the ethnological imagination's second analytical moment. Although advocating the admission of a certain cultural gap between modern society and its "primitive" counterparts, Lévi-Strauss is well aware that this cannot, in and of itself, sustain cross-cultural research. Gaining a view from afar does not imply believing in pure alterity, which risks becoming a new form of obscurantism that would assume the complete unintelligibility of non-Western or nonmodern societies. Hence, the task of mediation between different sociocultural worlds necessarily follows the encounter with forms of alterity.[15] For him, in-betweenness is enacted through structural analysis, which demonstrates that, across time and space, the field of mythological narratives produced by societies is limited to a fixed and universal series of invariable codes, which are cognitively equivalent to one another.[16] As such, there is a basic functional identity between various forms of logic, which display equivalent levels of taxonomic sophistication and complex reasoning. Because they are equipped with similar cognitive capacities, all civilizations set about to resolve the same problem, that of organizing the world according to this finite number of categories. Hence, while the content of the answers may differ markedly, the form is roughly identical. According to Lévi-Strauss, then, each society is the manifestation of specific combinations of mental operations and logical rules among the bounded binary repertoire available to humankind. The impression of essential incommensurability between cultures can be countered by placing them along this plane of intelligibility; they may speak a different language, yet the formal principles underlying them, their distinct and variable ensembles of structural relations, can be decoded through structuralism.

By demonstrating the cognitive equivalence of modern and "savage" modes of thought, Lévi-Strauss is effectively arguing in favor of a widening of our conception of humankind. To convey this idea, he repeatedly employs the poetic image of the social anthropologist as a cultural "astronomer" (Lévi-Strauss 1968i, 378; 1987a, 66). Traveling across the earth's vast expanses, he or she comes to appreciate the range of human possibilities and the incredible multiplicity of ways to put the world into form. Since he evokes the considerable depths and widths of our sociocultural universes, Lévi-Strauss strives to comparatively situate the modern West; it is accordingly recast as one spoke among many others, not the axle around which the wheel of humankind rotates. Its established patterns of thinking and acting are thereby shown to be the outcomes of specific historico-cultural orientations, rather than the singular pinnacle of human achievement.[17] Moreover, I would contend that for Lévi-Strauss, the responsibilities of conservationism and custodianship, no less than those of cultural astronomy, befall the thinker dedicated to preserving humankind's rich diversity. Yet this tapestry is being threatened by the accelerating Westernization of the globe, which he portrays as a homogenizing disease that contaminates indigenous cultures by exterminating what makes them distinctive, thus destroying the accumulated store of human creation and wisdom that feeds us all. In a controversial essay, "Race and Culture" (1985b), itself a follow-up to his widely read "Race and History" (1977h), Lévi-Strauss goes so far as to defend the normality, and even the desirability, of xenophobia and cultural isolationism. The promotion of unrestricted communication between societies inevitably leads, in his mind, to the erasure of difference and the tyranny of a monolithic global civilization underpinned by mass culture. Because it would mark the entropic death of humankind, monoculturalism must be denounced. Cultural exchange may be invigorating, yet in the end, it produces homogenization, as smaller and politically weaker cultures are absorbed by larger and more powerful ones. Limiting contact between them ensures the survival of traditional customs and ways of life, but also of the Western world itself. The continued existence of the human species depends on the preservation of global cultural plurality.[18]

To borrow Rose's (1978) characterization of Adorno's thought, social anthropology is "the melancholy science." For Lévi-Strauss, too, the owl of Minerva flies only at dusk, since contemporary encounters with indigenous societies occur once their decline, brought about by colonialism and Westernization, becomes irreversible. Despite anthropologists' struggles for atonement, the Western world will not heed their warnings about the impending extinction of many small-scale communities. Lévi-Strauss himself must take on the pathos-drenched, redemption-seeking burden of being a "bearer of ashes" (Pace 1983) for the doomed cultures whose last gasps he is helplessly witnessing.[19] Efforts toward conserving cultural diversity must consequently be devoted to the dead rather than to the living. They are transformed into a purely analytical operation aimed at creating a comprehensive museum of the human mind, where mythological constructs and taxonomic systems take the place of political struggles or material artifacts. Thus can be understood the impetus behind Lévi-Strauss's gigantic enterprise and self-imposed mission to meticulously record, catalog, and analyze some 813 myths spread across the four tomes of the *Mythologiques*.[20]

At the beginning of this chapter, I argued that Lévi-Strauss's work can usefully be read as an anthropology of modernity, for in addition to the quest for otherness and the process of intercultural mediation, his writings encompass an inward turn that, in the introduction, was identified as the ethnological imagination's third component. Turning the comparative mirror onto Euro-American settings, our estrangement from them is made possible by an enlarged set of sociocultural horizons. We must therefore move away from the familiarity and immediacy of our surroundings, since "[k]nowledge lies on the outside" (Lévi-Strauss and Eribon 1991, 154).[21] After being created abroad, the view from afar is brought back home to enable an interrogation of the established social order. Already predisposed toward marginality, the anthropologically minded thinker is even more prone to feel like an outsider inside of her or his own society after returning from foreign lands. This is doubtlessly one of the sources of Lévi-Strauss's boundless admiration for Rousseau, who, through his position as a civilized savage and his mythical state of nature (see chapter 1), captured the predicament of the cross-cultural critic of Western modernity.[22]

This view from afar is devised to challenge the self-evident, naturalized, or necessary status of modern Western customs and beliefs, which, when envisaged from a comparative distance, appear to be culturally and historically contingent, even rather peculiar. The critical impact of such an exoticization of apparently normal, habitualized, or ordinary sociocultural patterns is most powerfully displayed in a passage from *Tristes Tropiques*, where Lévi-Strauss, revisiting the terrain first explored by Montaigne, subverts the taboo against cannibalism. In juxtaposing anthropophagy and anthropemy as merely two equivalent modes of managing individual deviance to maintain social cohesion, he performs a brilliant operation of ethnological reversal that is worth quoting at length:

> But above all, we should realize that certain of our own customs might appear, to an observer belonging to a different society, to be similar in nature to cannibalism, although cannibalism strikes us

as being foreign to the idea of civilization. I am thinking, for instance, of our legal and prison systems. If we studied societies from the outside, it would be tempting to distinguish two contrasting types: those which practise cannibalism [anthropophagy]—that is, which regard the absorption of certain individuals possessing dangerous powers as the only means of neutralizing those powers and even of turning them to advantage—and those which, like our own society, adopt what might be called the practice of *anthropemy* (from the Greek *emein,* to vomit); faced with the same problem, the latter type of society has chosen the opposite solution, which consists in ejecting dangerous individuals from the social body and keeping them temporarily or permanently in isolation, away from all contact with their fellows, in establishments specially intended for this purpose. Most of the societies which we call "primitive" would regard this custom with profound horror; it would make us, in their eyes, guilty of that same barbarity of which we are inclined to accuse them because of their symmetrically opposite behaviour. (1978a, 387–88)[23]

Can we do otherwise than stare at ourselves in the mirror, intensely questioning and contextualizing what seemed to be the definitive ethical standards and rules of conduct underlying "civilization"? To return to Lévi-Strauss's allegory of the social anthropologist as astronomer of the human condition, the earth has a different appearance when observed from another planet. It should never be forgotten that the Western world unleashed the evils of colonialism, cultural homogenization, and environmental destruction into the world. Accordingly, the ethnological imagination offers not simply another epistemological framework for the human sciences, but a wider field of vision within which to locate the particularities of modern society and to scrutinize the North Atlantic region's here and now.

Structuralism as Cultural Perspectivism

In the previous section, I suggested that Lévi-Strauss's view from afar provides a tremendously insightful version of the ethnological imagination. As a social theorist, however, he is primarily remembered as a structuralist, that is, a pioneer in applying the apparatus of structural linguistics to the sociocultural field. What I would like to emphasize here, and what is much less widely acknowledged, is the fact that his rendition of structuralism invents a novel mode of cross-cultural engagement that binds analytical and normative principles to one another in support of a form of cultural perspectivism. Lévi-

Strauss believes that structuralism achieves scientific rigor by formalizing analyses of human phenomena and being able to uncover the unconscious rules framing all mythological systems.[24] More important, structuralism strives to reconcile conceptions of equality and difference between cultures; as I have already pointed out, Lévi-Strauss demonstrates that all societies' cognitive structures are formally equivalent, though varying in content because of differing orientations to the world. Since neither the "primitive" nor the modern worldview is, as a whole, inherently superior to the other, social research should concentrate on studying the structural relations between the universally repeated patterns and configurations forming each of these worldviews (Hénaff 1998, 29–32).

To sow the seeds of cultural perspectivism, Lévi-Strauss attempts to clear the undergrowth composed of pejorative representations of non-Western peoples. Naturalism, the tendency to place indigenous societies in a state of nature somehow removed from sociohistorical forces, is squarely dismissed.[25] Of greater concern to him is the resilience of social evolutionism, the misguided legacy of which still hovers over the human sciences. Lévi-Strauss contends that evolutionary theories epitomize ethnocentric and homogenizing thinking because they effectively deny humankind's sociocultural pluralism by constructing a singular model of historical development. All too easily, "primitive" societies are assumed to correspond to earlier or backward stages of the modern West's own evolutionary process.[26] He deems such beliefs to be part of a common "archaic illusion" (1969a, 84) that, instead of establishing a lateral field of comparison along which all cultures stand as contemporaneous to one another—something advocated by structuralism—legitimates Euro-American domination over the rest of the world. Being treated as a mythological construct, evolutionism's scientific pretensions are deflated.[27]

By contrast, Lévi-Strauss's brand of cultural perspectivism attempts to circumvent the Scylla of false universalism as well as the Charybdis of absolute relativism. In his opinion, the first position suffers from ethnocentrism, falsely universalizing what amounts to parochial speculations drawn from a narrow range of culturally similar settings to the rest of humankind. This is typified in contemporary Western philosophy, which, whether in the case of Sartre or Foucault, fails to situate its inquiries about the subject in time or space, while lacking openness toward the non-Western world. Tellingly, one of

Rousseau's (1966, 30) reproaches opens *The View from Afar*: "The great shortcoming of Europeans is always to philosophize on the origin of things exclusively in terms of what happens within their own milieu."[28] At the opposite end of the scale stands what Lévi-Strauss believes to be an equally ill-conceived extreme relativism. If adopted, it would render the assessment of other customs and ways of life impossible. The validity of unfamiliar patterns of thinking and acting would become wholly contextual and relative to their historical and geographical settings.[29] Contrary to the charges of some critics, then, Lévi-Strauss's perspectivist stance is not a sophisticated variant of absolute relativism.[30] As he repeatedly states, no society stands above reproach, whether from the inside or the outside. And if his writings do not reveal a sustained critique of non-Western societies, this should not be attributed to a supposedly latent primitivism or Occidentalism. Derogatory appraisals of such societies are abundant in the history of the modern intellectual, and to add to them is hardly the contemporary cross-cultural thinker's ethical duty (and even less his or her scientific project). Rather, the ethnological critic can compare the modern West to other civilizations and contextualize it vis-à-vis the accumulated wisdom of different epochs and places. When approached in this manner, the North Atlantic region appears neither as the zenith nor the nadir of humankind, but as one possible mode of social organization containing specific accomplishments and flaws.[31]

All in all, Lévi-Strauss's cultural perspectivism approaches all societies as complex ensembles of structures shaped by variable forms of interaction with the natural world. His first step is to advocate the recognition of multiple yet internally coherent sets of values and traditions, which may or may not find parallels elsewhere. In turn, this prompts a comparison of the normative and customary preferences of different societies, in order to devise a model of possible structural combinations. Storing the human species' universal patterns of thought and action, this model then serves to interpret and evaluate Western modernity. A new space for the ethnological imagination has been demarcated.

Anthropologizing Western Modernity

Having discussed the theoretical foundations of Lévi-Strauss's ethnological imagination, I would now like to consider how his view from afar is brought to bear on the modern West. It is knowledge of distant and unfamiliar cultural lifeworlds, I would argue, that enables him to "anthropologize" Euro-American societies by turning some of their defining traits into myths—that is to say, by treating them as sets of beliefs required to make sense of the world rather than necessary or accurate representations of it. In particular, Lévi-Strauss juxtaposes widely differing conceptions of reason, history, and culture, with the intent of estranging Western modernity as a sociohistorical constellation. Deprived of its sense of innate preeminence, it is situated in time and space; it cannot be taken for granted, but must be explained as the outcome of human action.

The Cult of Rationalism

For Lévi-Strauss, as for many others, the rationalist revolution launched in Western Europe during the seventeenth century marked one of the intellectual entry points into modernity. Establishing a rupture with faith in divine revelation as the ultimate source of authority, as well as with the more practical rationality of the preceding century's intellectual Renaissance, the Age of Reason witnessed the rise to prominence of abstract logic—in a word, the victory of Descartes over Montaigne. The ideals of universalism, objectivity, systematicity, and parcelization of reality displaced older religious, holistic, or pragmatic traditions of thought (Toulmin 1990, 30–35). Lévi-Strauss reacts to such a situation by recognizing the comparative distinctiveness of Cartesian rationalism, while stripping it of its claims to inherent superiority over other cognitive systems. The cogito is thereby situated within the wider context of human logic; rather than the pinnacle of thinking, it is rendered a historically and culturally specific version of humankind's universal mind.

Before reaching such a conclusion, Lévi-Strauss must take widespread misconceptions about "primitive thought" to task. He attributes Western science's failure to translate the "savage mind" into the language of modern rationalism to the latter's ethnocentrism, rather than to the former's supposedly illogical or alogical character. In fact, his writings counter any notion of "primitive" cognitive inferiority or complete incommensurability, found notably in Lévy-Bruhl's (1966) "law of participation." Evolutionary explanations, according to which the crudeness, affectivity, and incoherence of "primitive" ways of thinking give way to the sophistication and abstraction of modern ones, are equally problematized. Relatedly, Lévi-Strauss denounces a kind of functionalist naturalism that reduces the mental activities of indigenous peoples to products of biological stimuli or raw emotions.[32] Consequently, he shifts the burden of explanation from indigenous societies' shoulders to those of the modern West. It is not they who must account for their intellectual customs in rationalist terms, but the human sciences that must transform themselves to decipher other traditions. If "primitive" mental patterns remain incomprehensible or opaque to the Western mind, the fault lies with the inadequacies of our existing analytical methods—inadequacies that structuralism aims to remedy. For instance, in one of his more concise works, Lévi-Strauss (1963) criticizes the idea of totemism by portraying it as a fictional and erroneous discursive construct, a floating signifier without a referent. What he terms the "totemic illusion" does not designate an actual phenomenon observable among "savage" cultures, but an inversion of the modern West's self-identity:

> The alleged totemism pertains to the understanding, and the demands to which it responds and the way in which it tries to meet them are primarily of an intellectual kind. In this sense, there is nothing archaic or remote about it. Its image is projected, not received, it does not derive its substance from without. If the illusion contains a particle of truth, this is not outside us but within us. (1963, 104)[33]

Similarly, in a section of *The Jealous Potter*, Lévi-Strauss (1988, 185–86) boldly inverts the main claim of Freud's *Totem and Taboo* (1990 [1913]): it is not "savages" and neurotics who share similar mental processes, but "savages" and psychoanalysts. Illustrating Western modernity's unconscious reliance on mythical thinking, the Freudian version of the Oedipal story represents a psychoanalytical reworking of "primitive" narratives. The illusion of the West's purified and ex nihilo rationalism is shattered, for Lévi-Strauss insists that it stems from a specific sociohistorical orientation to the world. Moreover, instead of searching for the seeds of the cogito in other settings, he urges us to use non-Western modes of reasoning as the basis for a universal model of the human mind. This is possible because scientific thought has been present since the Neolithic age, during which time the great arts of civilization (pottery, agriculture, and cattle raising) were invented. Furthermore, the construction of coherent and detailed taxonomic schemes operating according to a binary logic of classification exists in all societies. "Primitive" thought is neither rationality's other, nor its childhood, but its essence.[34]

Of what, then, does "primitive" logic consist? Lévi-Strauss provides a culturally perspectivist answer to this question: when properly contextualized, the forms of rationality harbored by indigenous societies can be understood as perfectly adapted to their needs and realities. The "savage mind" contains a way of thinking that satisfies its own logical criteria, at the same time that it is well suited to the relationships that these cultures have established with the natural world. Therefore, I would contend that Geertz's (1973) description of Lévi-Strauss as a "cerebral savage" is an apt description of "primitive" thought more generally. "In the same way we may be able to show that the same logical processes operate in myth as in science, and that man has always been thinking equally well; the improvement lies, not in an alleged progress of man's mind, but in the discovery of new areas to which it may apply its unchanged and unchanging powers" (Lévi-Strauss 1968f, 230). Bricolage is what characterizes the "savage mind," which acts by combining and recombining a fixed number of mythological components; contrary to modern scientific reasoning, it is not geared to go beyond the given order of things, instead forming variable mental patterns within a stable framework that reproduces established representations of the world. Although capable of abstraction and speculation, the "savage mind" privileges practical reason, concreteness, and induction. Further, it is holistic because it is searching to integrate the cosmos's various levels—something that, according to Lévi-Strauss, is exemplified in Mauss's (1988) idea of the "total social fact." The "savage mind" strives to achieve an equilibrium between the different levels of existence: nature and culture, the emotional and the rational, and the sacred and the profane, as well as the normative and the analytical.[35]

For Lévi-Strauss, the cognitive model arrived at through analysis of the "savage mind" serves as the benchmark against which to interpret modern Western thought. Instead of looking on the intellectual activities of other epochs and cultures from the heights of the supposed zenith of reason, he thereby relativizes the cogito and mythologizes the Euro-American cult of rationalism. From this perspective, *The Savage Mind* (Lévi-Strauss 1966) can be read as an attempt to move Cartesianism off the center stage of world history by situating it as a historically and culturally peculiar manifestation of our universal mind. His memorable polemic against Sartre in the last chapter of the book gives us the tone of this argument:

> It is precisely because all these aspects of the savage mind can be discovered in Sartre's philosophy, that the latter is in my view unqualified to pass judgment on it: he is prevented from doing so by the very fact of furnishing its equivalent. To the anthropologist, on the contrary, this philosophy (like all others) affords a first-class ethnographic document, the study of which is essential to an understanding of the mythology of our own time. (1966, 249)[36]

When perceived in this manner, the rationalist revolution appears less as an absolute advance in the development of humankind's intellectual faculties than a path taken by some societies to suit their orientations to the world and types of social order. Modern rationalism, which Lévi-Strauss variously designates as corresponding to the "domesticated," "cultivated," or "tamed" mind, has a marked preference for cognitive engineering over bricolage.The cogito's propensity to instrumentalize the external world encourages manipulation of given structural relationships, yet also the invention of frameworks beyond those already existing—an imperative that does not find parallels in other ages or cultures. In addition, Euro-American science draws its considerable power from its talent for cumulation, the capacity to systematically collect disparate elements into a coherent totality and build on past achievements. Nevertheless, the tendency toward abstraction, the use of deductive logic, and the fracturing of reality into isolated parcels hamper the modern scientific outlook.[37] Ultimately, Lévi-Strauss topples the pedestal upon which Western rationalism has stood, for he establishes a common cerebral ground where all instances of the human intellect meet. Simultaneously particularized and estranged, Cartesianism loses its aura of indisputability. As one mode of acquiring knowledge about the world among others, it appears as a specific derivation of humanity's accumulated store of mental patterns.

The Fables of History

The murder of Clio, that great goddess of the modern West, is probably the most common intellectual crime laid at the doorstep of Lévi-Straussian structuralism because of its favoring of synchronic over diachronic aspects of the human experience. Yet I would contend that

Lévi-Strauss's purpose is not to deny that humanity dwells in time, but rather to comparatively estrange and put into question the teleological, progressivist "regime of historicity" (Abélès 1999, 44) that has become integral to Western modernity's self-identity. In other words, he aims to put History into myth by proposing an alternative model of temporality, as well as by juxtaposing the "primitive" and modern historical consciousness.

Going back to the Enlightenment—whether from Voltaire (1963a, 1963b [1756]) to Condorcet (1955 [1795]), or from Kant (1991a [1784]) to Hegel (1975)—one can find the intellectual roots of the North Atlantic region's dominant regime of historicity, namely its notions of progress and of humankind's irresistible ascent over time. However, instead of taking these conceptions for granted, Lévi-Strauss seeks to cross-culturally locate and problematize them in a manner that is reminiscent of the conclusion that Nietzsche (1983, 66) famously drew: "Our valuation of the historical may only be an occidental prejudice." Far from being an objective or necessary perspective about the world, historicism is an ensemble of beliefs and customs that certain societies have adopted to organize events chronologically. Moreover, the modern West has fetishized History, which appears as a transcendental being moving of its own volition. Such a myth conflates the universal passing of time [history] with a particular philosophy of history [History]; the connection between the latter signifier and the former referent is tenuous, if not completely arbitrary. As Lévi-Strauss (1978c, 38) concisely puts it, "The problem is: where does mythology end and where does history start?"[38]

In this light, progress comes to represent a peculiar bias attributing a unique direction and destiny to the Western world: the teleological and highest realization of human civilization. All too frequently, Lévi-Strauss contends, this myth becomes a device for establishing unwarranted cross-cultural hierarchies. His own writings are intended to break with such conceit, for, despite its considerable achievements, the modern West cannot be conceived as the apotheosis of history. By the same token, other sociohistorical constellations have not existed in order to prepare the advent of Western modernity, nor will they necessarily walk down the trail we have blazed.[39] Reminiscent of both Rousseau and Marx, Lévi-Strauss identifies another modern historicist doctrine, the ontologization of change, which posits constant flux as both necessary and desirable as such.[40] He employs the term "hot societies" to convey this idea, namely, Euro-American societies' conviction about their being of history, as well as in history. Like steam engines, they function according to a thermodynamic principle: expending a great deal of cultural energy to maintain themselves in movement and thus entrench self-transformation by gradual or revolutionary means. Disorder becomes an inevitable feature of modernity, requiring hierarchical cleavages within the body social to maintain itself.[41] Revisiting Nietzsche's (1983, 60, 83) diagnosis, one could say that the distinctive sickness of the modern soul is to be afflicted by the "consuming fever of history," the "oversaturation of an age with history." There is one additional feature of this strange sickness that Lévi-Strauss strives to question, faith in human control over history. Borne out of an anthropocentrism placing subjectivity at the center of the universe, a credo according to which time can be bent to our will makes its appearance during the modern epoch in the West. When viewed from afar, the supposed taming of Clio appears to be exceptionally foolish; the illusion of our historical omnipotence can only seem oddly arrogant when compared to other perceptions of time.

Lévi-Strauss's desire for this kind of cross-cultural juxtaposition is what explains his fascination with "primitive" understandings of temporality, which destabilize the self-certainty of History. To be able to interpret them, however, the human sciences must sidestep the ethnocentric trap already mentioned with respect to rationality; the inability to account for other regimes of historicity is due to a misleading cultural self-referentiality, not the absence of temporal change in different sociocultural settings. This is where structuralism comes into its own, for it is designed to take into consideration such settings' substantially different techniques of structuring and preserving time—techniques that do not include written documents or a collective narrative of linear and upward movement (the organizing of events along a progressive past-present-future chain). Against the idea of unilinear ascent, Lévi-Strauss underlines the fact that virtually all mythological systems refer to an original fall, a rupture of humanity's harmony with the cosmos symbolizing the passage from nature to culture. In a more cyclical vision of history, then, one longs for a return to a primordial state of equilibrium, rather than a forgetting of the past and a transcendence of the present to realize a teleologically posited future. Additionally, he claims that "primitive" peoples prefer stability, even homeostasis, to the modernist credo of incessant change. They live in "cold societies" that endeavor to neutralize, and eventually absorb or recuperate, all historical disturbances (known to us as events) within their existing modes of sociocultural organization. Because mythology acts as an "instrument for the obliteration of time" (Lévi-Strauss 1969b, 16), the basic configurations of these societies can be reproduced across the ages. Rather than being subjects without history, stagnant or childlike because not carried by the chronological tide, indigenous peoples are those who do not share the West's historicizing inclinations. They are organized against change, but not ontologically without change; they are in history, yet choose not to be of history.[42]

Inspired by such alternative conceptions of time, Lévi-Strauss produces a structuralist vision of history grounded in the civilizational tension between the dynamics of chronological rise and decline. Accordingly, he envisions societies as complex and contradictory constellations following a plurality of routes that lead toward comparative advancement or backwardness in each sphere of social life. The modern West's historical path is not one of innate ascent over other cultures and ages, for if it is marked by remarkable intellectual and technological achievements, it has also institutionalized forms of domestic and global domination to an unprecedented extent; exploitation and colonialism, Lévi-Strauss reminds us, are no less part of the Euro-American heritage than modern science and art.[43] At another level, his structuralism is supported by a deep-seated historical agnosticism. The passing of time has no inner meaning that human reflection could reveal, and to search for such significance is to mistakenly impose arbitrary perceptions onto what is an objective and ultimately senseless process. Relatedly, Lévi-Strauss believes that the modern conceit regarding the human capacity to predict or influence the course of history is a mystification. The modern West, and the persons living in its midst, must abandon the will to power over the temporal dimension of existence. Humankind does not create a meaningful world for Chronos; on the contrary, it is the indifferent flow of time that constitutes us. One recognizes here Lévi-Strauss's much-heralded antihumanism: human beings are not agents of historical change, but spectators witnessing the unfolding of their destiny. Our fate is always already inscribed on the parchment of time, which we are unable to decipher; it writes us, we do not write it.[44]

To agnosticism must be added the tremendous sense of pathos that submerges Lévi-Strauss's scheme of history. Humanity stands by as it is condemned to vanish from the face of the earth. Its temporary presence is, cosmologically speaking, a mere speck of time. Hence the significance of preferring synchrony over diachrony, which enables structuralism to extract general and more durable patterns out of comparative analysis of social relations and discourses within a fixed slice of time. Implicitly, his synchronic prejudice also points to what he has called a "conspiracy against time" (Lévi-Strauss 1981, 606–7), an end of History that would result in a quasi-Hegelian eternal present putting a stop to the fatal processes currently unfolding before our very eyes: the destruction of indigenous societies and the simultaneous advance of Western monoculturalism. With its orientation toward permanence and its bias against change, the "savage mind" understands this objective, and thus attains a kind of wisdom and reconciliation with the world that can only remain fleeting in the modern West.[45]

The Subjugation of Nature

After the cogito and History, the third component of the modern Western project that Lévi-Strauss radically casts into doubt is Man himself, who has regarded the natural environment as his dominion since placing himself at the crossroads of the universe.[46] Modernity unleashed an unabashedly hubristic humanism, according to which the human species became the self-styled measure of all that surrounds it; anthropocentric excess elevated humankind to the position of an immanent god, a sovereign roaming unrestricted throughout the universe. Prometheus is totally unbound, *techne* being the means through which society can overcome all natural limits to freedom. This striving for human omnipotence, Lévi-Strauss believes, results in an understanding of nature that reduces the latter to the status of an external obstacle needing to be overcome or conquered for the realization of our will. No higher instance of this conjunction of anthropocentric narcissism and Prometheanism can be found than industrialism, with its accent on mechanized production and its callousness toward the natural world—which is instrumentalized, converted into a series of raw materials, and accordingly devastated through intensive exploitation. In addition to constituting a form of ontological violence, such an instrumental conception of nature has wreaked havoc on the earth's fragile ecological diversity and, as a result, impoverished our social ecology.[47]

Much of Lévi-Strauss's body of work seeks to put into question this doctrine of cultural mastery of nature. Indeed, his investigations of indigenous societies, which have developed alternative conceptions of the relationship between humanity and the natural world, are meant to challenge the institutional entrenchment of and intellectual attachment to such a creed; a different conception of our place in the cosmos is unearthed, while the comparative oddity of the Western world's engagement with nature is exposed. At the same time, Lévi-Strauss is careful not to idealize these alternative conceptions, which have frequently and erroneously been translated into arguments about "primitives" or "savages" living in a precultural state of nature. The refusal to perceive humankind as distinct from nature should not be conflated with the absence of culture as such. In fact, locating the "primitive" in nature intentionally rules out worldviews forcing a complete reassessment of the modern West's common sense.[48]

Lévi-Strauss's writings reveal that indigenous peoples do not imagine themselves in nature, but instead that their reflexive move into the cultural realm is demarcated by a series of mythological narratives expressively symbolizing the social rules proper to the establishment of society. For example, *The Elementary Structures of Kinship* (1969a) analyzes the incest prohibition as one such narrative, whereas the adoption of various arts and conventions of civilization (the passage from raw to cooked, from naked to clothed, and so forth) is similarly studied in the *Mythologiques* (1969b, 1973, 1978b, 1981). On the other hand, these societies do not perceive themselves as being against nature, since they deliberately avoid distinguishing themselves from, or believing that they stand above, their environmental surroundings. The rupture with the natural world, inherent in the transition to society, is managed through foundational myths registering the trauma of the event while helping to make sense of it. Hence, the fear of losing one's traditional place in the cosmic order, of becoming alienated from other animate and inanimate beings, is tamed through narrative repetition; the act of telling, retelling, and transmitting a particular story reasserts bonds shared with the earth and the creatures that people it. Indigenous beliefs and rituals actively cultivate humanity's dwelling in the bosom of nature, which enjoys ontological primacy. From a cross-cultural perspective, then, anthropocentrism becomes a strange article of faith; the belief in a firm nature/culture divide can itself be interpreted as a sociocultural construct.[49] A striking passage from *The Origin of Table Manners* should be cited in full:

> When they assert, on the contrary that "hell is ourselves,"[50] savage peoples give us a lesson in humility which, it is to be hoped, we may still be capable of understanding. In the present century, when man is actively destroying countless living forms, after wiping out so many societies whose wealth and diversity had, from time immemorial, constituted the better part of his inheritance, it has probably never been more necessary to proclaim, as do the myths, that sound humanism does not begin with oneself, but puts the world before life, life before man, and respect for others before self-interest: and that no species, not even our own, can take the fact of having been on this earth for one or two million years—since, in any case, man's stay here will one day come to an end—as an excuse for appropriating the world as if it were a thing and behaving on it with neither decency nor discretion. (1978b, 507–8)

From this "lesson in humility," Lévi-Strauss is able to devise his own societal ethos: not an antihumanism, as some commentators have swiftly dubbed it, but a "moderate" and "universal humanism"—or as Bourdieu (1990, 2) nicely terms it, a "scientific humanism"—intended to put an end to the modern Western glorification of Man and advocate appreciation of all peoples, yet also to respect other living beings and rediscover the sublime grandeur of nature.[51] Thus, Lévi-Strauss's version of humanism decenters the self, for the idea that existence stems from the cogito ("I think, therefore I am"), or that human beings inject meaning into the world, begins to appear as historically and culturally aberrant. The notion of a hermetic and abstract subject independent from her or his natural surroundings, of an inner self without an outer universe, can begin to be viewed as either self-delusional arrogance or environmental autism. In fact, the subject, "that unbearably spoilt child who has occupied the philosophical scene for too long now" (Lévi-Strauss 1981, 687), is much more akin to a conduit of natural forces than an agent ruling over them. Further, as structuralism aims to prove, the very act of cognition is by no means sui generis; humankind's universal mental patterns emerge out of and reflect preexisting natural relationships.

Put differently, Lévi-Strauss seeks to substitute a "philosophical ecology" for philosophical anthropology (Clément 1996, 11). We should consider ourselves to be no more and no less than living beings, sharing the same right to survival as other species. In light of this cross-cultural reformulation, our most cherished values need to be understood differently. Western modernity's conventional notion of liberty has been pushed in a disproportionately and excessively anthropocentric direction, since it is not balanced out by a sense of restraint and responsibility toward the natural environment—conditions present in all other societies and during all previous epochs. Lévi-Strauss displaces the locus of ontology, ethics, and justice from attributes believed to distinguish humankind from other species (reason, morality, and so forth), to one that we share with them: life itself. Our rights are grounded in the principle of survival, which poses an intrinsic limit on human action; claims to freedom are valid to the extent that they respect the right of all other living beings to survive. To be free, Lévi-Strauss contends, is to do as one pleases if, and only if, the well-being of other species is not endangered in the process. A new categorical imperative is introduced, that of preserving the diversity of different forms of life. Emulating the vast majority of societies throughout history, those of the North Atlantic should entrench the principle of human responsibility for nature while abandoning that of our inferred rights over it. As Clément (1985, 50) remarks, Lévi-Strauss fleshes out the well-known phrase with which Kant concludes his *Critique of Practical Reason* (1996 [1787], 191): *"the starry heavens above and the moral law within."* More than a reunification of the two poles distinguished by Kant, however, Lévi-Strauss's philosophical ecology derives the moral law within from the starry heavens above (or rather, in a posttranscendental world, from a nature that surrounds us).[52]

Lévi-Strauss's point of view does not end with the restoration of a normative balance between humankind and the natural environment. In order to realize a genuinely universal humanism, philosophical ecology steers us away from hierarchical thinking in the sociocultural domain. He reminds us that, once the primacy of humankind over other living beings is established, it is but a short step to assert the inequality of societies themselves; the domination of culture over nature can easily be converted into the logic of domination of some cultures over others. Consequently, intercultural equality is premised on the disalienation of Euro-American societies from the natural world, as well as their reconciliation with other forms of life. For Lévi-Strauss, only then can an authentic humanism, combining modern Western scientific knowledge with the indigenous respect for our natural surroundings, embrace each and every culture around the world.[53] Humankind is reassigned to what Lévi-Strauss holds to be its proper place in the universe, that is, of being one species among others instead of the self-anointed master of all things and beings. The finale of many of Lévi-Strauss's books evokes our birth and passing as a temporary, even insignificant, event in the earth's history. The universe will continue to exist, indifferent as ever to a human presence fated to end with an echoless whimper.[54] By announcing the death of Man, Lévi-Strauss hopes to redeem Western modernity. Liberated from the vestiges of its last metaphysical illusions (namely, its presumed omnipotence and omniscience), modern Western societies can move forth on the condition that they remember the greatest lesson from other parts of the world: humility toward and harmony with the mineral, the animal, and the vegetable worlds that envelop and are part of us.

Conclusion

Lévi-Strauss is the rightful heir to a distinguished French tradition of cross-cultural social theory that, as argued in previous chapters of this book, has also coalesced in the work of Rousseau and Durkheim. I would argue, however, that he has pushed the ethnological imagination in two directions that his forebears on either side of the Rhine left underdeveloped. In the first instance, his structuralist brand of cultural perspectivism has irreversibly severed the ties binding comparative social research to naturalism and evolutionism. Largely thanks to his work, cross-cultural thinking could no longer, in the latter half of the twentieth century, position indigenous societies in a state of nature or "backward" stage of human evolution; Lévi-Strauss's work has unequivocally demonstrated how and why such ideas are both analytically mistaken and ethically abhorrent. Instead, the ethnological imagination's role becomes that of juxtaposing societies that are geographically distant and culturally other, yet historically contemporaneous and normatively equivalent. Second, if he has explored well-trodden aspects of Western modernity, Lévi-Strauss has been able to put them into myth through a fuller, more complete engagement with indigenous societies than our other five contributors. Accordingly, the cult of the cogito is contextualized in relation to the "savage mind," historicism is relativized by way of the contrast between "hot" and "cold" societies, and the domination of nature is questioned through a comparative philosophical ecology.

Lévi-Strauss's critical hermeneutics of the modern West, then, proceeds in two steps: dissolving its sense of preeminence over other sociohistorical constellations, and then denying humanity's predominance over the natural world. This double move provokes a reversal of the cross-cultural gaze, which trains its sights on what appears necessary or universal, and what has become habitulized and naturalized, at home. From a comparative distance, such anthropologies of modernity estrange and radically put into doubt the familiar and the strange. In this respect, Lévi-Strauss represents one of the vital links between the classics of intercultural theorizing and their contemporary offspring. One of the most prominent among them would have to be Foucault, whose quest for an outside through which to defamiliarize the existing social order owes a great deal to Lévi-Strauss's view from afar.

Six

An Ethnology by Other Means: Foucault's Critique from the Outside

Our journey across the ethnological imagination's intellectual landscape ends with Foucault, not because I intend to present his work as a culmination of cross-cultural thought in the modern West, but because it captures something of Euro-American social theory's current predicament with respect to cultural alterity. Though by no means immune to exoticism and ethnocentrism,[1] Foucault's writings demonstrate an awareness of these pitfalls, as well as the complexities of discovering an outside to Western modernity from which to spur a critical hermeneutics of our present condition. If the actual extent of his engagement with non-Western realities is modest, the theoretical benefits of an ethnological sensibility, in terms of estranging the here and now of the established social order, are not lost on him—as the following characterization of his project, put forth during an interview in 1967, indicates:

> I could define it [my research] as an analysis of the cultural facts which characterize our culture. In this sense, it would be something like an ethnology of the culture to which we belong. Indeed, I am attempting to situate myself outside of the culture to which we belong, to analyze its formal condition in order to critique it, not in the sense where it would be a matter of reducing its values, but to see how it has effectively constituted itself. (Foucault 1994a, 605)[2]

Using this quotation as my starting point and following the work of certain commentators, I would thus like to argue that Foucault's oeuvre can be read as an ethnology of modernity in Euro-American societies.[3] His writings strive to provoke a rupture with the self-evident or necessary status of proximate and familiar sociocultural universes by juxtaposing them to seemingly distant places and epochs; in this manner, the doxa of taken-for-granted ways of thinking and acting can accordingly be shattered.

The non-Western world's limited and flawed appearances in Foucault's writings—most notably, Borges's Chinese encyclopedia in *The Order of Things* (1970 [1966]), the "Oriental" *ars erotica* in the first volume of *The History of Sexuality* (1978 [1976]), as well as Japanese and Iranian society in articles and interviews published between 1978 and 1979—belie the significance of the stimulus that cross-cultural reflection provoked for his own quest for critical distance. Indeed, such a quest is representative of a larger trend within French social theory in the second half of the twentieth century, the cultivation of an "inverted ethnology" (Fuchs 1993) that takes the modern West as its principal object of study.[4] Due in no small part to the impact of Lévi-Strauss's thought, the reversal of the ethnological perspective is now so complete, and its application so wide ranging, that Western modernity is defamiliarized, and hence made to appear culturally strange. Foucault, then, renders the past and present into foreign territories, much like the cultural anthropologist who exoticizes distant societies. Historiography is "anthropologized," while the ethnological imagination's inward turn (or moment of reflexivity) can be decoupled from the creation of non-Western alter egos.[5] Working in a post-exoticist context where the conventional and facile devices of comparative research have become intellectually problematic, Foucault points to the possibility of throwing out the bathwater of naturalism and evolutionism, yet retaining the baby of intercultural perspectivism. If the non-Western world cannot be expediently envisaged as existing in a state of nature or an earlier stage of the North Atlantic region's sociohistorical development, it can nevertheless indicate a panoply of other modes of social organization that combat the present and the proximate's dehistoricizing naturalization.

Therefore, to discuss how Foucault invents a critical ethnology by other means, I will proceed in two steps. The first part of this chapter analyzes the gradual role that cross-culturalism assumes in his search for an outside to Western modernity. In turn, the second section is devoted to examining the ways in which he applies this comparative historicization to question Euro-American societies' processes of exclusion, rationalization, and subjectivation. Accordingly, Foucault can be placed in the lineage of his illustrious predecessors, for all six figures have been similarly inspired to employ the ethnological imagination to produce a critical hermeneutics of the here and now.

The Quest for an Outside

In the previously cited quotation, why does Foucault himself select the metaphor of ethnology to characterize his intellectual project? His explanation, that of trying to "situate himself outside of the culture to which he belongs," merits further consideration, since it responds to a challenge that other contributors to the ethnological imagination have faced—namely, that of approaching their own settings critically so that familiar patterns of thought and action can be thoroughly interrogated rather than taken for granted. Like them, he realizes that this can be accomplished by acquiring a sense of comparative detachment from the modern West; the Lévi-Straussian *technique de dépaysement* and view from afar invite just such a reversal of outlook. At the same time, Foucault's quest for an outside is framed by an attempt to preserve the ethnological effect of cultural estrangement without grounding it in substantial research about non-Western societies. To explain how he searches to resolve this tension, I propose a reconstruction of Foucault's oeuvre.

The ground for Foucault's eventually explicit recognition of ethnology proper is already cleared by his first major work, *Madness and Civilization* (1965 [1961]), as well as by a series of essays on the French literary avant-garde dating from the 1960s.[6] This early work is clearly preoccupied with finding a cultural outside to Western modernity, for which the experiences evoked by madness and literature—and even more so by the meeting of the two in some rare instances—stand as exemplars. Foucault therefore employs archaeological or aesthetic means to temporarily dispel the aforementioned tension. Opting to study what exists at the margins of the Euro-American world, he invokes a series of limit-experiences that outline the latter's boundaries from a certain distance. Thus, to move away from the empire of the modern Western cogito, Foucault seeks to return to a historical "zero point" when madness and reason shared the same universe of discourse. To estrange reason, he pursues an archaeology of the process through which the two counterparts were split off from one another and madness silenced by way of the science of psychiatry.[7] Similarly, I would contend, the literary experiments of Blanchot, Artaud, Breton, Bataille, Leiris, Roussel, and other *avant-gardistes*—who themselves find their roots in the accursed heritage of Hölderlin, Nietzsche, Rimbaud, and Sade—attract Foucault because they cultivate cultural defamiliarization and critique by repeatedly dwelling in that which is alien to everyday existence. The voices transcribed therein evoke not the self-certainty of autonomous subjects who express themselves transparently through language, but a troubling opacity and ambiguity of meaning, as well as the proliferation of difference, irreducible alterity, and irrevocable excess for their own sake.[8] By transgressing the bounds between what the modern West upholds at its core and what it has rendered beyond the pale, by retrieving a moment of a-rationalism or amorality, archaeology and literature can precipitate a rupture akin to that which cross-cultural thinking spawns. Accordingly, the phrase that Foucault chose to characterize Blanchot's work, "the thought of the outside" (Foucault 1998b), bears a striking resemblance to his description of ethnology in *The Order of Things* (1970 [1966]).[9] Both aim to shatter the doxa of our lifeworlds and in so doing, to expose to scrutiny deeply buried normative and cognitive assumptions undergirding taxonomic systems and practices of exclusion that are made to appear peculiar by being situated historically and culturally.

Despite what seems to be Foucault's initial resolution of the difficulties inherent in creating an inverted ethnology without an outward turn, two recurring problems remain. First, as he implicitly realized, the literary longing for a pure outside is characteristically modern and can thus hardly be considered transgressive in and of itself. By the same token, its more aesthetic and linguistic grounding could not serve as the main point of orientation of sociohistorical investigations of Western ways of thinking and acting. Second, a performative contradiction in Foucault's early quest for radical difference was brought to light by Derrida's (1978a) pointed critique of *Madness and Civilization*. Madness either expresses itself in its own tongue and thereby remains unintelligible to us, or it loses its otherness by virtue of entering our field of cognition and speaking our language; in neither case can it act as a pure outside.[10] More generally, Foucault is made aware of the fact that Western modernity cannot self-generate its own lines of total escape.

Having pondered Foucault's preliminary efforts to construct an estranged vantage point vis-à-vis his time and place, I would now like to consider his use of the field of cultural anthropology for the same purpose. *The Order of Things* (1970 [1966]) is accordingly pivotal, since this is where Foucault most explicitly advances his vision of an ethnology by other means and acknowledges his debt to the discipline that, with psychoanalysis and linguistics, forms a structuralist and antihumanist triumvirate.[11] In the Lévi-Straussian variant of cultural anthropology, Foucault discovers a domain that observes Western modernity from a distance without being mired in aesthetically ungrounded or archaeologically contradictory obstacles. It supplies the vantage point of the outsider inside that blends involvement and detachment. Hence, Foucault transforms the ethnological imagination by seizing on its ability to exoticize the familiar while discarding the element of encounter and comparison with other societies. *The Order of Things'* interest in cultural anthropology stems less from the latter's concrete ethnographies and inquiries about "primitive" universes than its epistemological skill at developing a critical perspective about the established social order:

> One can imagine what prestige and importance ethnology could possess if, instead of defining itself in the first place—as it has done until now—as the study of societies without history, it were deliberately to seek its object in the area of the unconscious processes that characterize the system of a given culture. (379)[12]

Partially fashioned after Lévi-Strauss's structuralist geology of human cognition, Foucault's archaeology of the human sciences applies an inverted ethnological gaze to unearth the internal grammar and buried logic of our systems of thought. From afar, then, their necessity can be contested. Detached from the biases and prejudices of his or her worldview, the ethnological critic can scan its taxonomic terrain as though it were itself a foreign landscape; our structures of classification and modes of organizing the world are relativized and interrogated as culturally and historically contingent constructs because deprived of their "naturalness," timelessness, and universality (a point to which I will return in the second part of this chapter).[13] According to Foucault, the modern West's threefold taxonomy of human activity is neither inherited nor self-evident, for the categories of life, labor, and language do not reflect a preexisting order of things. Instead, they reflect a particular way of putting the world into form.

The Order of Things' inverted ethnology is also visible in its prophecy of the death of Man, whose progenitor, for Foucault (1970, 379), is Lévi-Strauss. As discussed in the previous chapter, Lévi-Strauss pursues a substantive outward turn in order to undermine anthropocentrism: non-Western societies are shown to cultivate an entirely other perception of humanity's place in the universe, making our own preoccupation with Man seem parochial by comparison. Foucault, for his part, seizes on cultural anthropology's capacity to excavate the discursive rules of biology, political economy, and linguistics, which produce Man. Its great merit is to reveal the cognitive structures that exist underneath humankind's will and consciousness without seeking supposed truths about human nature.

This brings us to the historiographic component of Foucault's search for an outside to Western modernity, a search whose archaeological and genealogical modes of inquiry display a strongly ethnological slant.[14] Like structural anthropology, archaeological analysis contains much more of a spatial than a chronological sensibility. Accordingly, Foucault's version of archaeology conceives of history as an excavation of the sociocultural strata of past ages, whose shifting soil has been buried beneath temporal layers so as to appear frozen to us today. He approaches historical periods as synchronic blocks of time rather than as diachronic chains pointing to the present, preferring to draw out formal relations between structures within different epochs rather than denoting the developmental tendencies linking them to one another. To use his own metaphor, archaeology studies written archives as "monuments" rather than "documents."[15] Historians should not be conceived as guardians of their societies' collective memory, since their role is closer to that of explorers discovering the artifacts of an unknown civilization. And despite Foucault's shift toward genealogy, his investigations preserve this ethnological will to observe social life from a distance. Indeed, originating in Nietzsche's (1983; 1996) writings, his genealogical conception of history foregrounds the alienness of the past in order to recover that of the established social order. This is accomplished by discarding both philosophical anthropology, with its belief in an unchanging human nature across time and space, and the philosophy of history, which holds that time has an inner meaning to be discovered by human consciousness and that the present is a necessary outgrowth of the past.[16]

Foucault's "ethnologization" of history becomes clear when considering how its procedures parallel those of the ethnological imagination's three analytical moments. The outward turn corresponds to his exoticization of the past, which, if encountered on its own terms, takes on the appearance of being spectacularly uncanny and surprisingly alien. In his hands, historical research is transformed into a Lévi-Straussian *technique de dépaysement*, a disorienting journey to an unrecognizable land where the observer is confronted with a cabinet of curiosities containing an endless repository of mysterious customs and beliefs. Historiography becomes a discipline concerned with the then and there's radical alterity and the decentering of one's own horizons rather than, as is the case in conventional models and philosophies of history, a reduction of earlier epochs to the status of imperfect or undeveloped ancestors of the here and now (Veyne 1978)—something that effectively legitimizes the latter as the teleological fulfillment of the past. Practicing genealogy is an unsettling experience, for it underlines the gap between historical ages and the potential incommensurability between them. It represents a "counter-memory" (Foucault 1984b, 93); staring into the looking glass of time, we may not be able to recognize the reflection cast by those who preceded us. It is thus the existence of a gap between the present and the past, instead of the presumption of a continuous lineage, upon which Foucault focuses. One is reminded, for instance, of the unfamiliar, jarring character of the following images: the medieval ship of fools in *Madness and Civilization* (1965), *The Order of Things*' (1970) astonishing proclamation of the absence of Man in the West before the nineteenth century, the frequent use of torture as a public spectacle up until the end of the eighteenth century in *Discipline and Punish* (1977a), and *The History of Sexuality*'s (1978) evocation of a classical erotic art.

Foucault's juxtaposition of the past and the present can be related to the ethnological imagination's moment of in-betweenness. The aforementioned images are contrasted to current practices and beliefs in the Euro-American world (e.g., the confinement of the mad, the fetishization of Man, the imprisonment of criminals, and the scientificity of sexuality), with the French Revolution serving as the great threshold and caesura between what he terms the classical and the modern ages. Foucault takes visible pleasure in standing in the space of this caesura, the point at which our present is decentered and estranged by contrast to what preceded it.[17] The established social order is therefore situated within the vast field of historical possibilities out of which it emerged. From this perspective, we can readily grasp the fact that, before they became "commonsensical" due to their institutionalization and widespread diffusion from the nineteenth century onward, many of our ways of acting and thinking would have been considered shocking, or at the very least, odd.

Such a realization prompts a widening of our horizons of sociocultural possibilities, which itself fosters something akin to the ethnological imagination's inward turn: the reflexive questioning and historicization of the modern West's current state of affairs. By returning to points of rupture in the past, Foucault compels us to ponder moments of contingency and indeterminacy when the present was still being born and thus could be perceived as but one possible configuration of sociocultural relations, among others. In turn, the recovery of forgotten or discarded possibilities of existence underlines the comparative newness and incongruity of the existing social order, which results from the narrowing down of a plurality of conflicting tendencies through the exercise of power. "[H]istory serves to show how that which is has not always been; that is, the things which seem most evident to us are always formed in the confluence of encounters and chances, during the course of a precarious and fragile history" (Foucault 1998f, 450).[18] Given that what is cannot be considered the only path that the Euro-American world could have taken, the self-institution of society is revealed. We are not trapped in a system inherited from the past or decreed by metaphysical forces, dwelling instead in a self-created universe that has been—and can be again—remade.

No example of Foucault's ethnological historiography is more striking than the opening passage from *Discipline and Punish* (1977a), where the 1757 public quartering of Damiens in Paris for regicide is recounted. Here, Foucault occupies a position similar to that of Montaigne four centuries earlier, his narrative and its intended effect being reminiscent of early European travelers' accounts of cannibalism among so-called "savages." Initially, because of the visceral character of the corporeal punishment, the haphazard nature of the proceedings, and the casual tone of the sources quoted, we recoil in horror at the barbarism of the execution. We are thus confronted with a set of norms and customs that are internally coherent and described as habitual, yet are utterly different from our own; adding to the sense of disorientation, readers gradually recognize that these practices and beliefs do not exist in a faraway land, but in the West barely a few hundred years ago. Foucault then proceeds to contrast Damiens's quartering to an 1838 prison timetable, a familiar arti-fact of contemporary penology that encapsulates the chasm dug in less than a century. The aim of his procedure is akin to Montaigne's (1948a, 152) famed comment about the relativism of barbarism, namely to encourage critical perspectivism. By temporarily stepping outside of the bounds of the immediate and the proximate, our nor-mative standards and sociocultural assumptions can be reexamined, for if the past is deprived of legitimacy and becomes aberrant to our eyes, the same must be considered possible regarding the present from the point of view of another time or place. *Discipline and Punish*'s subtitle is therefore carefully chosen. The prison is born rather than given, recently created rather than eternally or naturally entrenched. What Foucault (1977a, 23) calls "its exorbitant singularity," cannot but be probed and problematized.

Up to this point, I have claimed that the development of Fou-cault's thought was marked by three distinct steps toward the es-trangement of Western modernity: the allegorical otherness provided by madness and avant-garde literature; the epistemological principles of structural anthropology; and the ethnological historiography pro-duced by archaeology and genealogy. Nonetheless, his rendition of the ethnological imagination does not entirely dispense with cross-cultural juxtaposition. After the first volume of *The History of Sexu-ality* (1978 [1976]), Foucault comes across a perspectival problem: what he calls the classical age (the ancien régime of the seventeenth and prerevolutionary eighteenth century) cannot provide an outside to its modern (that is, postrevolutionary) counterpart in the domain of sexuality because both epochs are bound to one another by a com-mon and overarching Christian worldview. The challenge then be-comes finding sets of practices and beliefs that are external to Chris-tianity, something that Foucault eventually resolves by turning to Greek and Greco-Roman antiquity in the second and third volumes of *The History of Sexuality* (1985; 1986 [1984]). What has barely been commented on, however, is that Foucault's turn toward classical civilization was preceded by forays beyond the West, specifically through visits to, and minor publications about, Japan and Iran.[19]

While I will return to the substance of his findings in the second part of this chapter, it should be noted here that both Zen Buddhism and the Iranian Revolution—the two specific objects of Foucault's reflections—play the role of cross-cultural alter egos to Western modernity. Foucault thus explicitly, albeit briefly, became interested in the possibilities for critiquing the here and now afforded by intercultural contrast; Christianity could be estranged when compared to Buddhism or Shi'ite Islam. Japanese and Iranian societies could be employed to carve out a vantage point of insider/outsider in relation to the Euro-American world: "For me, from the point of view of the technology, of the lifestyle, of the appearance of the social structure, Japan is a country extremely close to the Western world. And, at the same time, the inhabitants of this country seemed to me on all levels a lot more mysterious in relation to those in all other countries of the world. What impressed me was this mix of proximity and remoteness" (1994g, 619). Neither one of these brief ventures into non-Western realities was pursued, nor can references to them be found in Foucault's principal writings. Apart from the political fallout from his Iranian misadventure,[20] another reason for withdrawing from such projects stems from the realization that Japan and Iran's total otherness makes them genealogically ineffective. Because Foucault perceives them to be instances of radical alterity in sociohistorical terms, Asian modes of thinking and acting cannot be made to represent buried or forgotten genealogical possibilities for the West; their almost total remoteness does not permit an enlargement of the North Atlantic sociocultural universe. They are therefore of little assistance in problematizing the latter's current social order.

Hence, instead of turning to Asian civilizations for comparative purposes, the second and third volumes of *The History of Sexuality* draw upon Greek and early Greco-Roman antiquity as partial outsides to the Christianized West. It is their articulation of strangeness and familiarity, what Nietzsche (1983, 60) terms the "untimely" character of classical studies, that interests Foucault. As such, then, his ethnological imagination is yet again put to use, for ancient Greece and the Greco-Roman world are claimed to embody a mix of sociocultural

proximity and distance strongly reminiscent of non-Western societies. Antiquity is treated less historically than cross-culturally: it is
not the "cradle of civilization" or the "childhood of the West," but
a partial outside whose otherness is meant to be jolting. Foucault
reconstructs ancient Greek and Greco-Roman styles of life as exotic habits, customs, and creeds that put into relief current Euro-
American sexual prejudices and norms while putting into doubt the
necessity of existing sociocultural institutions.[21] This discovery of
antiquity's relative alienness is the final move in his search for an outside, his last attempt at pursuing an ethnology by other means.

I would like to conclude the first section of this chapter by sum-
marizing Foucault's contribution to the ethnological imagination.
Like the other theorists examined in this book, he formulates a cultural and historical perspectivism that interrogates Western modernity by contrasting and situating it in relation to other sociohistorical
constellations. Yet by virtue of principally dedicating himself to the
task of uncovering the processes through which the modern West's
modes of social organization and systems of thought were established, as well as firmly positioning them in time and space, Foucault
pushes the ethnological imagination's critique of naturalism and false
universalism further than do his counterparts. Other ages and societies, to say nothing of "domestic" figures of alterity, such as madness,
serve to problematize the necessity and "self-evidentness" of a here
and now that must be understood as socially constituted and thus lia-
ble to be transformed. And in prompting the familiar to be estranged
and the proximate to be viewed from a distance, he compels us to
recognize that our contemporary state is exceptional rather than
normal, uncanny rather than commonplace, relatively recent rather
than eternal, parochial rather than global, and most significantly,
arbitrary rather than necessary. In this vein, his insistence on the
modern condition's underside is not, as is frequently alleged, an expression of Occidentalism or wholesale condemnation, but a means
of critique that effectively deprives Euro-American societies of their
sense of civilizational superiority by complicating triumphalist narratives about the victory over ignorance and oppression as well as the
teleological march of freedom and equality. His various ethnologies
by other means urge us to view ourselves differently, to consider possibilities for individual and collective existence beyond the present's
one-dimensionality.

Foucault's Ethnological Critique of Western Modernity

If Foucault's quest for an outside has led him to formulate the theoretical grounds of an ethnology by other means, it also provides him with the means for substantively analyzing modern Euro-American societies. Indeed, for my purposes, what is striking is his pursuit of a reversed ethnology of Western modernity, which examines the latter from afar through an exoticizing *technique de dépaysement*. To bring this inverted ethnology to the fore, then, it can be argued that Foucault's project remains close to Lévi-Strauss's vision of an anthropology of home. Accordingly, and despite significant thematic shifts in his work, Foucault treats three of the modern West's sociocultural nodes of action and thought (rationalism, exclusion, and subjectivation) as peculiar sets of practices and beliefs; rationalism is thus viewed as an unfamiliar creed, while processes of collective exclusion and individual self-formation become strange rituals whose sociohistorical creation comes to the fore. In his hands, these cornerstones of the modern condition are distinctive when set against those of other times and places.

The Cogito as Creed

Foucault's ethnological treatment of rationalism underlines its fetishistic status, for its sociocultural roots have been made invisible because of the cogito's doxic hold on the modern Western outlook. In a 1972 interview, Foucault (1994c, 415) is explicit about his attempt to situate the Cartesian legacy in time and space: "I have wanted to do a history of sciences without referring to the history of sciences, to the universality of knowledges *[connaissances]*, but on the contrary to the historical, geographical singularity of learning *[savoir]*. The West was a small group of men at the end of the Middle Ages, again a small group of men during the sixteenth and seventeenth century."[22] Accordingly, he observes rationalism from afar, portraying it as an unexamined creed by exploring at least three metaphors of foreign worlds: madness, history, and Borges's Chinese encyclopedia.

Madness represents the first alien territory that Foucault visits to critically interrogate the cogito. In *The Order of Things* (1970, xxiv), he retrospectively explains the objective of *Madness and Civilization* (1965) along these very lines: "The history of madness would be the history of the Other—of that which, for a given culture, is at once interior and foreign, therefore to be excluded (so as to exorcise the interior danger) but by being shut away (in order to reduce its otherness)." Foucault's procedure recalls Lévi-Strauss's (1966) interpretation of the "domesticated" mind from the perspective of its "savage" counterpart. "At once interior and foreign," madness compels us to estrange rationalism from the viewpoint of the outsider inside.[23] Moreover, turning conventional knowledge about madness on its head, Foucault tackles rationalist discourse as a myth not unlike that of totemism, which Lévi-Strauss (1963) dissected. Madness is not given in and of itself, but constituted as a pathological condition via the cogito; no natural, timeless, or universal correspondence exists between the experience of unreason (the referent) and the medical diagnosis regarding it (the signifier), for as he claims, "the Greek Logos had no contrary" (Foucault 1965, xi). Correspondingly, the cult of the cogito cannot be understood as innate to Western culture or inherited from a prerationalist past. What Foucault does, effectively, is to remind us of the historical and cross-cultural uncanniness of Descartes' *"Cogito, ergo sum,"* the seventeenth century's Age of Reason inaugurating a rupture vis-à-vis other periods and societies. The requirements of abstraction, universality, objectivity, and logical consistency introduce a kind of absolutism to Western thought, a fundamentalism that is as unprecedented as it is unheralded.[24]

In viewing the rationalist discourse about madness as self-referential, Foucault mirrors Lévi-Strauss's interpretation of totemism in another respect: this discourse reveals more about Cartesianism than insanity per se, being a negative outward projection that generates an alter ego to construct its own identity. Building on Canguilhem's (1966) argument about the derivation of the normal from the pathological as well as Lévi-Strauss's (1966) demonstration of the secondary status of the "domesticated" mind vis-à-vis its "savage" equivalent, Foucault inverts conventional wisdom: the cogito is neither self-sustaining nor sui generis, since it is constituted in opposition to the ravings and extravagances of human reason. To safeguard its fragile existence, rationalism must expel behavioral and mental patterns incompatible with the strict rules of logic outside of its universe—as though the possibility of non-Cartesian ways of thinking (whether incarnated in madness or the "savage mind") threatens the cogito's sovereignty. Thus, whole realms of human experience, as well as the individuals who embody them, are simultaneously pathologized and ostracized.

I would like to insist on the ethnological component of Foucault's analysis of the cult of rationalism by drawing a parallel between the silent condition of the mad and that of people without writing, since both groups become known through monologues about and representations of them. From a Lévi-Straussian perspective, "primitive" societies' graphic silence cannot be equated with an ahistoricity; the absence of written documents about the past must not be conflated with the absence of a past. The problem thus stems from the ethnocentric "graphocentrism" of modern Western frameworks of interpretation, which are incapable of making sense of oral traditions beyond the bounds of writing. Similarly, Foucault suggests that the silencing of the mad by psychiatric discourses must not be converted into an assumption about the a-rationality of madness; the failure or refusal to speak in the language of Cartesian rationalism is not identical to the inability to reason per se (that is, the capacity to give meaning to and reflect on the world). Matching Lévi-Strauss's invention of a structuralist method suited to primitiveness's oral forms of expression, *Madness and Civilization* is not devised "to write the history of that language [psychiatry's], but rather the archaeology of that silence" (Foucault 1965, xi). By reestablishing madness's dialogue with reason and thereby bridging the chasm between them, Foucault acts as a cross-cultural mediator of sorts who, like the anthropologist inverting her or his perspective to discover what non-Western societies can teach the modern West, studies insanity to learn about rationalism. The cogito is thereby decentered, transformed into a recently created and localized variant of reason. Abstract Cartesianism is portrayed as a rather odd creed, an enclosed model of the human mind verging on dogmatism because of the intolerance it manifests toward other expressions of our faculty of imagination.

After madness, the second exotic land that Foucault explores to estrange rationalism is history, or more specifically the modern West's image of its own past. Two notable instances of how his ethnological historiography puts into doubt the creed of the cogito can be discussed here. First, if Lévi-Strauss (1966) has studied the domestication of the "savage mind" in a cross-cultural fashion, *Madness and Civilization* (1965) aims to explain the historical process of taming Western reason. Hence, for Foucault, the European Middle Ages are akin to a remote society in which madness is considered one of the many permutations of reason, an alternative way of grasping reality rather than the Other of thought. By plunging us into another universe, he highlights the historical and cultural specificities of the splitting off and segregation of insanity from reason. Because it is specific to the West during the last three centuries (though consecrated since the nineteenth century via psychiatry), such a development cannot be considered as an inherently necessary, universal, or timeless phenomenon. Second, *The Order of Things* (1970) locates the cult of rationalism's newest product: the worship of Man, a late-eighteenth-century anthropocentric mutation that is just as comparatively uncanny as its Cartesian predecessor. Launched by Kant's question, *"Was ist Mensch?"*—which marks the birth of philosophical anthropology and, relatedly, of the human sciences—this new form of worship converts the human being into an object of study and a possible domain of knowledge. More important, Foucault believes, is rationalism's reconfiguration of the Western episteme. Barely more than two centuries ago, humankind was an insignificant presence at the edge of the world. Abruptly, human reason becomes its central point of articulation, out of which meaning radiates outward. However, when viewed from afar with historicizing tools that pierce his shell of naturalism and timelessness, Man becomes a novel and parochial concern.[25] Why, then, does it remain so entrenched in some societies? I would argue that Foucault explains the attachment to anthropocentrism by equating it to a rationalist fetish, whereby the power to give meaning to the world is projected onto the figure of Man (when the human mind is, in fact, constituted by structural rules of discourse existing outside of it). The cogito has spawned Man, this strange creature that will perhaps be "erased, like a face drawn in sand at the edge of the sea" (Foucault 1970, 387) once it is perceived to be one of the modern Euro-American world's most persistently unexamined dogmas. Then, the antihumanist dissolution of Man will be complete.[26]

Borges's evocation of a Chinese encyclopedia is the third alien trope that Foucault employs to defamiliarize the modern Western cult of rationalism. Opening *The Order of Things,* this celebrated image confronts the reader with an utterly different taxonomical system to which is juxtaposed our unquestioned adherence to Cartesianism:

> This book first arose out of a passage in Borges, out of the laughter
> that shattered, as I read the passage, all the familiar landmarks of
> my thought—*our* thought, the thought that bears the stamp of our
> age and our geography—breaking up all the ordered surfaces and
> all the planes with which we are accustomed to tame the wild pro-
> fusion of existing things, and continuing long afterwards to disturb
> and threaten with collapse our age-old distinction between the
> Same and the Other. . . . In the wonderment of this taxonomy, the
> thing we apprehend in one great leap, the thing that, by means of
> the fable, is demonstrated as the exotic charm of the another system
> of thought, is the limitation of our own, the stark impossibility of
> thinking *that*. (1970, xv)[27]

The ethnological strategy contained in this section of Foucault's text
should be explained, since he draws attention to the sense of bewilder-
ment and disorientation that Borges's passage induces. The *Celestial
Emporium* represents the negation of the Age of Reason's legacy, for it
seems to privilege particularity over universality, arbitrariness over
objectivity, and practicality over abstraction. It is, in other words,
comparatively baffling, appearing even to be absurd. Yet Foucault is
not content with this disconcerting effect, for equally interesting is the
internal coherence and systematicity of the Chinese encyclopedia.[28]
The possibility that another society could cultivate a self-sustaining
logic functioning perfectly well with criteria foreign to those of modern Western rationalism not only relativizes the latter, but makes its
dogmatic character surface. Could it be that its preeminence is due
to unexamined prejudices rather than any innate cognitive superiority? The very act of reflecting on this question historicizes and "culturalizes" the cogito, which descends from its pedestal to become a
product of the sociocultural beliefs and values of "our age and our
geography." Foucault thereby deprives it of its presumption to simply
reflect the preexisting, universal, and eternal order of things—of the
conviction that it is "the mirror of nature" (Rorty 1979), that it is itself universal and eternal. On the contrary, rationalism is a mere hermeneutical device, a way of ordering and giving meaning to the world
by organizing it in distinctive categories of thought and experience.

The Social Rituals of Exclusion, or Anthropemy

To foreground another aspect of Foucault's ethnological sensibility,
I would like to recall the previous chapter's discussion of *Tristes
Tropiques*'s distinction between anthropemic and anthropophagic

customs of social control; the first expels or vomits otherness outside of the body social, while the second consists of the cannibalistic absorption of alterity and deviance (Lévi-Strauss 1978a, 387–88). This insight is crucial to Foucault's analysis of modes of exercising power in the modern West, as will be seen in this section and the following.[29] Let us begin by considering anthropemic practices of exclusion, a theme that undoubtedly occupies a central place in Foucault's corpus,[30] where at least two specific manifestations of this social expulsion can be found: the spatial segregation of abnormal individuals, who are isolated from the rest of the population through specialized institutions (the asylum, the hospital, the prison, and so forth); and the accompanying silencing of these same individuals, who are spoken about by a range of expert knowledges and diagnostic techniques (e.g., medical, psychiatric, legal).

Foucault investigates the processes of rationalization of such knowledges and processes demarcating the modern West in relation to other ages and cultures.[31] At no other time or place are the devices for taming otherness as refined in their precision, uniformity, and efficiency, nor have they proliferated to any remotely comparable degree elsewhere or previously. During a 1970 lecture delivered in Japan, Foucault reveals the comparative underpinnings of his approach and simultaneously identifies the stunning specificity of modern practices of segregating the mad:

> In every society, or almost, the madman is excluded in all things and, depending on the case, he is given a religious, magical, ludic or pathological status.
>
> For example, in a primitive tribe of Australia, the madman is regarded as an individual to be feared by the society, a man endowed with a supernatural force. In other instances, certain madmen become victims of society. In any case, they are people who have behaviors that are different from the others, in labor, in the family, in discourse, and in games.
>
> What I would now like to address is the fact that in our industrial societies madmen are similarly excluded from ordinary society by an isomorphic system of exclusion and are assigned a marginal condition. (1998e, 337)[32]

What he terms the "great confinement," a movement beginning in the seventeenth century with the founding of the Hôpital Général in Paris and extended with the multiplication of asylums, represents an unprecedented way of dealing with the problem of madness in human society. Whereas the European Middle Ages dehumanized the mad yet allowed them to circulate relatively freely in the social body—either in exile on the "ship of fools" or roaming about as "village idiots"—an imperative of socio-spatial segregation previously reserved for lepers suddenly comes into being. According to Foucault (1965, 205), a "geography of evil" is thereby produced, the asylum taking the place of the sanatorium as an institutional site of exclusion. At the dawn of modernity, moreover, madness is transformed into a very precise pathological problem, about which rationalized psychiatric and medical discourses must speak the truth to tame its alterity.[33]

Discipline and Punish, for its part, points to the prison's exceptional character as an anthropemic mechanism. In the past and in other societies, the communal disorder introduced by criminality is controlled through various forms of punishment: retribution, banishment, physical branding, and, notably during the medieval epoch in Europe, publicly sanctioned and performed physical torture. Yet since it breaks with all these conventions, the prison is anomalous: it introduces a "new economy of the power to punish" (Foucault 1977a, 80), centered around the criminal's confinement within purpose-built institutions enforcing his expulsion from society.[34] Here again, Foucault locates the radical singularity of the modern West, as displayed through its techniques of social exclusion.

The Customs of Subjectivation:
Anthropophagy and Lebensführung

In addition to the creed of rationalism and the anthropemic rituals of social exclusion, the third axis of Foucault's inverted ethnology of Western modernity concerns itself with the comparatively peculiar processes through which we become subjects, the customs of formation of the self. As such, I would contend that we would do well to keep in mind a distinction that Foucault himself introduces: his earlier writings draw out more heteronomous and "negative" processes through which the self is produced by societal knowledges and institutions, whereas his later research tends to examine more autonomous and "affirmative" practices of self-constitution.[35] Notwithstanding these different emphases, the ethnological imagination remains one of the major sources of his insights into subjectivation.

Regarding Foucault's interrogation of more "negative" rites of socialization, the argument presented in the previous section should be revisited. Effectively, his analysis can be understood as a domestic application of Lévi-Strauss's characterization of anthropophagy (or cannibalism), thereby covering strategies of social control in modern Western societies. Foucault's writings suggest that anthropophagic rites are performed there through the assimilation and internal absorption of otherness. Nevertheless, lest any misinterpretation occur, three important differences between "primitive" and modern practices of anthropophagy need to be recognized. In the first place, the latter obviously do not involve the literal consuming of human flesh or organs, though the objective is much the same; through training and the inculcation of discipline, the body of the deviant individual is targeted only as a conduit to her or his soul, whose exceptional powers are captured and reabsorbed into society. Second, while this neutralizing assimilation is accomplished by other individuals, groups, or institutions in all settings and places, Foucault underscores what could be termed the auto-anthropophagic character of social control in the modern West: abnormal subjects are socialized to domesticate or altogether eliminate their own disorderly patterns of thought and action. In other words, external sources of anthropophagy are widespread in other contexts, but in Euro-American societies, the forces of moral neutralization penetrate into the self's very soul. Third, elsewhere and in previous epochs, normalizing morality carries a transcendental or sacred purpose that is absent from its more recent versions in the Western world. Reminiscent of the Weberian analysis of the secularized shell of the Protestant ethic, Foucault describes anthropophagic normalization as a rationalized, immanent, and self-referential entity through which cultural prohibitions and interdictions are geared toward "correct" behavior for its own sake in an anthropocentric and posttranscendental lifeworld.[36]

The previously mentioned contrast between an "Oriental" *ars erotica* and a modern Western *scientia sexualis,* which is found in the first volume of *The History of Sexuality* (1978, 57–58), represents a telling cross-cultural illustration of Foucault's probing of anthropophagic techniques of socialization. According to his passing remarks on the topic, the erotic arts privileged in Asian societies would be devoid of rationalized and moralizing considerations aiming to control the potential for social disruption that emanates from the pursuit of sexual pleasure; the latter is its own standard, an end to be maximized for its own sake. On the contrary, since the nineteenth century, the

Euro-American world has created a science of sexuality sustained by expert knowledges that have, in effect, medicalized and pathologized the poles of desire and pleasure; in the sphere of sexual practice, rationalized, systematic, and uniform prescriptions and interdictions have quite suddenly appeared in conversation with culturally and historically particular notions of truth and morality. The remnants of the Christian ritual of confession are with us today, to the extent that the self becomes a sexual being through self-regulation and that the sexual therapist has been substituted for the priest.[37] In the past, we positioned ourselves toward a religious discourse of sin, whereas the science of pleasure fills the existing moral space. From a comparative perspective, such a form of conduct of life is rather odd, since the subject becomes individually responsible for domesticating his or her desire—not by repressing it, but by channeling it into "normal" and "correct" sexual activities.

In both *Madness and Civilization* and *Discipline and Punish*, Foucault's rendition of postrevolutionary humanist reforms within hospitals, asylums, and prisons goes in a similar direction. The mad and the criminal incorporate moralizing medical and legal knowledges into their own identity, striving to neutralize tendencies toward deviance by pathologizing them. Originating from the subject's own conscience, self-regulation shifts responsibility for the assimilation of abnormality downward in a capillary fashion, from institutional sites to the individual. Processes of individualization, commonly perceived as one of the unique characteristics of Western modernity, are invested with moralizing power.[38] I would go so far as to argue that Foucault interprets modes of normalization as self-anthropophagic rituals directed toward making the governance and self-regulation of one's conduct (according to what is considered within the bounds of sanity or legality) habitual, a second nature of sorts. For him, therein lies the historical and cultural specificity of contemporary Euro-American forms of subjectivation. We have become self-regulating persons constituted through discursive and institutional sources of societal morality and truth. Whether aimed at corporeal or spiritual features of the self, socializing practices foster individuals who train themselves to avoid acting and thinking wrongfully or erroneously, for the good and the true enter into the depths of our souls. He depicts the historical and cross-cultural oddity of the modern West's secularized ethos, a rationalized and individualized version of anthropophagic moralization; the assimilation of deviance is not only realized through uniform proscriptions, but through specific rules and norms intervening into the conduct of each person in his or her everyday life.

I would now like to turn to a consideration of Foucault's investigations of more "affirmative" processes of subjectivation, a reorientation of his thought that followed the publication of the first volume of *The History of Sexuality*. Indeed, his later writings are animated by a concern for the exercise of autonomy and freedom, the self-constitution of subjects in relation to ethical and societal imperatives. The Weberian theme of the conduct of life *(Lebensführung)*, already described in chapter 3, nicely captures Foucault's preoccupation with forms of the self-production of subjectivity within the context of a posttranscendental sociocultural ethos.[39] However, given his earlier studies of the extent to which existing modes of subjectivation are colonized by Christianized "code-oriented moralities" (Foucault 1985, 30) and normalizing discourses in the modern West, he could hardly confine himself to his own historical and cultural horizons. The discovery of different and more affirmative possibilities for selfhood were to take him elsewhere, namely to Asia and to Greek and Greco-Roman antiquity, where he found styles of life valuing ethical self-formation. In Japan and Iran, he believed, such ethically oriented types of morality serve to construct an aesthetics of everyday life that has been mostly overlooked or forgotten in the Euro-American world. Zen Buddhism, for instance, garners his attention because of its centuries-long refinement of ascetic corporeal and spiritual exercises; their more "positive" quest for the good through self-mastery vividly contrasts to proscriptive Christian conceptions of the self.[40] At a different level, Foucault (1994r) views the Iranian revolution, in a paraphrase of Marx's (1974d, 244) famous critique of religion, as "the spirit of a world without spirit," the injection of a political spirituality as well as new forms of collective solidarity and popular will into the social fabric. Combined, these forces open up prospects for sociopolitical action that are quite other to the constraining subjectivities imposed by state apparatuses in the Western world since the nineteenth century.[41]

In the end, despite briefly venturing into Asia, Foucault's investigations return to the civilizational fold of the West for reasons already explained in the first part of this chapter. The last two published volumes of *The History of Sexuality* (1985, 1986) thus analyze the

techniques of the self prevalent in Greek and Greco-Roman antiquity, which Foucault treats as partially alien settings. The substantial
differences in rituals of conduct, customs, and beliefs that he observes then and there become pivotal because they offer a partial
outside to "Christianized" traditions of subjectivity. While careful to
trace the lines of filiation, borrowing, and appropriation binding the
ancient and Christian worlds, Foucault is principally interested in the
strong sociocultural contrast between them.[42] Rather than being
performed in response to proscriptive forms of moralization, the
arts of existence developed in Greece during the fourth century BC
and the Greco-Roman societies of the first two centuries AD have developed elaborate "spiritual exercises" (Hadot 1995) geared toward
mastery over subjects' desires. Austerity can be cultivated as a virtue,
yet without denying the pursuit of sexual pleasure. And because they
develop an ascetic ethos grounded in self-transformation rather than
abnegation, such forgotten or marginalized modes of care of the self
appear highly unusual to us today.[43]

In spite of the fact that Foucault did not complete his research
program into more "affirmative" rites of subjectivation, his work on
ancient Greek and Greco-Roman practices of care of the self gestures
toward the enlargement of the field of possible styles of life in Western
societies. This broadening of our horizons of being and acting is itself meant to put into doubt the narrowness of, and comparatively
relativize, predominant sociocultural practices and convictions. The
code-oriented moralities and rationalized dynamics of moralization
common today are in reality exceptional; a multiplicity of different
ways of conducting one's life has existed. In his final move, then,
Foucault excavates an ethically, rationally, and aesthetically grounded form of ascetic self-creation suited to the contemporary epoch in
the West.[44] This differently autonomous mode of existence of life can
offer another way of being in the world, inspiring us to rediscover the
pursuit of the beautiful, the good, and the true.

Conclusion

Throughout this chapter, I have claimed that Foucault's body of work
can fruitfully be understood as an inverted ethnology of Western
modernity, a form of critique of the modern condition in the North
Atlantic that employs an anthropology of home to both defamiliarize and interrogate seemingly self-evident modes of thought and
action. Although explicit cross-cultural reflection remains relatively

marginal to his enterprise, his historicizing mode of estranging the here and now represents a viable response to the traditional flaws of comparative research and, as such, a significant move for the ethnological imagination. Whether in archaeological or genealogical terms, his ethnological historiography renders the past into a foreign province whose exploration sheds light on the making of current Euro-American ways of thinking and acting while radically putting their necessity into question. In other words, Foucault's ethnology by other means has skillfully undermined the established social order's claims to universality and timelessness by demonstrating its cultural and historical specificity. Accordingly, the forms of rationalism, exclusion, and subjectivation predominating in the modern West can be treated as a set of comparatively peculiar creeds and rituals whose existence should not blind us to other possible ways of thinking, forms of social organization, and modes of life conduct invented elsewhere or in the past—and most crucially, remaining to be invented in the present and future.

Foucault's earlier interventions therefore simultaneously particularize and problematize the humanist conception of the subject as a cogito-centered and free being. Instead, they insist on the arbitrariness of the rationalist worldview, as well as the construction of disciplinary, normalizing institutions and discourses that produce the self through either anthropemic rituals of exclusion or anthropophagic mechanisms of self-regulation aimed at achieving docility. Through historical and intercultural juxtaposition, Foucault's later writings inquire into more "affirmative" conceptions of subjectivity, other ways of fashioning ourselves through the practice of freedom and the exercise of individual autonomy. For all of these reasons, I believe, Foucault's thought from the outside marks one way of reconceptualizing the project of an interculturally inspired critical social theory. He rightfully stands in the lineage of the five other figures discussed in this book, who, by engaging with representations of cultural alterity, have proposed some of the most insightful and radical analyses of who we have become, how we act, and what we believe.

Conclusion

The Ethnological Imagination
Then and Now

A Retrospective Glance

I began this book by calling on Western social theorists, notably those of a critical persuasion, to simultaneously recognize the impasse provoked by cultural pluralism in our global age and urgently respond to it. However, I went on to claim that most theoretical attempts to take up such a challenge remain ensnared by the misleading dichotomies between traditionalism and postmodernism, on the one hand, and false universalism and radical particularism, on the other. Rather than being condemned to this predicament, I then suggested that we can excavate a significant yet hitherto marginalized current of cross-cultural thinking that runs through the history of modern Euro-American social theory; in the writings of Rousseau, Marx, Weber, Durkheim, Lévi-Strauss, and Foucault, among others, we find a particularly salient and rich ethnological imagination at work. Of course, our ensemble of six figures does not—and should not be expected to—offer ready-made templates or ideal "solutions" to be directly superimposed onto our contemporary situation. Changed sociopolitical and intellectual conditions in the world today make the recasting of the ethnological imagination's project imperative. Nevertheless, the legacy of intercultural theorizing provides a solid foundation from which to reinvigorate a critical hermeneutics of Western modernity while eschewing the perils of either integrally protecting the canon's traditional orientation or dispensing with it altogether, or yet again, of falsely universalizing culturally and historically specific experiences or restricting oneself to the immediate and the familiar. Enacting principles of openness, mediation, and reflexivity, practitioners of the ethnological imagination have created mythical representations of non-Western realities to inspire their own telling diagnoses of the modern condition in the North Atlantic region. For comparatively minded social theorists, the encounter with other ways of being in the world has facilitated the process of decentering their own times and places. In turn, moving between different sociohistorical settings has expanded these same theorists' horizons of reference, stimulating a self-critique of the modern West's established social order. Yet before pursuing this line of thinking further by projecting it into the present, a recapitulation of the arguments put forth in chapters 1 through 6 is in order.

My reconstruction began with Rousseau, who stands as the quintessential early representative of the ethnological imagination in an epoch during which the so-called "discovery of the New World" belatedly occupied the center stage of European intellectual life. In chapter 1, I argued that two principal contributions to cross-cultural critique demarcate Rousseau's work from that of his contemporaries during the Age of Enlightenment. In the first instance, he converts the state of nature into a device of critical juxtaposition vis-à-vis the aristocratic and nascent bourgeois culture of prerevolutionary Paris. And second, he invents a stance of civilized savagery not only expressed through some of his most memorable fictional protagonists (namely Émile and St. Preux), but emblematic of his own life circumstances. As a "natural man" within society, Rousseau is one of modernity's first self-styled outsiders inside, who, from a certain distance, can observe his time and place differently. This partially detached vantage point allows him to detect one of the defining traits of the modern condition, a trait that also subsequently struck both Marx and Lévi-Strauss as comparatively distinctive: the ontologization of temporal change, the historicist self-consciousness blindly prizing the restless spirit of incessant flux, and the ephemeral generated by the social whirlwind. Rousseau is also deeply concerned by early modern Europe's perversion of humankind's primeval condition through the valorization of artifice in most of its existing scientific and artistic pursuits. Accordingly, he portrays the burgeoning modern self as constantly at risk of being corrupted by artificial forces that obscure our innately benign natural instincts. For Rousseau, then, the subject is being transformed into a shell emptied of authentic content, yet submerged by the requirements of performatively staging one's identity. Thus, like many contributors to the ethnological imagination who have followed in his footsteps, Rousseau provides an ambivalent assessment of modernity: its origins are to be found in a social contract instituted to protect private property, the entrenchment of which leads equally to moral progress (the possibility of individual autonomy) and to alienation when contrasted to the state of nature.

Rousseau's portrayal of the state of nature found echoes in Marx's concept of primitive communism, yet what was most significant was his predecessor's comparative denunciation of private property and questioning of the beginnings of bourgeois society. But quite aside from Rousseau's influence, Marx's version of intercultural theory stands at the crossroads of the Enlightenment's universalist teleologies and nineteenth-century evolutionist currents, and most significantly, shifts the ethnological imagination from the realm of naturalism to that of culturalism. I claimed that commodity fetishism is a key motif with which to underscore Marx's cross-cultural sensibilities, as is evident in his analysis of the Asiatic mode of production and the Russian question, as well as his late interest in anthropological material. Chapter 2 thus examined the defetishizing character of his critique of political economy: his denaturalization of capitalism through historical and intercultural contextualization, as well as his countering of the Robinsonades by an early labor ontology and, later on, a form of sociohistorical constructivism. Juxtaposing capitalist modernity in the West to previous modes of production and other regions of the globe greatly assists Marx's identification of its dialectical character, the phenomenon of worship of the commodity illuminating capitalism's Prometheanism, its breathless revolutionizing of productive forces, and its invention of new kinds of economic heteronomy, exploitation, and domination.

Albeit present in Rousseau and Marx, the comparative dimension of classical Euro-American social theory finds its highest forms of expression in the work of Weber and Durkheim during the late nineteenth and early twentieth centuries. Indeed, I contended in chapter 3 that Weber's comparative analysis of world religions, which is relatively unencumbered by teleological or evolutionary notions, guides his investigations of modes of life conduct *(Lebensführung)* in Euro-American societies. Juxtaposed to the Asian "magical garden" is the demagified and thoroughly rationalized lifeworld of the modern West, where purposive-instrumental rationality has become the dominant sociocultural logic. The Protestant ethic, that unique brand of inner-worldly asceticism capable of regulating daily behavior and decentralizing the management of the human soul, epitomizes Western modernity's civilizational distinctiveness; whereas most Asian spiritual doctrines promote the idea of the believer as a vessel of god, Puritanism sees him or her as a tool of the divine whose duty is to transform the sociocultural and natural environments. Consequently, Weber believes, the modern condition is defined by the dramatic break that it establishes with personalistic and charismatic forms of authority through the bureaucratization, formalization, and "deethicalization" of everyday life—to say nothing of the pluralization of meaning and the separation of the spheres of life. In his mind, to confront such realities requires the acquisition of a unique ethos of cultivated specialization, a difficult blend of responsibility and conviction never contemplated before or elsewhere.

Around the same time that Weber was developing the ethnological imagination's civilizational component, Durkheim was aligning cross-cultural social theory to cultural anthropology. Situated in a French tradition stretching from Montaigne to Montesquieu and Rousseau, his writings continue to move the ethnological imagination away from its previous dependence on naturalizing and evolutionary premises. Thus, if he sometimes understands "primitive" societies as simpler forms of human organization, his analyses also treat them as complex and historically contemporaneous collective entities. Like the other five figures examined in this book, Durkheim comparatively pinpoints Western modernity's favoring of scientific logic and modes of rationality as distinctive because he finds few equivalents in the past or elsewhere. Similarly, for him, the advent of industrialization introduces an unheralded problem: the production and maintenance of solidarity in a context where ties of kinship or functional similarity are no longer predominant and where, moreover, excessive individualism risks overwhelming the power of the collective. Durkheim's most striking diagnosis of the moral malaise afflicting modern existence, anomie, is found to this degree in no other sociohistorical setting, therefore prompting him to search for novel mechanisms through which to regenerate solidarity. The division of labor plays this role in his early writings, yet as I argued in chapter 4, his later work promotes the morally rejuvenating function of a republican civil religion whose rituals and beliefs combine the modern respect for the individual and middle-range institutions (such as guildlike professional associations) with the "primitive" creation of collective effervescence.

In the last two chapters, Lévi-Strauss and Foucault served as exemplars of the ethnological imagination's sustained vitality in French intellectual circles of the second half of the twentieth century. Like Rousseau and Durkheim before him, Lévi-Strauss critically interpreted the modern condition in the Western world through a perspective that encountered non-Western societies in an anthropological manner. I argued that the cultural perspectivism imbedded in his version of structuralism effectively liquidated the remnants of evolutionary thinking from cross-cultural social theory. Lévi-Strauss, then, is a comparativist in the universalist, Weberian mold, according to which all cultures can be placed on a lateral plane of analysis. And at a more substantive level, his evocation of the mythical character of "primitive" universes enables him to extend the same treatment to some of the pillars of Euro-American modernity, which themselves are transformed into myths deprived of necessary or natural standing. As he demonstrates, the expansion of abstract rationalism's significance in the West has promoted a distinctive cult of the Cartesian cogito there. Yet beyond such a diagnosis, shared by his interculturally minded forebears, Lévi-Strauss demonstrates the cognitive equivalence of the operations of the "savage mind" *(bricolage)* and those of its "domesticated" counterpart. His famed contrast between hot and cold societies serves to challenge the historicist self-consciousness of the modern age, something that both Rousseau and Marx had similarly denoted; for Lévi-Strauss, historical patterns of progress or flux, so central to Western modernity's self-identity, are but modes of interpretation of time. Most radically, his advocacy of a philosophical ecology displaces humankind from the world stage while underscoring the indigenous quest for harmony and equilibrium between the natural and cultural spheres of existence. Reminiscent of Rousseau's Romantic denunciation of artifice, this critique of the subjugation of nature additionally problematizes the latter's instrumentalization, an integral element of industrial capitalism and its attendant belief-systems.

In chapter 6, I completed the analysis of the ethnological imagination with Foucault, whose work is both influenced by Lévi-Strauss's view from afar and expressive of the contemporary dilemmas of ethnocentrism and exoticism. Foucault's ethnology by other means persistently seeks an outside from which to defamiliarize Western modernity's contours; as such, his archaeological and genealogical modes of reading history approach the past as a foreign territory. His passing interest in Asia as a site of difference vis-à-vis the Euro-American world is instructive, Borges's Chinese encyclopedia serving as a motif through which to estrange rationalism's peculiar hold on the North Atlantic consciousness. In addition, I claimed that the Lévi-Straussian distinction between anthropemic and anthropophagic practices could be used to understand how Foucault views the exercise of power and processes of subjectivity formation in the West. Correspondingly, many of his writings highlight rituals and mechanisms of exclusion through socio-spatial segregation, as well as through applications of spiritual and corporeal discipline aimed at achieving self-regulation. In his later writings, the discovery of more affirmative modes of subjectivity in other places and epochs (Japan, Iran, the ancient Greek and Greco-Roman worlds) inspires his quest for different possibilities of existence in the present, as well as for a reexamination of the limits of prevailing Christianized and state-derived modes of conduct of life in Euro-American societies.

Underlying our consideration of the ethnological imagination has been an argument about the considerable extent to which the modern West's self-constitution and self-understanding have been bound to the creation and depiction of mythical non-Western and nonmodern alter egos, as well as how sociocultural alterity has been essential to the project of a critical hermeneutics of Western modernity. At the same time, representations of cultural otherness have not always been identically or stably positioned within the field of North Atlantic comparative theorizing. In fact, six figures illustrate the development of the sense of other societies' temporal and spatial distance from the modern West's here and now (see Figure 1).

Despite considerable internal variations, it is possible to demarcate three major periods in the ethnological imagination's modern history. In the first epoch, stretching from the sixteenth to the late nineteenth

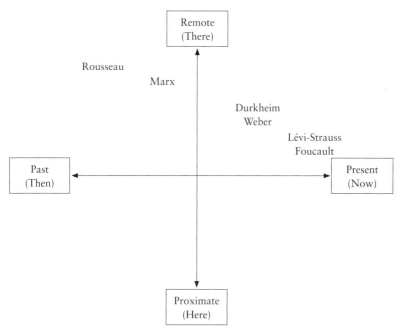

Figure 1. The development of the ethnological imagination.

centuries and encompassing both naturalism and evolutionism, non-Western peoples were considered either to be altogether outside previously known temporal and spatial bounds or to personify one of Europe's earlier stages that had persisted in faraway lands. Here one can think of Rousseau's state of nature or of Marx's conceptions of primitive communism and the Asiatic mode of production. The second era, which lasted from the late nineteenth to the mid-twentieth century, began to question—without ever entirely dispensing with—the truism that geographically remote and culturally different societies were historically backward.[1] Both Weber's analysis of various civilizations' forms of socioeconomic conduct and Durkheim's more anthropologically inspired writings about indigenous beliefs and rituals pointed in the direction of such cultural perspectivism. During the latter half of the twentieth century, contributors to the ethnological imagination's third period (among them, Lévi-Strauss and Foucault) advanced perspectivist ideas about the relative merits of all cultures, while recognizing their chronological simultaneity to a degree that had not been previously envisaged. Nevertheless, even if the conviction in the existence of historical and normative gaps between the West and the non-West has crumbled in recent decades, what has remained generally unquestioned in social-theoretical circles throughout the modern age is the belief in the spatial-cum-cultural remoteness of the world's societies.

Yet today, it is precisely this unexamined assumption that prevents Western social theorists from rediscovering their cross-cultural inheritance and dispensing with a number of flawed notions: the projection of mythical constructs of cultural otherness onto non-Western realities; "culture" as a self-contained, homogenous, and territorially bound entity; the clear-cut divide between the West and the non-West; and modernity as a singular and essentially North Atlantic phenomenon. Today, three major sociohistorical trends place such views on shaky ground: postcolonialism,[2] multiculturalism, and globalization. The struggles of Third World populations, as well as those of people of color and immigrants in the First World, have challenged the authority, legitimacy, and adequacy of Euro-American regimes of intercultural representation and understanding; alternatively, they have offered their own sociocultural interpretations and narratives. Further, albeit highly unevenly distributed and differently experienced—not least because of the impact of global capitalism—the intensification and acceleration of transnational flows of all kinds have resulted in "time-space compression" (Harvey 1989). This virtual shrinking of the globe has in turn fostered a growing sense of material and symbolic integration of previously remote territories. This is not to say that the world has become a McLuhanesque global village where neighbors live in harmony with one another because they are always and everywhere mutually appreciative of and thoroughly conversant with each other's beliefs and practices, nor even that national or civilizational borders have totally dissolved. Still, even if it ranges anywhere from earnest sensitivity to grudging acknowledgment, a generalized awareness of the existence of an astonishing multiplicity of ways of life around the world has been encouraged by global interconnectedness. And bolstered by shifting demographic and immigration trends, the "multiculturalization" of many regions has complicated that to which "culture" refers, appearing more and more to constitute a fragmented, deterritorialized, and internally heterogeneous ensemble of forces. Taking all these factors into consideration, then, the ethnological imagination must turn toward the elaboration of a fourth epoch in its history. It can be guided in this endeavor by an emerging body of literature in the human sciences, which can assist it in resolving the impasse within which it finds itself in order to pluralize modernity and complicate the West/non-West divide.[3]

The Ethnological Imagination's Prospects

Throughout the preceding chapters, I have asserted that the cross-cultural legacy left behind by Rousseau, Marx, Weber, Durkheim, Lévi-Strauss, and Foucault has supplied social theory with a vibrant yet underappreciated source of a critical hermeneutics of Western modernity. At the dawn of a nascent century characterized by postcolonial, multicultural, and global influences, what shape can the ethnological imagination's fourth period take? As already mentioned, it must conceive of all parts of the world as existing in the same historical moment and participating in an integrated geographical space, as well as diversifying modernity's sociocultural referents. Additionally, it should steer clear of a binary logic forcing it to choose between postmodernism's complete rejection of the canon and traditionalism's purely historicist defense of it, or between the ethnocentrism of false universalism and that of radical particularism. Jettisoning exoticizing and hierarchical perspectives, intercultural theorizing must still preserve the effect of comparative estrangement and self-critique sparked by encounters with other ways of thinking and acting. To further elaborate on these points, we can return to the three analytical aspects of the ethnological imagination proposed in the introduction: the outward turn or moment of openness, "in-betweenness" or the moment of mediation, and the inward turn or moment of reflexivity.

The Outward Turn

First and perhaps most noticeably, sociopolitical and intellectual transformations have considerably modified the terrain of cross-cultural engagement. After the end of formal empires and the attainment of political self-determination on the part of formerly colonized peoples, a process of intellectual decolonization of the Western human sciences has gradually followed suit. In particular, postcolonial critics and critical anthropologists have led the way in exposing the ties between Euro-American power and knowledge about the Third World (including representations of it). While this tendency has sometimes fostered a certain intellectual reductionism, it has usefully put into question the frequently unexamined capacity and authority of North Atlantic thinkers to speak for non-Western peoples through prejudicial, denigrating discursive and representational conventions. Today, notwithstanding the survival of sociocultural evolutionism and civilizational chauvinism in certain pockets of Western scholarship, the battles to discard flawed ideas about the inherent inferiority, backwardness, stagnation, or simplicity of Third World societies have largely been won in progressive circles.[4] Whether for purposes of self-critique or self-legitimization of Euro-American modernity, even the invention of mythical constructs of cultural otherness has come under scrutiny for drawing on exoticizing, reductionist, and instrumentalizing views of such societies. Creating a "primitive," a "savage," or an "Orient" as empty canvasses onto which to project a set of mirrorlike alter egos, figures of total negation or signifiers of absolute alterity that have little or nothing to do with the actual lifeworlds and self-conceptions of their supposed referents—and this solely for the purposes of assisting the modern West's self-understanding—is analytically flawed and normatively objectionable.[5]

In short, and despite the persistence of global Euro-American hegemony, exoticism may be dying. Cultural perspectivism enables us to grasp the fact that the world's peoples enact different yet legitimate manifestations of the human condition, grounded in the cultivation of morally valid traditions and complex types of sociopolitical organization. Cultures mingle and coexist in a condition of contemporaneity, perpetually engaged in dynamic processes of exchange and self-transformation; they are full participants in the great human adventure rather than bystanders, remnants of bygone eras, or second-class passengers. While the demise of exoticism should be welcome, it must not serve as a pretext for ending cross-cultural engagement. Complacently or timidly retreating to the familiar and the close at hand leaves the intellectual terrain open to the ethnocentric temptations of false universalism and radical particularism, which always lurk in the shadows. To use another metaphor, the baby of intercultural critique must not be thrown out with the bathwater of exoticism, nor can the Western human sciences be allowed to parochially close in upon themselves by ceasing to investigate other worldviews, subjectivities, and modes of social organization. As Clifford (1997, 91) argues:

> [W]hen criticizing specific legacies of travel, one should not come to rest in an uncritical localism, the inverse of exoticism. There is truth in the cliché, "Travel broadens." . . . Sojourning somewhere else, learning a language, putting oneself in odd situations and trying to figure them out can be a good way to learn something new, simultaneously about oneself and about the people and places one visits. This commonplace truth has long encouraged people to engage with cultures beyond their own.

I would only add that broadening also needs to travel, namely that the considerable merits of openness to the diverse ways of putting the world into form must become widely accepted by critical theorists.

For this to be possible, the ethnological imagination must strive to cultivate a form of dialogical cosmopolitanism that situates itself in time and space, as well as being committed to studying the world at large and being willing to embrace the provocation of cultural difference. Today, the fact that alterity is no longer being externalized or kept at bay, that it is seen as existing just as much in the North Atlantic region as "out there," or around the corner and within oneself as across the oceans, presents us with renewed intercultural opportunities. What becomes both possible and imperative is the act of listening to others speak, and indeed speaking back, with voices that express their standing as subjects of history and authors of alternative narratives—rather than as objects of Western monologues. In the same vein, the interpretive labor of making sense of others' self-representations, of striving to understand different ways of thinking and acting on their own terms, must be undertaken.[6] The acknowledgment that cross-cultural interpretation is fraught with difficulties, that it cannot but be partial because of the impossibility and undesirability of completely divesting oneself of familiar lifeworlds in order to be entirely submerged by different ones, does not relieve us of the task of persistently looking beyond the here and now. The corresponding effect of cross-cultural disorientation can expose to scrutiny, or go so far as to put into doubt, deeply held Euro-American norms, beliefs, and practices.

Developing and preserving a genuine sense of openness, however, is not synonymous with granting non-Western perspectives inherent and absolute validity, nor with the longing for unadulterated manifestations of the "Other" (such as the "discovery" of an isolated community untouched by the vagaries of Western civilization). The assimilationist postulate of complete identity and the exoticist one of authentic alterity are but the opposite sides of the same reductionist coin, as are unqualified veneration and condemnation of cultures. Instead, the challenge consists, first, of recognizing the diverse, multidimensional, and complex character of non-Western subjects and societies, which, in a global and increasingly integrated age, constitute hybrid blends of the commonplace and the unknown; and second, that these same subjects and societies can, just like their counterparts in the West, be ambivalently understood as combining the valid and the questionable. The subaltern speaks in polyphonic voices; one should listen to her or him not as a representative of pure otherness (e.g., holism, traditionalism, stability) or truth, but as someone who is simultaneously similar to and different from "us," embedded in sociocultural environments that are not the opposite of "ours," but offering alternative models of mediation and articulation between universal tendencies. I would argue that this kind of acknowledgment, coupled with the commitment to glimpse into and partially enter different cultural universes, amplifies the possibilities for and the extent of cultural estrangement. In fact, far from being compromised, the latter is much more likely to be sustained by a dialogical cosmopolitanism attuned to the presence of multiple sites of sociocultural difference in the world, as well as the impossibility of attributing a single or essential identity to non-Western societies. An incessant dialogical process, whereby knowledge aimed at rendering other peoples' worldviews and practices is set in conversation with their own self-understandings, compels us to reformulate and reexamine our theoretical premises and conclusions. In some instances, one can even realize that sets of beliefs and forms of social action believed to be analogous to one's own actually dwell beyond the bounds of that which was imagined to be possible, or conversely, that what seems incommensurable is not inevitably so.[7] Cross-cultural reality, especially in its nonreductionist forms, is often stranger than fiction.

"In-Betweenness"

If postcolonialism, multiculturalism, and globalization have transformed the conditions under which cross-cultural encounter takes place, they are similarly affecting the ethnological imagination's understanding of mediation in a culturally pluralistic world. As a result, Western social theory must jettison a characteristic alluded to at the opening of this book, namely, the attachment to an intrinsic correspondence between nation-state, society, and culture, or to put it differently, to conceptions of culture as nationally and territorially bound, discrete and homogeneous. Here again, social theorists can move in this direction by incorporating some of the insights of recent intercultural research in the human sciences, which proposes new linguistic tropes and analytical perspectives to reflect changing sociocultural realities. Though not themselves entirely unproblematic, notions of transnationalism, diaspora, hybridity, and creolization, among others, are designed to capture the porousness, diversity, and deterritorialization of cultures—that is to say, the global unhinging of and disjuncture between cultural, societal, and geographical entities.[8]

The proliferation and intensification of various transnational flows have blurred cultural and civilizational boundaries, for people from different backgrounds and parts of the world share an increasing number of material and symbolic spaces. Hence, due to this overlap and interpenetration between most societies, what was formerly assumed to be an absolute gap between insular and uniform cultures cannot hold. Under such conditions, "in-betweenness" becomes both more urgent and more complicated than ever before, its very character changing from a contrast between binary oppositions ("primitive"/ modern, West/East, and so forth) and the bridging of chasms to movement amidst patchworks of resemblance and divergence—a movement that cannot attain perfect translation or identity. Furthermore, mediation must also foreground the asymmetrical nature and effects of globalization processes. One does not need to adhere to a crude, homogenizing thesis equating the latter with Americanization to recognize the vast differences between rates of diffusion of, say, U.S. and New Guinean Highland popular culture. And of course the circulation of images across the planet does not in and of itself guarantee greater cross-cultural understanding; in fact, quite the opposite case could be made. "In-betweenness," then, also involves the scraping away of long-held or newly acquired cultural prejudices, stereotypes, and misunderstandings, about which critical social theorists must be perpetually vigilant.

Comparative thought can move to destabilize cultural dichotomies by adopting a perspective that searches for axes of similarity and difference between fluid and permeable sociocultural lifeworlds.[9] Mediation therefore takes place among "multiple" or "alternative modernities" (Eisenstadt 2000, Gaonkar 1999, Taylor 1999). Cross-cultural interface is rarely characterized by a straightforward, unilateral substitution of one set of sociocultural orientations (the exogenous, the secular, the individual) for another (the indigenous, the religious, the collective). Much more commonly, modernity consists of the formation of heterogeneous "fields of tensions" (Arnason 1990) structured by the dialectical relationship of, for instance, system and lifeworld (Habermas 1987b), rationalization and subjectivation (Touraine 1995), rational mastery and autonomy (Castoriadis 1997a), or liberty and discipline (Wagner 1994). Accordingly, all sociohistorical configurations are syncretic because they are forged out of the violent and/or benign processes of amalgamation of numerous local, regional, and global forces within the human condition's vast range of possibilities; one can thus usefully refer to Islamic and Indian modernities, East Asian forms of capitalism, or South American aesthetic modernisms.[10] By the same logic, the determination of a given society's specificity cannot be derived from abstract and universal models of modernity. Instead, one should assess the distinctive manner in which a society institutes itself through processes of selecting, reconciling with, and "creatively adapting" to differing cultural tendencies, as well as patterns of thought and action grounded in specific historical, economic, and political circumstances (Taylor 1999). In addition, one should consider the extent to which the shifting amalgam, resulting from an articulation of such tendencies and patterns into a society's self-understandings, is accepted or disputed by people living within and outside of it.

I would contend that the kind of outlook favoring multiple and intersecting syncretisms over binary dualisms is better suited to the cultivation of a contemporary ethnological sensibility. To put it succinctly, it views cultures as processes rather than things, actively created and recreated on the basis of appropriation, imposition, and negotiation over time and in different places. Rather than permanently fusing together what are considered to be distant, static, and self-contained entities—a process that relies on essentialized representations of cultures—mediation can create a space of changing interconnections between cultural beliefs and practices in an expanded, globalized field of analysis. This form of "in-betweenness" would also stand as a viable alternative to radical particularism's parochial nominalism and to false universalism's ahistorical and acultural homogenization. In a syncretic world, a cross-cultural broadening of horizons is attained less through the search for a nonmodern or non-Western radical outside than by comparatively decentering and situating North Atlantic types of modernity within the transnational context of multiple modernities. When coupled with the erosion of the West/non-West divide, intercultural pluralization does much to expose us to other possible modes of social organization while prompting us to ask how different societies have attempted to resolve tensions constitutive of the modern condition.

The Inward Turn

By concurrently altering the ethnological imagination's object of study and its method of comparative analysis, the phenomena of postcolonialism, globalization, and multiculturalism have modified the terms under which reflexivity and a critical hermeneutics of Western modernity can be performed. To be sure, the rethinking of cross-cultural critique presents us with novel opportunities for breaking with the doxic common sense of Euro-American societies, since it becomes exceedingly difficult to take the existing social order for granted in the age of global cultural pluralism. The presence of the Third World in the First World, as well as the blending of the West and the non-West, transform the domestic into a site where heterogeneity and likeness are woven into mosaic patterns; "home" and "here" cannot intrinsically stand for sociocultural familiarity or sameness. In other words, once it is recognized that alterity lives within, the proximate and the ordinary cannot but be estranged. Accordingly, the sources of the modern West's "core traditions" must be reimagined as diverse, fragmented, and disputed because born out of sociopolitical relations with other civilizations and peoples.

The sort of dialogical cosmopolitanism to which I have already referred situates, and thereby "provincializes," the North Atlantic region in a manner that underscores its historical and cultural specificity (Chakrabarty 2000). This specificity originates neither from a clear-cut rupture with its own past, nor from the uniqueness of certain characteristics and principles (e.g., reason, freedom, secularism, individualism), but more to the point, from the particular character of its hybrid versions of modernity; Euro-American societies are the perpetually contested outcomes of, among other things, purposive-instrumental and communicative rationality, liberation and domination, and secular and religious tendencies, as well as individualistic and collectivist orientations (Gaonkar 1999, Taylor 1999). Because different constellations of these factors exist in other parts of the world, the institutional forms that surfaced in the West over the modern era cannot be considered natural, universal, or necessary. Their striking oddity requires explanation, piercing through the veil of the self-evident in pointing toward an inescapable query: why and how has this way of life become widely accepted, and should it be? Cross-cultural theorizing combats the ubiquitous threat of one-dimensionality, the dehistoricizing and ethnocentric closure of alternative ways of acting and thinking. If other modes of social organization are possible, then the present can be otherwise. What comes to light is the self-instituting of society, the processes of collective struggle and relations of power through which it has been created.

A Few Parting Words

In the preceding pages, I have urged social theorists to rediscover the ethnological imagination as a mode of critique. Apart from constituting a lively and diverse tradition that has vitally nourished the project of a critical hermeneutics of Western modernity, cross-cultural theory provides us with some of the tools for reformulating intellectual work in an ever-more pluralistic and integrated world—and this, despite the frequent manifestations of exoticism and civilizational chauvinism that have marked social-theoretical encounters with cultural otherness. Admission of the gravity of historical errors and of the prevalence of lingering dangers on the intercultural terrain must not serve to justify the retreat to apparently safer, albeit ethnocentric, ground. As I have already indicated, most Euro-American responses have done just that, embracing the misleading alternatives of traditionalism or postmodernism, on the one hand, and of false universalism or radical particularism, on the other. Yet Western social theory cannot afford to provincially close in on itself, either by exclusively focusing on what is nearby and commonplace or by generating ahistorical and acultural models of social life based on what is observed from within its own sociocultural horizons. Nor can it be seduced by facile normative and cultural inversions, such as Occidentalism (the wholesale condemnation of the West) or nativism (the idealization of non-Western societies), as correctives for the abuses and mistakes of the past. At the same time, the ethnological imagination cannot pass over in silence the ever-expanding socioeconomic gulf between the Northern and Southern Hemispheres, the origin of many of the most pervasive obstacles to the fostering of a genuine cross-cultural dialogue among the world's peoples. Were we to succumb to any of these temptations, both the relevance and the worth of theorizing would be seriously jeopardized in the human sciences.

The ethnological imagination offers a different route. It insists on the importance of enlarging our horizons in order to engage with, to be open to the provocation of, and to learn from other ways of being and thinking in the world. In addition, it seeks to mediate between diverse sociohistorical constellations and thereby to widen the scope of what is possible within the bounds of humankind. And it "culturalizes" and comparatively situates the established Euro-American order of things to an extent that undermines the latter's appearance of "naturalness," inevitability, and universality. The associated troubling of the ordinariness of the categories of the "West" and "modernity" can only be welcome. Cross-cultural perspectivism, then, counters the narrowing down of the array of possibilities for individual and collective existence just as it stimulates reflection about alternative forms of social organization. This could prove vital to the future of critical social theory, which would be considerably enriched by incorporating interculturalism into its better-established modes of philosophical and historical interrogation of what is. Denoting both the comparative merits and flaws of the modern West without falling prey to either indiscriminate triumphalism or the denunciation of it, dialogical cosmopolitanism nurtures precisely the kind of ambivalence that is sorely needed today. Such is the spirit animating the ethnological imagination, which compels us to return to Gauguin's haunting queries: "Where do we come from? What are we? Where are we going?" These are fundamental questions about the intricate play of similarity and difference that gives birth to the human condition— questions, it should not be forgotten, that have been sparked by cross-cultural encounter time and again.

Notes

Preface

1. See, among others, Hobsbawm (1987), Said (1978, 1993), Wallerstein (2000), and Wolf (1982).

2. For instance, etymologically speaking, "primitive" initially designated whatever was considered original, basic, or primal in a given society. Yet dating back to Greek antiquity, such traits rapidly came to be attributed to particular peoples who deviated from the predominant standards of what was considered civilized life. Since the Enlightenment, but more strongly since the mid-nineteenth century under the impact of various progressivist and, later, evolutionary modes of thought, "primitive" has come to connote indigenous societies claimed to be historically and culturally backward. The erroneous and prejudicial belief in their lack of development in various spheres of life (intellectual, moral, economic, technological, political, cultural, and so forth) has legitimated their supposed inferiority vis-à-vis the modern Western world.

Introduction

1. See, inter alia, the following writings: Appadurai (1996), Bauböck and Zolberg (1996), Baudrillard and Guillaume (1994), Benhabib (2002), Bennett (1998), Bernstein (1992), Bhabha (1994), Calhoun (1992, 1994, 1995), Chakrabarty (2000), Clifford (1988, 1997), Dallmayr (1996), García Canclini (1995), Gilroy (1993, 2000), Goldberg (1994), Gunew and Yeatman (1993), Gutman (1994), Habermas (1996, 2001), Hall (1990, 1991), Hannerz (1992), Kozlarek (2001), Kymlicka and Mesure (2000), Morley and Chen (1996), Ouellet (2000), Papastergiadis (2000), Robertson (1992), Schnapper (1998), Spivak (1988a, 1988b, 1993, 1999), Todorov (1993), Touraine (1997), Wieviorka (1996), and Young (1990). Even the authoritative *Report of the Gulbenkian Commission on the Restructuring of the Social Sciences* has

weighed in: "The question that is consequently before us is how to take seriously in our social science a plurality of worldviews without losing the sense that there exists the possibility of knowing and realizing sets of values that may in fact be common, or become common, to all humanity" (Wallerstein 1996, 87).

2. This is not to suggest that cross-cultural thinking is unique to Euro-American societies during the modern era. It has existed at different times and places, going back as far as Herodotus's *Histories* (1996) in the fifth century BC and is found in both ancient and medieval conceptions of the savage, the barbarian, and the wild man (Bartra 1994, 1997; Boas 1948; Lovejoy and Boas 1935). Intercultural reflection has also played an important role in non-Western settings; in the case of Japan, for instance, see Miyoshi (1991) and Tanaka (1993).

3. See Mohanty et al. (1991), Spivak (1988b, 1993, 1999), and Trinh (1989).

4. See Bhabha (1994), Chakrabarty (2000), Said (1978, 1993), Spivak (1988b, 1999), and Young (1990).

5. See Asad (1973), Clifford (1988), Clifford and Marcus (1986), Ellingson (2001), Fabian (1983), Kuper (1988), and McGrane (1989).

6. See Derrida (1976, 1978a, 1978b), Foucault (1965, 1998b), and Irigaray (1985a, 1985b), among others.

7. See Calhoun (1997), Hall (1991), Giddens (1990), Gilroy (1993), Touraine (1992), and Wallerstein et al. (1996). This correspondence is in part derived from nineteenth-century European nationalism, according to which the right of peoples to self-determination was tied to the belief that each linguistically and/or territorially identifiable culture should be recognized through the creation of the matching institutional structure of a nation-state.

8. It should be noted that the mapping out of the intellectual terrain proposed here is not intended to suggest that specific theorists perfectly fit within its categories or wholly subscribe to one camp or another. Rather, their work is best seen as situated along a continuum whose opposing poles (the four positions suggested above) are ideal types.

9. For historicist positions, see Camic (1997), Poggi (1996), and Skinner (1969).

10. For a more detailed critique of historicism along the lines presented here, see Alexander (1987b).

11. The category of "postmodernism" is intended here to be much more restrictive than the catchall meaning it has acquired in the English-speaking world—a meaning that, among other things, conflates the postmodern with the poststructural.

12. See Game (1991), Game and Metcalfe (1996), Lyotard (1985), Seidman (1991b), and Trinh (1989).

13. As Said (1989) put it, even the contemporary discipline of anthropology must consider the possibility that it remains nothing more than "a partner in domination and hegemony" (225).

14. See Chakrabarty (2000), Clarke (1997), Marcus and Fischer (1999), Rorty (1991c, 219), and Spivak (1999, 6–9).

15. Schnapper (1998) makes a like-minded distinction between assimilationism and differentialism, which correspond to false universalism and radical particularism, respectively.

16. To be explicit, the problem lies neither with Haraway nor Geertz, but with radical particularists who have appropriated their work.

17. See also Ouellet (2000, 99–119).

18. See, for instance: Bhabha (1994), Said (1978, 1989, 1993), Spivak (1988b, 1999) and Young (1990) for postcolonialism; Bartra (1997), Chinard (1934, 1978), Dudley

and Novak (1972), Fairchild (1961), Marouby (1990), Mason (1990, 1998), Meek (1976), Todorov (1984, 1993), White (1978, 150–96), and Whitney (1934) in the history of ideas; Barkan and Bush (1995), Goldwater (1987), Gombrich (2002), Rubin (1984), and Smith (1989, 1992, 1994) in art history; Asad (1973), Ellingson (2001), Fabian (1983), Kuper (1988), Marcus and Fischer (1999), and McGrane (1989) in cultural anthropology; and di Leonardo (1998) and Torgovnick (1990) in cultural studies.

19. Elias's ability to generate a distancing effect vis-à-vis the modern West is also implicitly grounded in cross-cultural juxtaposition, as he indicates in an interview where he discusses the influence of the years he spent in Ghana (Elias 1994b, 68–72).

20. See Kögler (1996, 216–19) and Marcus and Fischer (1999).

21. Marouby (1990) prefers the expression "anthropological imagination" to designate a similar idea. However, I believe that "ethnological" is more suitable for two reasons: it is not circumscribed to what has come to be known as the discipline of social and cultural anthropology in the English-speaking world, referring instead more generally to cross-cultural forms of critical thinking in the human sciences; and it aims to avoid possible conflation with philosophical anthropology, the German tradition of reflection on human nature.

22. The translation is my own. More recently, Jullien's writings on the philosophical study and uses of China for a self-critique of the West strongly capture Merleau-Ponty's insight. See Jullien (1989, 1995, 1999) and Jullien and Marchaisse (2000).

23. I partly follow Eliade (1960, 23–24) in using the notion of myth not in contradistinction to truth or reality, but in the widest philosophical-anthropological sense: a narrated set of beliefs that is viewed as a truthful, sacred, and repeatable explanation of the origins of humanity. A myth serves to make sense of, give meaning to, and transmit specific versions of the past, the present, and the future of a society to its members.

24. See Calhoun (1995, 43), Schnapper (1998), and Todorov (1993). For a more detailed description of this intellectual field, with specific reference to the "primitive," see Kurasawa (2002).

25. See also Toulmin (1990, 28).

26. See Chinard (1934), Gay (1966, 168–70), Marouby (1990), and Todorov (1993).

27. For more detailed discussions of the French (or Durkheimian) School, see Besnard (1983), Dumont (1986, 1–6, 183–201), Karady (1995), Kurasawa (2003), Lévi-Strauss (1971), and Wacquant (1995).

28. Bourdieu's advocacy of an epistemological break with the "doxa" of modern society demands a constant back-and-forth movement between alien and familiar settings, something the ethnological imagination makes possible. See Bourdieu (1979, 587–88; 1990, 18, 20), and Bourdieu, Chamboredon, and Passeron (1991, 251).

29. For a detailed discussion of the role of the idea of America for French intellectuals, see Mathy (1993).

30. However, as I will explain in the conclusion, the rigid modern/traditional dualism is itself problematic.

31. See Faubion (2000, 245–47) and Schnapper (1998, 14–18). By the early 1970s, Gouldner (1973, 344–45) merely repeated what had come to stand as conventional wisdom: "The very activities of the anthropologist require him to go to more exotic and romantic locales; sociology, however, remains, for the most part, a study of the familiar, the everyday, and the commonplace. . . . The anthropologist writes about extraordinary locales that have color and vividness, in contrast to the sociologist's

greater proclivity for the matter-of-fact and the prosaic." In a similar vein, Elias (1987b, 40n4) commented that "[a]nthropologists, in most cases, study societies to which they do not belong, other sociologists, mostly societies of which they are members."

32. The publication of Fields's meticulous retranslation of *Elementary Forms* (1995) has gone some way toward rectifying the standing of Durkheim's magnum opus. And despite the efforts of scholars such as Nelson (1991a, 1991c) and Schluchter (1981, 1996), Weber's comparativist credentials remain underappreciated.

33. Much the same can be said of the English-language reception of Bourdieu's work. Anglo-American commentators rarely consider the importance of his early ethnological work among the Kabyle in Algeria for the elaboration of his theoretical apparatus and subsequent studies of French society.

34. As Geertz (1973, 347) has said: "Every man has a right to create his own savage for his own purposes. Perhaps every man does. But to demonstrate that such a constructed savage corresponds to Australian Aborigines, African Tribesmen, or Brazilian Indians is another matter altogether."

35. See Dallmayr and McCarthy (1977), Gadamer (1976, 18–43; 1992), Habermas (1988, 143–70; 1992), Kögler (1996), Ricoeur (1981b), and Warnke (1993).

36. Arbitrating the debate between Gadamer and Habermas, Ricoeur (1981c, 144) has drawn a similar conclusion: "[W]e can no longer oppose hermeneutics and the critique of ideology. The critique of ideology is the necessary detour which self-understanding must take." See also Arnason (1992, 259), Bauman (1978, 225–46), Bernstein (1978), Calhoun (1995, xviii), Horkheimer (1972, 208), Kögler (1996), Taylor (1985a), and Thompson (1981).

37. Although Gadamer limits his remarks to the idea of distance in time, he also indicates that a more general conception of distance—one that could incorporate geographical and cultural distance—is entirely feasible: "[I]t is distance, not only temporal distance, that makes this hermeneutic problem solvable" (1994, 298n228). His numerous comparisons between interpretation and translation further suggest that he is aware of the intercultural implications of his argument.

38. See Bauman (1987, 9), Calhoun (1995, 8–9, 44), Clastres (1977, 17), Diamond (1974, 100), Eliade (1960, 9), Gadamer (1994, 97), Ricoeur (in Lévi-Strauss 1970, 64, 66; Ricoeur 1974, 51), Taylor (1985b, 129–30), and Walzer (1987, vii). It is in this spirit that Nietzsche (1974 [1882]) has the *Gay Science*'s wanderer declare: "If one would like to see our European morality for once as it looks from a distance, and if one would like to measure it against other moralities, past and future, then one has to proceed like a wanderer who wants to know how high the towers in a town are: he *leaves* the town." I thank Charles Ambrose for drawing my attention to this passage.

39. On this point, see Dumont (1977, 18, 36; 1986a, 8–9), Merleau-Ponty (1953a, 114–15), and Taylor (1985b, 129).

40. This is not to say that these figurative and literal modes are independent of one another. The person who "goes abroad" to study a non-Western society already carries with her or him a particular set of imaginary expectations, preconceptions, and representations, while the one who "stays at home," yet participates in the creation of Western modernity's cultural alter egos, is invariably influenced by firsthand accounts of other sociocultural settings.

41. As Taylor (1998, 111) explains: "When we escape from the prison of our perspective, the ground shakes under our feet."

42. This is why Winch's (1970) widely debated late Wittgensteinian position regarding the ultimate untranslatability and unintelligibility of "primitive" institutions

from a modern Western perspective remains unconvincing. Incommensurability is a possible outcome of cross-cultural work, yet should not be presumed as always already present.

43. See Arnason (1992, 256), Calhoun (1995, 48–49, 80–82), Dumont (1977, 15–16), Gadamer (1994, 387–88, 537), Kögler (1996, 128–44), Merleau-Ponty (1953a, 100, 114; 1953b, 166; 1960, 153), Rabinow and Sullivan (1987, 19), and Ricoeur (1981a, 62).

44. Dumont echoes Elias's sentiment: "Ethnology, or more precisely social anthropology, would have only specialist interest if the subject of its study—'primitive' or 'archaic' societies and the great civilizations of other countries—revealed a human kind quite different from ourselves. Anthropology, by the understanding it *gradually* affords of the most widely differing societies and cultures, gives proof of the unity of mankind. In so doing, it obviously reflects at least some light on our own sort of society" (1972, 36). See also Bourdieu (1990, 15), Bourdieu, Chamboredon, and Passeron (1991, 19–20), Diamond (1974, 100, 211–12), Dumont (1977, 18), Eliade (1960, 9–12, 38), Elias (1978, 104), Merleau-Ponty (1953a, 113, 117, 121; 1953b, 166; 1960, 150), Mills (1959, 6–8, 132–34), Park (1950, 253–54), Ricoeur (1974, 52), Taylor (1994, 67), and Wolf (1974, xiii).

45. See Elias (1987b, 13), Gadamer (1994, 14, 114, 268–70, 299, 441–42, 447–48), Kögler (1996, 169, 174–75, 183–84, 212–13), Merleau-Ponty (1953a, 115; 1953b, 163), Ricoeur (1981a, 62), Taylor (1985a, 54, 57), and Walzer (1987, 39, 61–62).

46. The history of sociology is replete with representatives of outsiders inside the modern West: Simmel's (1950) stranger combining "nearness and remoteness," Park's (1950, 51) "marginal man," who "lives in two worlds but is not quite at home in either," Du Bois's (1995) description of African-Americans' "double consciousness," as well as the many feminist theories about women's distinctive standpoint at the margins of patriarchal society (e.g., Collins 1991 and 1998; Smith 1987 and 1990). I would like to thank Vince Marotta for bringing to my attention the similarities between Simmel's and Park's ideas, on the one hand, and the viewpoint carved out by cross-culturally oriented social theorists, on the other.

47. See Arnason (1990, 206), Bourdieu (1977, 168, 233n16; 1990, 14), Bourdieu and Wacquant (1992, 73), Calhoun (1992, 258; 1995, 48–49, 84), Eliade (1960, 7–10, 38), Gadamer (1994, 17, 299), Merleau-Ponty (1953a, 114–15; 1960, 150), Mills (1959, 146–52), Taylor (1985a, 54; 1985b, 131), and Winch (1970, 78, 94, 99). Castoriadis makes a similar argument: "[I]t unsettles our tendency to confine ourselves to what we are given as the average and usual type of man and society—and, quite especially, to our own society and to the individuals we encounter therein. . . . In other words, people think that living in a society where everything can be challenged goes without saying, whereas that is the thing that goes without saying the least of all. This possibility therefore shakes up our banal and false sense of self-evident truths" (1997b, 101).

1. On Civilized Savagery

1. Cassirer (1954, 36) contends that "Rousseau was the first thinker who not only questioned this certainty [of the eighteenth century] but who shook its very foundations. He repudiated and destroyed the molds in which ethics and politics, religion as well as literature and philosophy were cast." Shklar (1969, 1) abounds in the same direction: "His denial was comprehensive, embracing civilization as a whole. And in his tone of undeviating contempt for all he saw around him, he was singularly

consistent. . . . His enduring originality and fascination are entirely due to the acute psychological insight with which he diagnosed the emotional diseases of modern civilization." See also Gay (1954, 28) and Shklar (1969, 30). Though Rousseau was writing and living in the mid-eighteenth century, his analysis is not circumscribed to ancien régime societies, for it anticipates many of the dilemmas of social life in the postrevolutionary modern world.

2. I have let myself be guided by Cassirer's (1954) and Starobinski's (1971) important studies, which adopt a hermeneutical approach to reconstructing Rousseau's thought.

3. See Bénichou (1984, 126–27), Gay (1969, 319), Marouby (1990, 124–25), and Symcox (1972, 224–25, 229–30).

4. See also Rousseau (1964a, 12; 1966, 30) and Todorov (1993, 10–12). Whenever possible, I have used Cole's standard English translation of Rousseau's *Social Contract and Discourses* (1973). However, I have also referred to the authoritative five-volume edition of Rousseau's *Oeuvres complètes* published in Gallimard's Bibliothèque de la Pléiade (1959–95), edited by Gagnebin and Raymond. The above footnote by Rousseau is omitted in the Cole translation; I have thus quoted from Cranston's translation of *The Discourse on Inequality* (1984).

5. The translation is my own. See also Rousseau (1984, 160–61), Marouby (1990, 155–56), Symcox (1972, 225–26), and Todorov (1993, 11–12, 351–52, 390–91). Here I disagree with Cassirer when he claims that "[t]he expansion of the spatial-geographical horizon can help us as little as the road back to prehistory. Whatever data we may gather in this area remain mute witnesses unless we find in ourselves the means of making them speak. The true knowledge of man cannot be found in ethnography or ethnology. There is only one living source for this knowledge—the source of self-knowledge and genuine self-examination. And it is to this alone that Rousseau appeals; from it he seeks to derive all proofs of his principles and hypotheses. In order to distinguish the '*homme naturel*' from the '*homme artificiel*,' we need neither to go back to epochs of the distant and dead past nor take a trip around the world" (1954, 50). Cassirer revises this judgment in his later work: "Often enough he [Rousseau] confused his role as educator, as social critic and moral philosopher with the role of the historian. . . . And in the final review Rousseau gave of his whole work in his *Rousseau Judge of Jean-Jacques*, he maintained this interpretation: he here describes himself as the first truthful 'historian of human nature'" (1963, 24). For Rousseau, introspection and cross-cultural encounters are not mutually exclusive; on the contrary, they are complementary routes for arriving at a "true knowledge of man." On this point for the Enlightenment in general, see Gay (1969, 174–75, 319–20).

6. See Diamond (1974, 219–20), Lévi-Strauss (1977b, 33–35, 43), Lovejoy (1948, 17–18), and Symcox (1972, 230–31, 243–44).

7. See Cassirer (1954, 76–78; 1963, 45), Diamond (1974, 219–20, 331), Gay (1954, 27–28; 1966, 141–42, 150, 185), Rousseau (1973b, 48; 1973d, 169–70; 1973e, 182; 1974, 10–11, 173, 176, 244–45), Shklar (1969, 31–32), and Symcox (1972, 225–26).

8. See Cassirer (1954, 95; 1963: 9, 11–12), Rousseau (1953, 214, 332, 374–76, 384, 589–91; 1959, 789–90, 813, 824–25, 866; 1979, 129–33), and Starobinski (1971, 52–53, 222–23, 341, 378–79).

9. The emphasis is mine. See also Berman (1970, 320), Cassirer (1954, 42–43), Derathé (1984, 116–17), Rousseau (1959, 669–71; 1979, 27, 30–33, 52–53, 58), Starobinski (1971, 16, 52–53, 56–59, 152–54, 160–61, 354–55, 423), and Symcox (1972, 235).

10. "The same man who would remain stupid in the forests should become wise and reasonable in towns, if he were merely a spectator in them." (Rousseau 1974,

217). See also Cassirer (1954, 123; 1963, 9), Derathé (1984, 110–11), Rousseau (1974, 205–6), Starobinski (1971, 354), and Symcox (1972, 237).

11. "I must begin by observing everything among the first [people] among which I find myself; then gradually assign differences as I travel across the other countries; compare France to each of them, like the olive-tree is described in relation to the willow and the palm-tree in relation to the first, and delay judging the first people observed until I have observed all the others" (Rousseau 1964a, 242–43) The translation is my own.

12. The state of nature is by no means the only other sociocultural constellation that Rousseau contrasts to early Western modernity: ancient Greece and Rome, as well as Geneva (and thus, to a certain extent, the pastoralism of the European medieval world) also operate as lenses through which the here and now are evaluated. For my purposes, only the first motif will be examined.

13. See Rousseau (1964a, 241–46) and Starobinski (1971, 154).

14. Here and throughout this chapter, I deliberately use the masculine pronoun without its feminine equivalent when referring to Rousseau's notion of the "savage" in order to underline its gendered character.

15. See Berman (1970, 123, 134), Cassirer (1963, 26), Colletti (1972, 155, 157, 161–63), Gay (1969, 537–38), Rousseau (1953, 306; 1964c, 969; 1964d, 605–6; 1964f, 909–10, 914–16; 1973b, 44, 52–53, 63–64, 80, 92; 1973e, 187; 1974, 148, 167, 197–98), Shklar (1969, 25, 30–31, 34–35), and Starobinski (1971, 274, 347–49).

16. The emphasis is mine. See also Bénichou (1984, 126–27, 129), Cassirer (1951, 270–71; 1954, 49–50), Colletti (1972, 149), Durkheim (1960, 69), Gay (1969, 96, 538), Lovejoy (1948, 17–18), Marouby (1990, 155–56), Rousseau (1953, 362, 595–96; 1959, 668–69, 828–29; 1973a, 20; 1974, 438), Shklar (1969, 2–3, 6, 36, 44), Starobinski (1971, 26, 342–44, 380, 382–83), and Symcox (1972, 244).

17. Among others, Voltaire (1995) and Condorcet (1955, 54) were the originators of the primitivist misinterpetation of Rousseau. His writings should be compared to the actual primitivism of Diderot's polemical *Supplement to Bougainville's Voyage* (1972 [1796]), which unfavourably juxtaposes the artificiality and old age of Europe to the youthful purity of Tahiti. A more convincing and nuanced reading of Rousseau has since been provided by many commentators; see Berman (1970, 153), Lovejoy (1948), Marouby (1990, 114), Starobinski (1971, 344–45), Symcox (1972, 236), and Todorov (1993, 277–82). Lovejoy's (1948, 25, 35) influential treatment tends to go too far, arguing that Rousseau is not only a firm advocate of progress, but one of the first evolutionists.

18. See Berman (1970, 129–31, 149–53), Cassirer (1951, 269–70; 1954, 78, 105), Gay (1969, 536), Lovejoy (1948, 36), Rousseau (1953, 50; 1964c, 971–72; 1973b, 43, 51, 54, 86–87, 91; 1974, 411; 1979, 61; 1995b, 379, 428–29), Shklar (1969, 45), Starobinski (1971, 38–39, 44, 245–47, 357, 366), Symcox (1972, 239–40), and Todorov (1993, 280). Rousseau proposes an intermediary period between the state of nature and civil society, a state of savagery where nature and culture are perfectly balanced because technology and artifice are neither underdeveloped, nor overdeveloped while morality is nascent (Rousseau 1973b, 91; Starobinski 1971, 348–49, 370–71; Todorov 1993, 280). This is what Lovejoy (1948, 31) has identified as the third stage of Rousseau's history of humanity, which corresponds to Lévi-Strauss's image of the Neolithic era.

19. See Rousseau (1964c, 969–70; 1973a, 6, 9–10, 14; 1973b, 46–47, 60–61, 70–71; 1995b, 396, 400–401), and Shklar (1969, 44).

20. See Cassirer (1954, 57), Rousseau (1959, 805–6, 890–91; 1964a, 57, 78,

479–83; 1964c, 965–66; 1973b, 56; 1974, 221–22, 261; 1979, 109–11, 116–17; 1995b, 384, 414–15, 419, 424–27; 1995c), Starobinski (1971, 176–80, 364–65, 368–69, 375), and Taylor (1989, 358).

21. See Berman (1970, 130), Derathé (1984, 119–20), Rousseau (1995a, 15–16, 43, 52–53), Taylor (1995, 47), and Trilling (1972, 62–65).

22. See Berman (1970, 146, 151), della Volpe (1978, 22–23), Rousseau (1959, 668–69, 864–65; 1964b, 826–27; 1964f, 905, 911–12, 917; 1973b, 60–62, 79-80; 1974: 44–45, 191), Shklar (1969, 28–29, 55), and Starobinski (1971, 23–24, 39–40, 139, 260, 324, 340, 361–62, 387–89).

23. See Berman (1970, 150–51, 167–68; 1988, 17–18), Rousseau (1964b, 815–16; 1964d, 605–6; 1969, 551; 1973b, 43; 1974, 44–45, 373–74; 1979, 123–24), Shklar (1969, 28–29), and Starobinski (1971, 132–33, 388–89).

24. See Colletti (1972, 150–51), Rousseau (1959, 670–71, 854–55, 864; 1964c, 969–70; 1964d, 612; 1973b, 71–72; 1995b, 380–81), Shklar (1969, 48), Starobinski (1971, 22–23, 359), and Symcox (1972, 233–34).

25. Berman (1970), Ferrara (1993), Taylor (1989, 1991) and Trilling (1972) all provide an analysis of the centrality of authenticity to Rousseau's thought. As will be discussed in chapter 6, Foucault's antihumanism, manifest in his work on self-regulation through "passive" processes of subjectivization, aims to dissolve the very idea of authenticity. For Foucault, there is no true self to be discovered, and attempts to do so lean toward normalization.

26. See Berman (1970, 140, 143–44; 1988, 18), Durkheim (1960, 103–4), Gay (1969, 541), Rousseau (1964a, 255–56, 273, 298, 300; 1964d, 611–12; 1973d, 169–70; 1979, 123–24), Starobinski (1971, 42–43, 62), and Taylor (1995, 48–49).

27. See Berman (1970, 133), Cassirer (1951, 25960; 1954, 75), della Volpe (1978, 88–90), Rousseau (1964a, 584; 1964d, 601–2, 611–12; 1973b, 50, 96–97, 116–17; 1973d, 176), and Starobinski (1971, 35–51). Lovejoy's (1948, 26–28) claim that Rousseau's vision of human nature is both derived from and essentially identical to that of Hobbes appears mistaken. Macpherson's argument goes in the same direction as my own: Hobbes's and Locke's conceptions of the state of nature are fictional constructs employed to help understand and justify dawning social order in Europe, notably the existence of a sovereign state and a private market economy (Macpherson 1962, 18–21, 68–70, 197–98, 208–211, 235–38).

28. See also Bénichou (1984, 141), Berman (1970, 85), Cassirer (1951, 270–71), Rousseau (1953, 387; 1959, 824–25; 1964d, 603–4; 1973a, 6; 1973b, 57–58, 92, 102–5; 1979, 101, 153–54; 1995b, 400–401), Shklar (1969, 29–44), and Starobinski (1971, 344–46, 361).

29. See also Colletti (1972, 174–75, 179–80), Derathé (1984, 111–12), Shklar (1969, 3, 5), Todorov (1993, 21–23), and Weil (1984, 13, 31). Regarding Rousseau's impact on Kant, see Starobinski (1971, 46–47, 345), Taylor (1989, 363–64), Weil (1984, 17–18), Cassirer (1954, 58, 82) and, more generally, the latter's "Kant and Rousseau" (Cassirer 1963, 1–60). In turn, regarding Cassirer's own neo-Kantian reading of Rousseau, see Gay (1963, xi–xii).

30. See Berlin (1969, 138, 142), Cassirer (1951, 261–62, 272–73; 1954, 55–56, 58, 62, 96, 104–6, 123), Colletti (1972, 174–75), Durkheim (1960, 84–85), Gay (1969, 547–48), Kant (1991c, 227–28), Rousseau (1959, 671–72, 864; 1973e, 195–96; 1974, 243–44, 252, 408; 1979, 49, 61, 73, 96, 101, 123–24), Shklar (1969, 13), Taylor (1989, 359–60; 1991, 27–28), Todorov (1993, 23), Trilling (1972, 66), and Weil (1984, 32–33). It should be pointed out, however, that Rousseau's (and Kant's) notion of autonomy excludes women, who are deemed incapable of moral maturity.

31. See Berman (1970, 182), Cassirer (1951, 260–61, 272–73; 1954, 54–56, 62–65; 1963, 26), Colletti (1972, 151–52), Derathé (1984, 121), Durkheim (1960, 89–91, 142–43n2, 143n3), Gay (1969, 549), Kant (1991c, 227–28), Rousseau (1964e, 806–7, 842, 891; 1973c, 132–34, 147–48; 1973e, 190–92, 196, 207–8; 1974, 48–49, 424–25; 1979, 96), Shklar (1969, 31–32), Starobinski (1971, 62, 345), Taylor (1995, 48–50), and Weil (1984, 16).

2. Disenchanting the Commodity

1. Postone's (1993) work has the merit of combining the historicist insights of humanist Marxism and the social constructivism of structural Marxism. However, his insistence on the immanent and historically specific character of Marx's critique of capitalism underplays the transcendent or outside role played by noncapitalist societies in this critique, and thereby overlooks the ethnological imagination's presence.

2. It should be noted that Marx's transcendent critique of the capitalist social order is also realized through the positing of a communist future, as well as the use of literary reference points; on the latter, see Prawer (1976). These themes, albeit important, fall outside the immediate purview of my consideration of the ethnological imagination. The notion of Asiatic or Oriental despotism does make its appearance in Marx's *Critique of Hegel's Doctrine of the State* (1974a [1843], 91), yet this is but a passing reference wholly indebted to Hegel's own use of the concept in his *Philosophy of Right* (1952 [1821]) and *Lectures on the Philosophy of World History* (1975 [1840]).

3. See Habermas (1987b, 341), Hobsbawm (1964, 46–47), Honneth (1995b, 22–23, 26), Marx (1974a, 148; 1974f, 317–19, 323; 1976a, 113, 183–88), and Marx and Engels (1976, 66).

4. See Beilharz (1992, 8) and Testard (1985). At that point, Marx's knowledge of the "primitive" condition is largely derived from travel books (Fabian 1983, 155–56; Marx and Engels 1976, 303).

5. Anderson (1974, 472) presents an exhaustive taxonomic reconstruction of the intellectual sources of Marx's conception of Oriental despotism, while the first chapter of Krader's *The Asiatic Mode of Production* (1975, 19–79) provides a historical overview of the idea in European thought. Hindess and Hirst (1975, 201–2) offer a clear exposition of the essential traits of the Asiatic mode of production, while Bailey (1981) provides a useful review of the massive secondary literature on the topic written during the 1960s and 1970s (C.E.R.M. 1969, Godelier 1977, Hindess and Hirst 1975, Krader 1975, Said 1978, Sawer 1977, Thorner 1990, Turner 1978, Wittfogel 1957). For a famed critique of Marx's Orientalism, see Said (1978, 153–56).

6. The theses about Oriental despotism and Asian socioeconomic stagnation appear again in the *Grundrisse* (Marx 1973, 473), as well as in the first and third volumes of *Capital* (Marx 1967b, 331; 1976b, 479, 791).

7. See Marx (1968a, 88–89; 1968b, 125–31) and Turner (1978, 14–16).

8. See Anderson (1974, 477, 483), Bloch (1983, 34, 36–39), Dunayevskaya (1981, 176), Godelier (1977, 100), Hobsbawm (1964, 25), Krader (1975, 96–105, 115, 119–20, 131–35, 177), Marx (1973, 107, 225–26, 242–45, 471–99, 511–12), Melotti (1977, 30, 49, 56), Thorner (1990, 451), and Wittfogel (1957, 373, 376).

9. See Benhabib (1986, 106–8), Honneth (1995b, 24), and Márkus (1980).

10. See Krader (1975, 122–23), Marx (1967b, 326–27, 331, 334, 614–15, 726, 783, 786–87, 790–93, 818, 831, 877–78; 1976b, 273, 452, 477–79, 951), and Thorner (1990, 452–53).

11. Somewhat rhetorically, *The Communist Manifesto* (Marx and Engels 1969a, 112) also contains a scenario about the universalization of capitalism.

12. See also Dunayevskaya (1981, 185–87), Shanin (1983, 6), and Wada (1983, 44). Engels added a note to the 1888 English edition of *The Communist Manifesto* suggesting that Marx's sustained engagement with anthropological material occurred relatively late: "In 1847, the pre-history of society, the social organization existing previous to recorded history, was all but unknown. Since then, Haxthausen discovered common ownership of land in Russia, Maurer proved it to be the social foundation from which all Teutonic races started in history, and by and by village communities were found to be, or to have been, the primitive form of society everywhere from India to Ireland. The inner organization of this primitive Communistic society was laid bare, in its typical form, by Morgan's crowning discovery of the true nature of the *gens* and its relation to the *tribe*" (Marx and Engels 1969a, 108–9). In Engels's opinion, the implications of these cross-cultural findings are sufficient to warrant amending the famous formula from *The Communist Manifesto*, "The history of all hitherto existing society is the history of class struggles," by adding in the footnote quoted above, "that is, all *written* history" (Marx and Engels 1969a, 108).

13. See Anderson (1974, 477–85), Bloch (1983, 45–47), Godelier (1977, 101), and Thorner (1990, 455–56).

14. Nevertheless, Engels's work neglects the qualifications and criticisms of Morgan's *Ancient Society* (1964 [1877]) contained in *The Ethnological Notebooks*. In particular, Engels's enthusiasm in "The Origin of the Family" for Morgan's work is more pronounced than in Marx's own preliminary assessment (Dunayevskaya 1981, 179–87; Krader 1972, 11, 77–78).

15. See Bloch (1983, 44), Godelier (1977, 101), Hobsbawm (1964, 49–51), Krader (1972, 5–6), and Shanin (1983, 6–7, 15, 29). See also the "Preface to the Russian Edition of 1882" in *The Communist Manifesto* (Marx and Engels 1969a, 100–104); on how the latter partially revises Marx's position in the drafts of his letter to Zasulich, see Wada (1983, 70–71).

16. Of course, as we will see in the next chapter, this is precisely the question that Weber asks a few decades later.

17. See Marx (1975, 203, 485; 1976a).

18. Vico's *New Science* (1984 [1744], 62, 91) is among the major works whose argument about the inherently societal character of human existence preceded Marx's own sociocentric position. See also Habermas (1973, 242–44). Marx's notion of species-being is taken from Feuerbach. See, inter alia, the latter's "Towards a Critique of Hegel's Philosophy" (1972a, 92–93).

19. See Habermas (1987a, 34), Hobsbawm (1964, 12–13), Krader (1972, 58–61, 69–70, 75; 1975, 303, 323–24; 1979, 166–69), Löwith (1982, 75, 83, 96n11), Márkus (1978, 16), Marx (1969a; 1973, 496; 1974e, 265–66; 1974f, 350; 1974g, 418–19; 1976b, 443–44, 447), and Marx and Engels (1975, 131; 1976, 44).

20. The predominance of evolutionary thinking during the Victorian epoch is evidenced in such major works as Darwin's *Origins of Species* (1968 [1859]) and *Descent of Man* (1981 [1871]), Morgan's *Ancient Society* (1964 [1877]), Spencer's *Principles of Sociology* (1969 [1876–96]), and Tylor's *Primitive Culture* (1974a, 1974b [1871]). Of course, this is not to suggest that evolutionism is a homogenous paradigm of analysis, since it regroups diverse and even competing schools of thought (e.g., polygenist and monogenist, biological and cultural). See Stocking (1968, 1987).

21. See Hobsbawm (1964, 32–33, 36–38), Krader (1975, 115, 136–37), Melotti (1977, 25–27), and Shanin (1983, 5, 15, 29). Though heavily influenced by Althusserian

structuralism—and thereby offering an ahistorical and clinically abstract rendition of Marx's thought on the subject—Hindess and Hirst (1975) carefully enumerate the characteristics of different precapitalist modes of production mentioned in his writings (primitive communism, ancient, slavery, Asiatic, and feudal).

22. See Althusser and Balibar (1970, 178–79), Castoriadis (1987, 24–29), Dumont (1977, 200–203), Lukács (1971, 235–36), and Merleau-Ponty (1973, 35–36).

23. A fuller treatment of Marx's thought would examine his historically specific concept of value, and notably the fact that he intends the labor theory of value to be applicable solely to capitalism rather than being transhistorical and universal (Postone 1993). However, such a discussion would take us well beyond the scope of this chapter and the central focus of this book. For an overview of recent poststructuralist uses of Marx's notion of fetishism, see Pietz (1993, 122–29).

24. See Carver (1975, 11, 175), de Brosses (1988, 11–15, 110), and Pietz (1993, 130–35). I am indebted to Peter Beilharz for drawing my attention to de Brosses and Carver.

25. See also Langer (1984, 104), Marx (1973, 156–65, 221–22, 469–71; 1974c, 239), and Marx and Engels (1975, 82).

26. Lukács comments: "Thus we see that the road to an understanding of precapitalist societies with a non-reified structure could not be opened up until historical materialism had perceived that the reification of all of man's social relations is both a product of capitalism and hence also an ephemeral, historical phenomenon. (The connection between the scientific exploration of primitive society and Marxism is no mere accident.) For only now, with the prospect opening up of re-establishing non-reified relations between man and man and between man and nature, could those factors in primitive, pre-capitalist formations be discovered in which these (non-reified) forms were present" (1971, 237–38). This is not to say that reification and commodity fetishism are identical in Marx's mind, since Márkus (1982, 149) demonstrates that the former concept includes both objectification ("the externalization and material fixation of human activity in the product") and fetishization ("the transformation of relations between men into relations between things").

27. Marx's fragmentary remarks about the Asiatic mode of production suggest that social formations ruled by "Oriental despotism" do not necessarily find their sources of legitimation in nature or God, but also in the person of the ruler. Nevertheless, this is also a case of heteronomy, the ruler acting as the personification of an all-powerful state, which embodies divine or natural forces outside of civil society.

28. On Marx's philosophical anthropology and his labor ontology, see, inter alia, Arendt (1958, 86, 98–99), Beilharz (1992, 7), Benhabib (1986, 55–58), Dumont (1977, 185–86), Habermas (1987a, 27–29, 43; 1987c, 64, 341–42), Heller (1976, 31), Honneth (1995d, 146), Honneth and Joas (1988, 20–21), Joas (1996, 91–92), Krader (1972, 80–82; 1975, 165, 177–78, 300), Langer (1984, 110–11), Lefebvre (1968, 8, 20), Márkus (1978, 3–7, 14–15, 26–27, 50), Marx (1969a, 14; 1969d, 503; 1969e, 13–14; 1969f, 14; 1973, 271–72, 360–64, 611–12; 1974e, 265–66; 1974f, 328–29, 389–90; 1974g, 418–19; 1976a, 165–66, 170; 1976b, 128–34, 270, 283–91, 308, 998), and Marx and Engels (1975, 39, 130–31; 1976, 36–37, 41–42, 82).

29. See Marx (1904, 69–70; 1973, 83; 1976b, 169n31). Marx's comments are aimed at political economists' use of the Crusoe allegory rather than Defoe's original story, where it is clear that the main protagonist does not act out of natural instinct, but because of his prior socialization in eighteenth-century England (Defoe 1972 [1719]; Prawer 1976, 274).

30. See Benhabib (1986, 109–10), Castoriadis (1987, 24), Colletti (1972, 188–89),

della Volpe (1978, 144), Dumont (1977, 193), Hobsbawm (1964, 14–15), Márkus (1978, 16–17, 21–22, 37), Marx (1904, 69–70; 1969a; 1973, 83–85, 496; 1974a, 147; 1974c, 220, 233–34; 1974e, 266–67; 1976b, 169n31), Marx and Engels (1975, 113), Prawer (1976, 273–76), and Rosanvallon (1989, 189–91).

31. See also Marx (1976b, 175). It should be noted that Marx attributes to political economy the ideological qualities that Feuerbach (1972b, 114) unearths in religion.

32. See Bloch (1983, 2–3, 11–16, 42–43), Castoriadis (1987, 33), Geras (1972, 295), Godelier (1977, 158), Heller (1976, 28–29, 33, 74–75, 80–81), Langer (1984, 105), Lukács (1971, 229–32, 241, 245), Marx (1967a, 225; 1967b, 818–19, 830–31, 877–81; 1973, 97–98, 102–7; 1974f, 322–23; 1976a, 112–14, 162, 165–66, 183–85; 1976b, 96, 174–75, 273–74, 771–72, 874–76, 918, 925–26), Marx and Engels (1975, 32; 1976, 48), and Taussig (1980, 8–10).

33. For analyses demonstrating the indelibly historical and cultural character of market capitalism, see Dumont (1977), Macpherson (1962), Polanyi (1944), and Rosanvallon (1989). As will be discussed in the next chapter, this also represents an important part of Weber's project.

34. See Dumont (1977, 207–8), Godelier (1977, 171–75), Heller (1976), Hindess and Hirst (1975, 43, 51), Lefebvre (1968, 14–15), Löwith (1982, 82–83), Lukács (1971, 84–86, 91–92, 237–38), Marx (1967b, 806; 1973, 226, 245, 471–72, 489–95; 1976b, 170, 452, 457–58, 471–72, 477–80, 643–44, 880–81; 1989b, 366), Postone (1993, 171–72), and Trilling (1972, 123). Of course, this is not to say that, for Marx, social relations in noncapitalist environments are transparent. His writings are careful to study the sociopolitical ideologies obscuring the actual power relations and structures in all social formations (Godelier 1977, 172–76; Marx 1967b, 831; 1974a, 178). Diamond (1974) exemplifies the pitfalls of a simplistic primitivism, which highlights Marx's assessment of the positive traits of primitive communism while ignoring his equally critical judgment of its serious flaws.

35. See Benhabib (1986, 110), Heller (1976, 44–45), Lukács (1971, 233, 241), Márkus (1978, 13–14, 31, 83; 1982, 151), Marx (1967b, 596–97, 793–94; 1968a, 88–89; 1968b, 131; 1969b, 236–37; 1969c, 478–80; 1974e, 274; 1976b, 172–73, 927–28; 1989b, 351, 366), and Merleau-Ponty (1973, 35).

36. See Berman (1988, 101, 127), Castoriadis (1987, 17), Marx (1969b, 213–14; 1969e, 20; 1976b, 618, 637–38), Marx and Engels (1969a, 113–14, 119), and Prawer (1976, 24, 27, 31). Marx believes that the growth of productive forces is eventually limited by capitalist social relations and immanent contradictions within the mode of production (e.g., the falling rate of profit). Furthermore, capitalism's dialectic plays itself out on Marx's grand stage of history: the bourgeoisie steps forth as the Faustian sorcerer's apprentice, having unleashed forces that will eventually lead to its downfall.

37. See Benhabib (1986, 115, 372n16), Habermas (1973, 218–19; 1987c, 60), Löwith (1982, 70), and Marx (1967b, 830–31; 1976b, 171–73).

38. See Lukács (1971) and Postone (1993, 30–31, 125–26).

39. See also Benhabib (1986, 108, 114–15), Carver (1975, 177–78), Geras (1972, 286–87, 293), Godelier (1977, 7–8, 158–59, 163–64, 170–71, 176–79), Habermas (1987a, 59–60), Lefebvre (1968, 62–63), Löwith (1982, 77), Lukács (1971, 83–86), Marx (1967b, 392–93, 399, 826–27), Postone (1993, 62, 70, 168–73), and Taussig (1980, 26–33).

40. See also Habermas (1973, 221–22), Marx (1967a, 29; 1967b, 41; 1969a, 216; 1969e, 13; 1973, 305–8, 364, 497–99, 502–3, 514–15; 1974f, 330–32; 1976b, 271–74, 280, 424–25, 486, 716, 719, 723–24, 874–76), and Marx and Engels (1976, 78–79).

41. See Benhabib (1986, 116), Habermas (1973, 221; 1987b, 334–36, 340–41; 1987c, 349–52), Heller (1976, 26–27, 38–39, 48–57), Honneth (1995b, 23), Langer (1984, 107), Löwith (1982, 69, 78–81), Lukács (1971, 88–92, 231–32), Márkus (1978, 81), Marx (1967a, 110, 116–17; 1967b, 617–18; 1973, 145–51, 156–65, 221–26, 232, 242–45, 693–95, 699–700, 704–6; 1974e, 260–61, 268–70; 1974f, 317–19, 337, 340–41; 1976a, 186–88; 1976b, 128–29, 138–39, 159–60, 165–69, 182–83, 187, 203–5, 209, 254–55, 457–58, 501–3, 526–27, 545–49), and Marx and Engels (1976, 63, 73, 86–87, 230).

3. The View from the Magical Garden

1. A reminder about the broad meaning of the expression "ethnological imagination" is in order here, since Weber's intercultural contrast is established with Asian civilizations (specifically, India and China), rather than with indigenous societies (the conventional object of the discipline of cultural anthropology). Of course, Weber also employs Greco-Roman antiquity, ancient Judaism, and the European Middle Ages as points of contrast and comparison, yet they are not viewed in the same manner as the "Eastern" Other. In Weber's mind, the former are part of the Western world's civilizational past. For the purposes of this chapter, I will not be dealing with the historical or sociological accuracy of Weber's portrayal of non-Western cultures. Van der Sprenkel (1964) and Molloy (1980) discuss both the flaws and the merits of Weber's writings on China. Said's (1978, 259) claim that "Weber's studies of Protestantism, Judaism, and Buddhism blew him (perhaps unwittingly) into the very territory originally charted and claimed by the Orientalists" is overly hasty in lumping him together with other thinkers of the turn of the century.

2. What Parsons titled the "Author's Introduction" to *The Protestant Ethic and the Spirit of Capitalism* is in fact the introduction to Weber's *Collected Essays in the Sociology of Religion (Gesammelte Aufsätze zur Religionssoziologie)*.

3. See Bendix (1960), Eisenstadt (1991), Kalberg (1994, 1997), Schluchter (1981, 1987, 1996), Tenbruck (1980), and Turner (1974, 1996); for Weber's global framework of analysis, see Arnason (1997) and Eisenstadt (1986, 1987a, 1987b, 2000).

4. For a more detailed but related critique of Parsons's interpretation of Weber's writings on China, see Molloy (1980).

5. For a discussion of Tolstoy's influence on Weber's outlook, see Roth (1971a, 25–30) and Scaff (1989, 100–102). Weber's explanation hinges on the interaction between the institutional and existential dimensions of capitalist rationalization. However, I will follow Gordon (1987), Hennis (1988), Owen (1994), and Schluchter's more recent writings (1996) in insisting on Weber's primary interest in the second aspect: modern Western capitalism's impact on the conduct of life, the self's regulation of his or her personality and mentality.

6. See Scaff (1989, 59–61), Weber (1979), and Marianne Weber (1988, 129–30).

7. See Käsler (1988, 36–38), Nelson (1991c, 97–98), and Marianne Weber (1988, 329).

8. See Nelson (1991a, 217–21; 1991c, 98–99), Schluchter (1981, 8–9, 149), Seidman (1983, 237–42), Tenbruck (1980, 326–31), and Marianne Weber (1988, 326, 331–32). *The Protestant Ethic* was originally published in 1904–5, whereas its revised edition came out in 1920. Another passage inserted into the later edition also underscores the contribution made by intersocietal comparison: "Capitalism existed in China, India, Babylon, in the classic world, and in the Middle Ages. But in all these cases, as we shall see, this particular ethos was lacking" (1930b, 52).

9. See Weber (1949b, 81) and Scaff (1989, 86).

10. See Bendix (1971, 297–98), Habermas (1984, 153–54), Mommsen (1991, 119–20), Roth (1971d, 254–56; 1979, 195), Scaff (1989, 83), Schluchter (1981, 10–11), Weber (1949b, 76–81, 84–87, 111; 1976, 385), and Marianne Weber (1988, 310–13).

11. See Weber (1949b, 51–52; 1980, 449n4).

12. See Bendix (1971, 286), Hennis (1988, 160), Scaff (1989, 65, 68–71, 113), Schluchter (1979a, 50–51n137), and Weber (1949a, 27–28, 32–35, 39; 1949b, 85–87, 139; 1980, 436–38).

13. See Arnason (1982, 6), Castoriadis (1992, 246), Giddens (1987, 184), Habermas (1971, 63), Merleau-Ponty (1973, 19–22), Nelson (1991a, 221–23; 1991c, 96–97), Roth (1971d, 257–58; 1979, 196), Scaff (1989, 20, 63), Schluchter (1979a, 21; 1981, 5, 10–12, 175), Seidman (1983, 238–42), Weber (1930a, 29; 1946c, 294; 1949b, 67, 76–77, 80–81, 111–12; 1949c, 155–56; 1971, 256; 1976, 37–45), and Marianne Weber (1988, 312–13, 338, 677).

14. See also Schluchter (1987, 95) and Weber (1949b, 81).

15. See Weber (1980, 437) and Merleau-Ponty (1973, 21–22).

16. See Bendix (1971, 291–96), Eisenstadt (1991, 9–10), Hennis (1988, 41–42, 84–85), Löwith (1982, 42–43, 102), Molloy (1980, 390–91), Schluchter (1987, 97–98), Weber (1930a, 26–28; 1930b, 90–91; 1946c, 267–70, 284, 293–94; 1978b, 1111–13), and Marianne Weber (1988, 326, 331–32).

17. See Habermas (1984, 202–4), Schluchter (1981, 157–60; 1987, 103), and Weber (1946c, 285–86; 1946e, 324–25, 340; 1951, 178–87, 235–40, 248; 1958, 206–22, 331–33, 337–39; 1978a, 497–98, 542–51). Although not discussed in this chapter, Weber's analysis of ancient Judaism demonstrates the latter's importance for the creation of theocentrism and the rationalized cultural ethos that was to characterize the modern West. Nonetheless, Weber believes that Protestantism's crucial point of distinction (i.e., inner-worldly asceticism applied to daily economic behavior) is no less absent in ancient Judaism than in other world religions. See Weber (1952; 1978a, 611–16, 1201–4; 1981, 360–61).

18. Weber portrays the Hindu Brahmans as an intensely ascetic social group, but one whose otherworldliness and orientation toward magic prevent the transition into a fully rationalized conduct of life. Instead, according to Weber's rather Orientalist understanding, ascetic Hinduism veers into magical, contemplative, and apathetic mysticism (Nelson 1991c, 102–4; Weber 1946c, 292; 1946e, 323; 1958, 59–61, 123, 139, 147–52, 162–67, 172, 178, 184–91; 1978a, 544–51).

19. Weber presents Confucianism as possessing an inner-worldly, practical, and rational inclination hostile to contemplation, magic, and mysticism (Weber 1951, 144–47, 155–57, 228–29), yet this is not converted into asceticism. Despite similarities with the Protestant ethic, Confucianism's "relentless canonization of tradition" (Weber 1951, 164) directs it away from constructing a systematically rationalized system of daily conduct. Inherited and customary patterns should be maintained as they are, lest the equilibrium of the cosmos be destroyed. The religious tension with the world is minimized since the universe is viewed as the unchanging container of the human condition—not raw material to be molded by us. Consequently, the onus is placed on humankind to adjust, to perpetuate a style of life and a culture adapted to the eternal shape of the cosmos (Habermas 1984, 208; Molloy 1980, 393; Nelson 1991c, 100–101; Schluchter 1979a, 31; 1981, 61, 163; Weber 1951, 87, 152–53, 156–57, 227–29, 235, 240, 243–44).

20. See Alexander (1987, 192–93), Habermas (1984, 206–7), Schluchter (1981, 161–65, 170–73), Seidman (1983, 232–34), and Weber (1930b, 79–81, 108–9, 158; 1946c, 290; 1946e, 326–33; 1951, 227–28, 237–38, 240, 247–48; 1978a, 546–51, 555–56).

21. See Weber (1930b, 58–59, 64–65, 161–63; 1946c, 277–78, 290–91; 1978a, 615–16; 1978b, 1112–15, 1124–25; 1981, 271, 367–68).

22. See Eisenstadt (1991, 4, 8), Hennis (1988, 31–32, 36, 39–40, 153), Merleau-Ponty (1973, 13, 15), Nelson (1991a, 217), Roth (1971c, 111–12), Schluchter (1981, 142–44, 156, 173), and Weber (1930a, 16–18, 23–27; 1930b, 42–44, 51–58, 90–91; 104–6, 118–19, 166–71, 288–89; 1946d, 309, 320; 1946e, 328–31; 1978a, 435–36, 462–63, 480, 575–76, 583–84, 587–89, 611–16, 624, 1199–1200; 1978b, 1121; 1981, 276, 313–14, 355–58, 364–65).

23. As Gordon (1987) has shown, this aspect of Weber's thinking anticipates several themes of Foucault's later work. The connection will be explored in chapter 6. Weber is fascinated by Benjamin Franklin, the figure who incarnates a novel type of human being in whom bourgeois consciousness is allied to ascetic faith.

24. See Weber (1951, 206, 208, 223–25, 229–30, 235–38; 1958, 216–22, 352).

25. See Weber (1930b, 97–98, 126, 133, 154; 1958, 338–39; 1981, 368).

26. See Habermas (1984, 164) and Weber (1930b, 104–5; 1946d, 320; 1978a, 430–32, 437, 543–44, 575–76, 603–4; 1978b, 1114–17, 1119, 1121). Nietzsche's *Daybreak* (1997 [1881], 162 § 331) contains an apt aphorism to this effect: "Asceticism is the right discipline for those who have to exterminate their sensual drives because the latter are raging beasts of prey." I am grateful to Charles Ambrose for drawing my attention to this passage.

27. See Alexander (1987a, 188–91), Habermas (1984, 228), Merleau-Ponty (1973, 15, 18), Seidman (1991a, 155), Marianne Weber (1988, 341–42), and Weber (1930b, 72–73, 174, 176, 180; 1946d, 307, 321–22; 1978a, 476–77, 575; 1978b, 1125, 1128–29; 1981, 368–69). My emphasis on Puritanism's sociocultural ethos is not intended to deny that Weber's analysis of the creation of rational capitalism in the West includes consideration of the role of institutional factors. Among them, he identifies the "free" organization of the forces of production (the sale of labor power and the circulation of capital), the invention of modern accounting techniques (bookkeeping), the emergence of a rational state administration with a solid legal system, mechanization and "technologization" of industrial activity, commercialization, as well as the separation of office from home (Habermas 1984, 158; Weber 1930a, 21–22, 24–25; 1978a, 165, 378–80; 1981, 276–78, 313–14). Weber maintains that some of these aspects may have existed in other societies, yet never in a systematically coordinated or formally entrenched way. For instance, some of the chief preconditions for the development of rational capitalism have been present in China: financial and commercial activity, the cultivation of a bureaucratic class (the so-called mandarins), an inner-worldly and rationalized cultural ethos (Confucianism), and so forth. Nevertheless, the continued dominance of patrimonial traditionalism and magic has resulted in the absence of an institutional configuration comparable to that of modern Western societies (Merleau-Ponty 1973, 17; Weber 1930a, 21–22; 1951, 12–13, 20, 84–86, 95–96, 100–103, 242–43; 1958, 113–14; 1978a, 237–41; 1981, 313–14).

28. See Weber (1951, 27–31, 34, 37, 47, 50, 60–62, 148–50, 236–37, 240–42; 1958, 49–50, 67, 325–26, 331–36; 1978a, 226–29, 237–41, 244–45, 816–23, 1006–7, 1010, 1020, 1029–31, 1041–44, 1049–50, 1068, 1085–86, 1112–17, 1394–95; 1981, 338–43).

29. See Habermas (1984, 246) and Weber (1946a, 93–94; 1946c, 271–72, 296; 1951, 27–29, 60–62, 95–96, 164–65, 178–79, 196, 200, 205, 224–27; 1958, 26–27, 49–50, 111–12, 342; 1978a, 406, 576–78, 630, 816–28; 1981, 355–61).

30. See Arnason (1982, 4–5), Benhabib (1986, 257–59), Habermas (1984, 163–64, 243–46; 1987c, 1, 112–13), Hennis (1988, 72, 101–2), Löwith (1982, 32), Scaff (1989, 72, 81–82, 91–93), Schluchter (1979b, 78–79; 1981, 45), Seidman (1991a, 154,

163–64), Weber (1946b, 139, 142, 147–48; 1946e, 342, 350–51, 356–57; 1949a, 15–18, 27–28, 34–35, 37–38; 1978a, 506), and Wellmer (1985, 41–43). For Weber (1946b, 148), both Baudelaire's *Les Fleurs du mal (The Flowers of Evil,* originally published in 1857) and Nietzsche's philosophy are emblematic of this cultural shift toward polytheism. Simmel's concerns, notably in "The Conflict of Modern Culture" (1971 [1918]) run parallel to those of Weber on this point. For a discussion of their mutual influence, see Frisby (1987) and Scaff (1989, 121–51). See also Weber's (1972) own fragmentary assessment of his colleague, whose study of money as a purely abstract measure of value and equivalence (Simmel 1990 [1900]) was important for the former's argument about rationalization (Weber 1978a, 86, 92).

31. For instance, Weber (1930a, 24–25) argues that mathematics has been used as the basis for rational accounting techniques in the Western world, a kind of practical outcome that was never sought in India despite its advanced mathematical knowledge.

32. See Hennis (1988, 98–100, 156), Scaff (1989, 167–71), Schluchter (1979a, 54; 1981, 53), and Weber (1946a, 78–79; 1946b, 155; 1946c, 293, 298–99; 1946e, 333–34; 1978a, 85–86, 107, 148, 215–20, 225–26, 666–67, 812–15, 841–48, 854–58, 880–84, 956–58, 973–75; 1979, 182, 190–91).

33. See Hennis (1988, 100–102) and Weber (1946a, 95; 1978a, 988, 1116–17, 1148–50, 1402–3).

34. See Alexander (1987a, 192–93, 197), Arnason (1982, 3–4, 8), Habermas (1971, 64), Hennis (1988, 45, 100–101), Löwith (1982, 43, 47–51, 58–59, 104), Merleau-Ponty (1973, 23), Nelson (1991a, 219–21; 1991b, 345; 1991c, 98–99), Scaff (1989, 32–33, 53–55, 88–90), Weber (1930a, 13–15; 1930b, 181; 1946a, 79–80; 1946c, 276; 1949c, 124–25; 1951, 247; 1978a, 26, 1115, 1133, 1146–47, 1402; 1978b, 1124–25; 1981, 366), Marianne Weber (1988, 333–34), and Wellmer (1985, 41–43). Parsons famously translated Weber's original German phrase, *"stahlhartes Gehäuse,"* as "iron cage," yet Kalberg's new translation of *The Protestant Ethic* uses the more etymologically literal and analytically accurate "steel-hard casing." For a convincing explanation of this choice, see Weber (2002, 245–246n129). Throughout this chapter, I nevertheless retain page references to Parsons's more widely known translation of the work (Weber 1930b).

35. See Bendix (1960, 116–25, 152–58) and Weber (1951, 107, 119–21, 125–27, 246–48; 1958, 338–39; 1978a, 1001).

36. "Specialists without spirit, sensualists without heart; this nullity imagines that it has attained a level of civilization never before achieved" (Weber 1930b, 182). Found toward the end of *The Protestant Ethic,* this sentence paraphrases the contents of Nietzsche's assault on the "last men" (Nietzsche 1954, 129–30, 399–400) and religious asceticism. About the latter, see the third essay of Nietzsche's *Genealogy of Morals* (1996 [1887], 77–136), entitled "What Is the Meaning of Ascetic Ideals?" In a passage from his *Sixth Letter on the Aesthetic Education of Man,* Schiller (1967, 35) expresses the effects of such a shift on the individual's style of life: "Everlastingly chained to a single little fragment of the Whole, man himself develops into nothing but a fragment; everlastingly in his ear the monotonous sound of the wheel that he turns, he never develops the harmony of his being, and instead of putting the stamp of humanity upon his own nature, he becomes nothing more than the imprint of his occupation or of his specialized knowledge."

37. For a discussion of Weber's concept of charisma as a modern counterweight to rationalization, as well as its relationship to notions of social action and creativity, see Arnason (1982, 4–5) and Joas (1996, 44–49).

38. See Alexander (1987a, 186–89), Benhabib (1986, 257–59, 371n12), Castoriadis (1992, 252), Habermas (1984, 247), Hennis (1988, 158–59), Löwith (1982, 38–40, 56–60), Roth (1971b, 56–57), Scaff (1989, 77–78, 81–82, 112–13, 170, 183–85, 224–27), Schluchter (1979a, 52–53), Seidman (1983, 231; 1991a, 159–64), Weber (1946b, 139–40, 148–49, 152–53, 156; 1946e, 336, 356; 1978a, 576–78), and Marianne Weber (1988, 319–20, 325, 684).

39. See Weber (1946a, 115, 117, 127–28; 1949b, 57–58).

40. Jaspers (1989, 34) attributes these exact qualities to Weber himself.

4. In the Shadow of the Other

1. Apart from Durkheim and Mauss, the French school included figures such as Henri Beuchat, Célestin Bouglé, Paul Fauconnet, Maurice Halbwachs, Henri Hubert, and Robert Hertz. Like others of the "Lost Generation" in Europe, many members of the school were sent to the battlefront (and some never returned). On the history and influence of the school in French intellectual circles, see the essays collected in Besnard (1983), as well as Bourdieu and Passeron (1967, 198), Dumont (1986, 1–6, 183–201), Karady (1995), Lévi-Strauss (1971, 1977c), Lukes (1985, 398–403), Vogt (1976), and Wacquant (1995). The French school of sociology and anthropology heavily influenced avant-garde artistic movements during the interwar period, notably the Collège de sociologie (which included figures such as Bataille, Caillois, and Leiris). See Clifford (1988, 117–51), Hollier (1988), Kurasawa (2003), and Richman (1990).

2. See Durkheim (1927, 163–64; 1975a, 77–78), Karady (1995, 142), and Lukes (1985, 159).

3. See Durkheim (1965a, 24–25; 1995, 5–6), Karady (1995, 150), Lacroix (1981, 126–27), Lévi-Strauss (1977c, 44–45), Lukes (1985, 180–81), and Thompson (1982, 94).

4. See Durkheim (1927, 148–49; 1956, 77; 1959; 36–50, 194–95; 1960, 66–71; 137–38, 143n3; 1965b, 55; 1970d, 234–35; 1975a, 80; 1984, 130, 331–32) and Lukes (1985, 285–87).

5. "We could not wish to be free of society without wishing to finish our existence as men. I do not know whether civilization has brought us more happiness, and it is of no consequence; what is certain is that from the moment we are civilized we can only renounce civilization by renouncing ourselves. The only question that a man can ask is not whether he can live outside society, but in what society he wishes to live" (Durkheim 1965b, 55). See also Durkheim (1952, 211–13, 246–52; 1956, 76, 133; 1957, 7, 11–13, 60–61; 1965b, 54; 1965c, 72; 1965d, 97; 1970i, 314; 1973, 6, 48–49, 51, 69, 71–73; 1984, xxxii–xxxiii, xliii–xliv, 331; 1995, 321, 351, 425) and Mestrovic (1988, 139).

6. It should be remarked that Durkheim's argument overemphasizes the significance of social cohesion and thus leaves little room for individual dissent; it veers very close to advocating conformity toward the established social order.

7. See Durkheim (1927, 100–106; 1960, 57–60; 1995, 1–8, 93–94, 110–11, 169), Lukes (1985, 456–57), and Karady (1995, 143–44). For a sample of Spencer's evolutionary views, see Spencer (1969, 8–10, 31, 152–55; 1971, 71, 75, 80–81; 1972, 39–40).

8. See Durkheim (1927, 144–47, 169–71; 1970a, 89–90; 1975a, 79–80), Lévi-Strauss (1977c, 47–48), and Thompson (1982, 73).

9. This is not to deny the significance of either Comte or Spencer for Durkheim's thinking. On their influence, see Gouldner (1973), Lukes (1985, 140–47), and Parsons (1937a, 307, 311–14).

10. See Durkheim (1960, 58; 1995, 1–3, 45) and Thompson (1982, 122–24). In a similar vein, Lévi-Strauss (1971, 515–17) establishes a distinction between the functionalist and historical components of Durkheim's thought: the analysis of social roles is not to be confused with a search for origins. Commenting on Mauss, Lévi-Strauss explains: "When he [Mauss] follows Durkheim in refusing to dissociate sociology and anthropology, it is not because he sees in primitive societies early stages of social evolution. They are needed, not because they are earlier, but because they exhibit social phenomena under simpler forms. As he once told this writer, it is easier to study the digestive process in the oyster than in man; but this does not mean that the higher vertebrates were formerly shell-fishes" (Lévi-Strauss 1971, 527).

11. See also Tylor (1974b, 410).

12. See Durkheim (1995, 1–3, 419–21) and Giddens (1978, 21).

13. See Durkheim (1978b, 147; 1995, 240), Lévy-Bruhl (1923, 433–34, 447; 1966, 7, 14–15, 22–23, 61–63; 1983, 50, 87–88), and Lukes (1985, 438–39). In 1925, Mauss, Lévy-Bruhl, and Rivet founded the Institute of Ethnology at the University of Paris. By 1927, however, Lévy-Bruhl had broken with the Durkheimian school and left the institute, where Mauss remained (Bunzel 1966, viii; Lévi-Strauss 1971, 510).

14. See Alexander (1988, 4–5), Bourdieu and Passeron (1967, 166–68), Dosse (1997a, 13), Durkheim and Mauss (1968a, 57, 67, 82), and Lévi-Strauss (1971, 530–31; 1987a). Horton (1995, 185) usefully contrasts Lévy-Bruhl's "contrast/inversion" schema with Durkheim's "continuity/evolution" model. Mauss repeatedly criticizes Lévy-Bruhl's strict opposition of modern and "primitive" mentalities for much the same reasons that Durkheim does (Karady 1968, xlv; Mauss 1969a, 126–27; Mauss 1969d, 563–64). In *The Notebooks on Primitive Mentality*, a work left unfinished at his death, Lévy-Bruhl substantially revises his position by rejecting the equivalence of prelogical with "primitive" and logical with modern. Instead, he opts for a continuum along which mystical and logical modes of thought are variably intertwined in different social contexts (Lévy-Bruhl 1975, 100–103). This late shift brings him much closer to the stance of continuity that Durkheim and Mauss favor.

15. See Durkheim (1927, 52, 146–47; 1960, 16–18; 1984, xxvi, 276; 1995, 1–3), Durkheim and Mauss (1968b, 454, 476), and Parsons (1937a, 371–72). Related points are made in *The Division of Labor in Society* (Durkheim 1984) and *The Rules of Sociological Method* (Durkheim 1927). Parsons's (1937a, 447) contention that Durkheim's thinking eventually slipped into a "complete ethical relativism" conflates cultural perspectivist and absolute relativist positions. A passage from *Montesquieu and Rousseau* makes this distinction explicit: "These writers disregarded history and failed to realize that men are not always and everywhere the same, that on the contrary they are dynamic and diversified, so that differences of customs, laws and institutions are inherent in the nature of things. Montesquieu, however, understood that the rules of life vary with the conditions of existence. In the course of his investigations he observed different kinds of society, all equally 'normal,' and it never entered his head to lay down rules valid for all peoples. He adapted his rules to each different type of society. . . . He did not approve of everything that has ever been done, but decided what was good and what was not on the basis of norms derived from the phenomena themselves and thus corresponding to their diversity" (Durkheim 1960, 18).

16. "These men of former ages were men like ourselves, and it is consequently impossible that their nature should be completely foreign to us. Similarly, there live in us, as it were, other men than those with whom we are familiar" (Durkheim 1977, 330). See also Durkheim (1952, 364–65; 1977, 326–28, 331–33; 1984, xxvi; 1995, 4, 418), Durkheim and Mauss (1968b, 451, 478–79), Durkheim and Fauconnet (1975, 150–52), Lévi-Strauss (1977c, 48), and Tiryakian (1995, 101).

17. See also Durkheim (1995, 5–6) and Dumont (1977, 16).

18. This position originates from Durkheim's sociocentrism, which is concisely expressed in the following sentence: "Society furnishes the canvas on which logical thought has worked" (1995, 149). See also Durkheim (1952, 375–76; 1973, 12, 69–70; 1984, xxvi, xxviii–xxvix, 238–39), Durkheim and Mauss (1969a, 13–16, 88), and Habermas (1987b, 83).

19. See Durkheim (1977, 326), and Durkheim and Mauss (1968a, 16–17, 78–87).

20. See Durkheim (1927, 97–100) and Lukes (1985, 74).

21. On this shift in Durkheim's outlook, see Alexander (1988, 2–3), Durkheim (1965a, 24–25; 1995, 231–33), Gane (1992b), Habermas (1987b, 51), Lukes (1985, 235–36, 423–24), and Tiryakian (1995, 111–12). Habermas highlights the communicative dimension of Durkheim's theoretical horizons, though he tends to reduce the latter to a linguistic phenomenon. Parsons's (1937a, 441–50) well-known claim of a misguided shift in Durkheim's writings from positivism to idealism misses this point.

22. See Durkheim (1977, 326, 328; 1995, 226–27, 240), and Durkheim and Mauss (1968a, 30, 57, 67).

23. See Durkheim (1956, 79; 1978b, 147; 1984, xxv; 1995, 8, 24, 205–6, 224–25, 421, 431–32, 446), Joas (1996, 51–52, 58), Lukes (1985, 73), and Vogt (1976, 38). Hubert and Mauss make a similar point about magic, which has in common with science a number of technical skills and forms of knowledge (Hubert and Mauss 1968, 56, 69, 134–35).

24. See Alexander (1982, 122), Durkheim (1956, 69, 117; 1984, 64, 83–85, 126–31; 1995, 5), and Thompson (1982, 70–71, 75–77). Durkheim terminologically and substantively inverts Tönnies's (1957 [1887]) analysis by arguing that the sources of a more vigorous sense of solidarity are created by the dynamics of the *Gesellschaft*. The *Gemeinschaft*, by contrast, depends on the less effective mechanism of nondifferentiation to ensure solidarity (Dumont 1986, 211–12; Durkheim 1984, 102–5, 123).

25. Bauman (1989, 170–75) has convincingly demonstrated the serious flaws of Durkheim's "societalization" of ethics, a move that risks making individual dissent and the exercise of one's conscience subordinate to the imperative of adhering to the prescribed social order's institutionally produced morality.

26. See Durkheim (1956, 77; 1984, 3–4, 333–35).

27. See Durkheim (1952, 254–55; 1957, 10–13; 1959, 37, 40; 1984, xxxii–iv, 165), Mestrovic (1988, 67), Thompson (1982, 150), and Vogt (1976, 40). This line of argument has been pursued more extensively in Mauss's *The Gift* (1988), where the economy is described as a series of moral transactions implicating the whole of social life. It has also acted as one of the mainstays of economic anthropology, stretching from Polanyi's *The Great Transformation* (1944) to Dumont's *Homo aequalis* (1977).

28. See Alexander (1982, 83), Dumont (1972, 42), Durkheim (1956, 64; 1977, 325; 1984, 84–85, 88–89, 117–18, 121–23), and Giddens (1978, 25). For an analysis beginning from similar themes to produce a cross-cultural history of the ideology of individualism, see Dumont's *Essays on Individualism* (1986).

29. See Douglas (1966, 20), Durkheim (1957, 28–29, 51–52; 1965b, 37–38, 58–59; 1965c, 72; 1970b, 212; 1970f, 266–67; 1975b, 25–26; 1984, 142–46, 288n16; 1995, 447), Giddens (1978, 10, 17–18), Habermas (1987b, 115–16), Lukes (1985, 80), Mestrovic (1988, 8–9), Parsons (1937a, 311–14, 346, 351–55), and Seidman (1983, 162–64).

30. See Durkheim (1952, 209–10, 213–14, 256–58, 363–64, 386–89; 1957, 11–12; 1970a, 109; 1973, 42–48, 68; 1984, xxxi–xxxiv, xliii), Lukes (1985, 221), and Mestrovic (1988, 66–68, 75).

31. See Alexander (1982, 122) and Durkheim (1952, 209–10, 214, 217–21, 363, 375–76).

32. I am deliberately translating Durkheim's *La Division du travail social* as *The Division of Social Labor* instead of the widely used *Division of Labor in Society*. The former title is more accurate and remains closer to the author's central argument—namely that the division of labor is a social and moral phenomenon, rather than a strictly economic one.

33. See Alexander (1982, 83, 138), Durkheim (1952, 363; 1957, 69–70; 1965b, 58–60; 1970f, 264–75; 1984, 122), Giddens (1978, 11, 17–18), Mestrovic (1988, 134–36), Seidman (1983, 174–75), and Thompson (1982, 44, 51–52, 83).

34. See Durkheim (1956, 78, 121–22; 1965b, 37–38; 1970a, 109–10; 1970f, 264–65; 1973, 59–60, 67–68, 72–73; 1984, xxxiii, xliii–xliv, 335–36; 1995, 274–75), Giddens (1978, 29–30, 84), Habermas (1987b, 84), Joas (1996, 59–60), Seidman (1983, 148–50, 171–74), and Thompson (1982, 147, 162). This is why Durkheim favorably regards Rousseau's notion of the general will (expounded in *The Social Contract* [Rousseau 1973e]), which, like his own idea of collective consciousness, is a source of integration and regulation of the members of society. The distinction between the individual and general will approximately corresponds to that between individual and collective consciousness (Dumont 1986, 89–90; Durkheim 1960, 103–4; Lukes 1985, 283–84). Nevertheless, Durkheim does criticize Rousseau for tying the general will (and morality) too closely to the state, whereas his own vision situates its locus within civil society (Durkheim 1970b, 212).

35. See Durkheim (1952, 373–74, 378, 380, 382–83; 1956, 69–72, 123–25, 133; 1957, 7, 12–15, 28–29, 46–48; 1970i, 329, 332; 1973, 13, 64–65; 1984, xxxiv–xxxv, xlii–xliii, lii–lvii; 1995, 231–33, 351–52), Giddens (1978, 62), and Gouldner (1973, 377). The growing emphasis on professional corporations vis-à-vis the division of labor is made explicit in the important 1902 "Preface to the Second Edition" of *The Division of Social Labor* (Durkheim 1984) and in a series of lectures posthumously published as *Professional Ethics and Civic Morals* (Durkheim 1957).

36. Further evidence of the significance of this problem for Durkheim's later work can be found in the fact that he left, upon his death in 1917, an unfinished manuscript entitled *Morality*; its introduction has been translated into English (Durkheim 1978c). Durkheim came to perceive morality as double-sided: positively, it includes social ideals and values toward which to strive; negatively, it is composed of rules and norms not to be violated. Discipline and attachment to social groups are its constituent parts; autonomy (individual self-mastery and societal self-determination) is its objective (Durkheim 1927, xx–xxin; 1957, 1–2, 14–15; 1965b, 35–36; 1973, 1995, 210–11n6; Giddens 1978, 65; Habermas 1987b, 48–49; Lukes 1985, 78, 421; Parsons 1937a, 382–83, 387).

37. See Durkheim (1927, 9–10, 15; 1952, 170; 1965b, 59; 1965d, 91–92; 1970c, 224–25; 1970g, 290; 1970h, 306–8; 1970i, 327–29; 1973, 62; 1975b, 24–27; 1995, 34–39, 150, 189–93, 208–21, 351–54, 386–87, 402–5, 410–11, 415–17, 424–30, 447–48), Douglas (1966, 20–21, 83, 387), Gane (1992a, 60), Joas (1996, 62–65), Parsons (1937a, 450), and Tiryakian (1995, 99, 120–22). Durkheim's argument is inspired by three principal sources: ethnographic material about Australian indigenous peoples, particularly Spencer and Gillen's (1899) pioneering research; Hubert and Mauss's (1964, 1968) studies of sacrifice and magic in "primitive" cultures; and Beuchat and Mauss's (1968) essay on the seasonal sacred life of the "Eskimos." As Karady indicates, Mauss links the sacred and the profane to society and the individual, respectively (Karady 1968, xxix). In his last major work, *The Elementary Forms of Religious Life*, Durkheim adopts a similar perspective (Lukes 1985, 27).

38. See Durkheim (1927, 6–10, 147–48, 150–52; 1952, 38; 1956, 72, 124–25; 1957, 15; 1965b, 54; 1965d, 93, 97; 1970f, 266–67; 1970h, 311–13; 1973, 6–11, 60–61, 65–66, 90–93, 121, 123; 1975b, 25–30; 1995, 16–17, 189–93, 207–33, 266–67, 274–75, 351–52, 367–75, 420–22, 427, 447–48), Giddens (1978, 67–68), and Parsons (1937a, 417). This is, I believe, a more convincing interpretation than Habermas's (1987b, 56–57, 60–61, 77–92) argument about Durkheim's "linguistification of the sacred," which overstates the latter's linguistic orientation at the expense of the more crucial republican, sociocentric, and extralinguistic dimensions of his thought. According to Durkheim, the public gatherings and rituals of modern societies derive their integrative and regulative power from symbolism and collective effervescence, neither of which is solely reducible to the linguistic aspect of communication. Habermas's formulation is nonetheless useful in explaining the fact that, for Durkheim, communicative action fosters solidarity by an intersubjective process of transmission of moral codes and ideals.

5. Mythologizing the Modern West

1. For all intents and purposes, the distinguished German tradition of cross-cultural critique, which stretches from Herder's *Outlines of a Philosophy of the History of Man* (1966 [1784]) to Humbolt and culminates in Weber's magisterial comparative sociology of life-conduct, has recently been neglected in its country of origin. Honneth (1985, 63) persuasively suggests three reasons for this phenomenon: after the First World War, German indifference toward French sociology (notably the Durkheimian tradition and its heavily anthropological orientation); the hegemony of American social science in Germany in the aftermath of World War II; and the lack of "strategic" interest in social anthropology, partly caused by the country's status as a minor colonial power.

2. On Lévi-Strauss's connection to the Durkheimian school, see Bourdieu and Passeron (1967), Dosse (1997a, 13–14, 26–31), Lévi-Strauss (1971, 1987a), and Merleau-Ponty (1960). Lévi-Strauss's introduction to a collection of Mauss's essays, *Sociologie et anthropologie,* was later published as a separate volume in English (Lévi-Strauss 1987a). At the very beginning of an essay on his intellectual trajectory, Bourdieu (1990, 1) declares that "[i]t is not easy to communicate the social effects that the work of Claude Lévi-Strauss produced in the French intellectual field." Later in the same text, he discusses the pathbreaking nature of Lévi-Strauss's thought in the France of the 1950s, which was consumed by the Algerian War: "Needless to say, in such a context, in which the problem of racism arose, at every moment, as a question of life or death, a book like Lévi-Strauss's *Race and History* (1952) was much more than an intellectual argument against evolutionism. But it is harder to communicate the intellectual and emotional impact of seeing American Indian mythologies analysed as a language containing its own reason and *raison d'être*" (Bourdieu 1990, 2).

3. See de Gramont (1970, 9), Dosse (1997a, xxi), and Roger (1999, 1). Despite this, a reassessment of the contents and merits of Lévi-Strauss's research has been taking place in France over the last few years. Indications of this return can be found, inter alia, in the publication of Hénaff's major study (1998 [1991]), the double issue of *Critique* (620–21 [1999]) devoted to Lévi-Strauss, and the special section on *Regarder Écouter Lire* in the *Magazine littéraire* (311 [1993]).

4. This interpretation follows the lead of Merleau-Ponty, whose essay "From Mauss to Claude Lévi-Strauss" (1960) captures the rich implications of Lévi-Strauss's inverted anthropology. Moreover, it is supported by Lévi-Strauss's own recent defense of his body of work, as well as by contemporary reinterpretations of it. Responding to

criticisms leveled at the lack of an anthropology of home in his writings (Delacampagne and Traimond 1997), Lévi-Strauss points to his consistent belief in a generalized (rather than geographically restricted) anthropological perspective (Lévi-Strauss 1998, 73–74). The first chapter of Hénaff's (1998) definitive study of Lévi-Strauss discusses his ethnologization of the here and now, while Abélès (1999, 43) recognizes that the current wave of anthropologies of the West was being encouraged by Lévi-Strauss as early as the 1950s.

5. This chapter will not concentrate on Lévi-Strauss's structuralist method, or on the ethnographic details of his analysis of "primitive" myths; both aspects have been amply covered in the secondary literature (see, inter alia, Hénaff [1998], Jenkins [1979], and Leach [1989]). Although the intellectual sources of structuralism are multiple and complex, ranging from Freudian psychoanalysis to cybernetics and structural linguistics (most famously exemplified by de Saussure's *Course in General Linguistics* [1959]), what is relevant for our purposes is the fact that Lévi-Strauss acknowledges his structuralist debt to two other contributors to the ethnological imagination. In his view, Marx's *Capital* (1976b [1867]) pioneers the "geologically" oriented search for the true essence of phenomena beneath surface appearances, while Durkheim's *Elementary Forms of Religious Life* (1995 [1912]) serves as a blueprint for structural analysis's construction of general comparative models of social reality on the basis of its fundamental components. Therefore, the echoes of Durkheim's magnum opus in the title of Lévi-Strauss's first major work, *The Elementary Structures of Kinship* (1969a [1949]), are hardly coincidental. It should be added that Mauss's *The Gift* (1988 [1923–24]) has also played a determining role in the development of Lévi-Strauss's structuralism.

6. See also Lévi-Strauss (1955, 1218–19) and Steiner (1970, 171–72).

7. While a detailed discussion of the affinities between Boas and Lévi-Strauss goes beyond the scope of this chapter, it should be remarked that the former's antievolutionism and cultural perspectivism influenced his French counterpart (a fact acknowledged by Lévi-Strauss himself). See, for instance, Boas (1940) and Dosse (1997a, 15–16).

8. See Augé (1999, 4, 12), Fabian (1983, 53–56), Leach (1989, 8), Lévi-Strauss (1969a, 463–64, 472; 1971, 527; 1978b, 206–7, 263–64, 396, 401; 1981, 37–38), and Merleau-Ponty (1960). In a review of the postwar French intellectual field, Bourdieu and Passeron (1967, 198n44) comment: "More broadly speaking, it is among a new generation of sociologists, who started out in philosophy and were schooled in ethnology, that there has been a reunification of the ethnological and sociological interests that had been completely dissociated by neo-positivism." Because of its radical implications, Lévi-Strauss's revival of the Durkheimian current's ethnologization of the modern West has met with both enthusiasm and resistance: "[O]ne has only to observe the furor aroused by the anthropological approach when, in keeping with the Durkheimian tradition, which made no distinction between ethnology and sociology, it is rigorously applied to familiar behavior and institutions, whether with reference to the functions of a university or to attitudes to works of art" (Bourdieu and Passeron 1967, 198).

9. See Lévi-Strauss (1955, 1194; 1968i, 347, 362–63, 378; 1977a, 15; 1977e, 62–63; 1978a, 332–33), and Pace (1983, 57–58).

10. See Clément (1985, 13), Lévi-Strauss (1977b, 35–37; 1978a, 376, 383), Lévi-Strauss and Charbonnier (1969, 17), Lévi-Strauss and Eribon (1991, 67), and Pace (1983, 36–37).

11. The quasi-religious language of sin, guilt, and atonement peppers Lévi-

Strauss's oeuvre. For instance, writing between 1989 and 1990 (on the eve of the celebrations marking the five hundredth anniversary of Columbus's voyage to the Americas), he states: "To recognize this as we are about to commemorate an event that—rather than the discovery—I would call the invasion of the New World, the destruction of its peoples and its values, is to engage in an act of contrition and devotion" (Lévi-Strauss 1995, xvii).

12. See Boon (1985, 163), Lévi-Strauss (1977b, 39; 1978a, 389), and Paz (1970, 145–46).

13. See Clément (1985, 94–95) and Lévi-Strauss (1977f, 272; 1978a, 86, 316, 335, 392).

14. See also Honneth (1995c, 138–39) and Lévi-Strauss (1955, 1218–19; 1968a, 19; 1977a, 31–32; 1977b, 35–40; 1978a, 326; 1995, 218–20).

15. See Bourdieu and Passeron (1967, 167), Clément (1985, 20), and Lévi-Strauss (1977i, 10; 1987a, 35–36).

16. This is what Geertz (1973, 351) aptly terms "a universal grammar of the intellect." See also Boon (1985, 162), Bourdieu and Passeron (1967, 201), Geertz (1988, 48), Hénaff (1998, 26–27, 109–17), Leach (1989, 21–22, 55–56), Lévi-Strauss (1968b, 65; 1968e, 202–4; 1968f, 230; 1968i, 347, 365; 1973, 401–2, 407–10, 413–14, 417, 446, 461–64; 1977a, 3–4, 8–9; 1978a, 58; 1978b, 17, 469; 1981, 229, 500–501, 537; 1978c, 8, 36; 1985e, 186, 191; 1987a, 33–35, 65–66; 1988, 204; 1995, 189–90), Lévi-Strauss et al. (1970, 66–67), Lyotard (1979, 84–85), Merleau-Ponty (1960, 150–54), Pace (1983, 143, 181), Paz (1970, 85, 88), and Steiner (1970, 173–74, 179–80).

17. See Clément (1985, 21), de Gramont (1970, 12), Delacampagne and Traimond (1997, 24), Hénaff (1998, 3–32), Honneth (1995c, 139), Leach (1989, 11), Lévi-Strauss (1955, 1190; 1968a, 17; 1977c, 47–48; 1977h, 326, 344; 1978a, 385–93), Merleau-Ponty (1960, 150), and Paz (1970, 146).

18. See Clément (1985, 21, 142–43), Hénaff (1998, 27), Lévi-Strauss (1955, 1198–1201; 1977d, 54; 1977h, 358–62; 1978a, 38, 86; 1978c, 20–21; 1985a, xiv–xv; 1985g, 267; 1987b, 24; 1993, 176), Lévi-Strauss and Eribon (1991, 146–54), Pace (1983, 60, 106), and Sontag (1970, 196).

19. "Can it be that I, the elderly predecessor of those scourers of the jungle, am the only one to have brought back nothing but a handful of ashes? Is mine the only voice to bear witness to the impossibility of escapism?" (Lévi-Strauss 1978a, 41). See also Boon (1985, 175), Clément (1985, 81–83), de Gramont (1970, 12), Derrida (1976, 134), Honneth (1995c, 137–38), Lévi-Strauss (1968g, 315; 1977d, 55; 1978a, 260, 293–94, 305; 1987b, 11; 1995, xvii), and Pace (1983, 58–59).

20. See Clément (1985, 24), Geertz (1973, 351–52, 355), Lévi-Strauss (1977a, 29–32; 1977d, 50–53; 1981, 654; 1987b, 12), Lévi-Strauss and Charbonnier (1969, 56), Lévi-Strauss and Eribon (1991, 145–46, 153–54), and Pace (1983, 62). Awkwardly translated into English as *Introduction to a Science of Mythology,* the four volumes are entitled *The Raw and the Cooked* (1969 [1964]), *From Honey to Ashes* (1973 [1966]), *The Origin of Table Manners* (1978 [1968]), and *The Naked Man* (1981 [1971]).

21. See also Aron (1970, 945), Hénaff (1998, 22, 28), Lévi-Strauss (1955, 1216–17; 1987a, 30–31; 1998, 73–74), and Merleau-Ponty (1960, 150–51).

22. See Clément (1985, 13, 43, 45–46, 90–91), Hénaff (1998, 24–25, 31–32), Lévi-Strauss (1955, 1215, 1217–18; 1968c, 117; 1977b, 35–40; 1978a, 55, 376–77, 383–84, 389–93), Lyotard (1979, 63–64), and Pace (1983, 64, 68–71).

23. See also Bauman (1993, 163), Clément (1985, 57–58, 72–73), Lévi-Strauss (1955, 1212; 1968a, 18–19; 1979, 111–20), and Pace (1983, 58).

24. According to Lévi-Strauss, conventional interpretive paradigms only analyze

conscious manifestations of the logic of indigenous societies. For instance, to make sense of a specific myth, functionalism would attempt to identify the need or function that its narrative fulfills within a particular society, while a phenomenological approach would search for the meaning the myth holds for the social actors themselves (i.e., the sender and the receiver, in a simplified model).

25. It should be mentioned that in *Of Grammatology*, Derrida (1976, 114–18) claims that *Tristes Tropiques* naturalizes indigenous peoples as noble savages in order to criticize Western civilization. Lévi-Strauss is accused of adopting an ethnocentric stance that always already assumes the absence of writing—and thus of violence, since the former is the product of the latter in his argument—among the Nambikwara. Accordingly, Derrida (1976, 110, 120–21, 135) claims that Lévi-Strauss privileges speech as the expression of a pregraphic innocence. Nevertheless, Derrida's criticisms fail to acknowledge that Lévi-Strauss culturalizes (rather than naturalizes) the democratic and nonhierarchical character of indigenous societies, which are not portrayed as being born as such, but on the contrary, as being reflexively organized to avoid institutional domination and subordination. Lévi-Strauss remains vulnerable on the count of assuming a civilizational divide between speech and writing (or peoples with and without writing). To my knowledge, he has never directly replied to Derrida on these matters.

26. See Lévi-Strauss (1955, 1191; 1968a, 3; 1968c, 103–4; 1971, 536; 1977e, 62–63; 1979, 93–94; 1985c, 26) and Pace (1983, 82, 87, 92–93). Even Durkheim's *Elementary Forms of Religious Life* (1995 [1912]) and Mauss's *The Gift* (1988 [1923–24]), which Lévi-Strauss considers landmark works, are chastised for their residual evolutionism—that is, their occasional slippage into a form of explanation that considers "primitive" communities to be both simpler and earlier instances of modern societies in the West (Lévi-Strauss 1971, 515–17; 1987a, 53–55).

27. Sociobiology combines naturalism and evolutionism in its analysis of non-Western peoples, whose behavior is claimed to be "racially" determined by their instincts, emotions, and primal needs. Needless to say, such biologically determinist ideas form one of Lévi-Strauss's ongoing targets (Lévi-Strauss 1969a, xxix, 485; 1977h, 323–24; 1981, 667–68; Lévi-Strauss and Eribon 1991, 106).

28. "It is true that, in my own past, what drew me away from philosophy toward anthropology was precisely the awareness that if you wish to understand man you must avoid becoming mired in introspection or limiting yourself to studying only one society—our own—or again to surveying a few centuries of the Western world" (Lévi-Strauss and Eribon 1991, 72). See also Clément (1985, 70), Lévi-Strauss (1955, 1193; 1973, 474; 1977a, 8–9, 27–28; 1977h, 328–29, 339–42; 1981, 640; 1985b, 10–11), and Young (1990, 43–44).

29. See Lévi-Strauss (1968h, 334–35; 1977h, 330–33; 1985b, 8–9), and Paz (1970, 142).

30. See Aron (1970, 944–47) and Todorov (1993, 62–65, 80–81).

31. Lévi-Strauss has consistently sung the praises of Western science vis-à-vis other kinds of cognition, although he has also been careful to state that this superiority in one domain cannot be generalized to an assessment of Euro-American civilization as a whole—for the latter's history is also filled with gigantic errors and sins (de Gramont 1970, 13–14; Honneth 1995c, 138; Lévi-Strauss 1955, 1188, 1204, 1211–12; 1968h, 334–35; 1977a, 26–27; 1977h, 344–46; 1978a, 385–92; 1978c, 13–24; 1985b, 8–9; 1995, 211).

32. See Leach (1989, 94), Lévi-Strauss (1963, 56–58, 69–71; 1966, 2–3, 40–42; 73–74, 219–20, 267–68; 1968g, 282; 1969a, 87–88, 94–96; 1971, 534–35; 1973, 474; 1977a, 25; 1978c, 15–16), and Pace (1983, 136–39).

33. See also Clément (1985, 53–54), Leach (1989, 42), and Pace (1983, 173–76).

34. See Clément (1985, 113), de Gramont (1970, 6), Delacampagne and Traimond (1997, 19), Hénaff (1998, 118, 141–43), Leach (1989, 97), Lévi-Strauss (1955, 1195–96; 1963, 89; 1966, 2–3, 8–10, 15–16, 35–36, 43, 71, 73, 133, 162, 164, 215–16, 267–69; 1968a, 21–23; 1969a, 63–64, 91–92, 97, 126–27, 495–96; 1969b, 1; 1973, 185, 304–5; 1977e, 65; 1978c, 11–12, 19; 1979, 123; 1981, 586; 1988, 204, 206), Lévi-Strauss et al. (1970, 59), Lévi-Strauss and Eribon (1991, 110, 123–24), Pace (1983, 131–43), Paz (1970, 99–100, 128–30, 150–51), and Ricoeur (1974, 40).

35. See Clément (1985, 137–38), Geertz (1973, 352–53), Hénaff (1998, 140, 151), Honneth (1995c, 147–48), Lévi-Strauss (1963, 26, 29; 1966, 7, 17–22, 25, 32–33, 37–38, 138–39, 166–67, 182–83, 218, 245; 1968d, 184; 1973, 260, 447, 472–73; 1978c, 17; 1987a, 24–26, 56–58; 1988, 194–95), Lévi-Strauss and Eribon (1991, 112), Pace (1983, 138–40), and Paz (1970, 88). It should be pointed out that, for Lévi-Strauss, the "savage mind" does not directly correspond to "primitive" thought; the former category is intended to be larger than the latter. Hence, if he claims that the "savage mind" predominantly exists in "primitive" societies (whereas the domesticated mind is associated with modernity), elements of it can be found in all cultures; see Hénaff (1998, 149–50), Leach (1989, 9), Lévi-Strauss (1966, 219–20, 269; 1969b, 300–301, 327–29, 334, 337–38; 1988, 13), and Lévi-Strauss and Eribon (1991, 110). Despite such statements—and apart from the parallels he draws between psychoanalysis and mythical thought—Lévi-Strauss's argument would have been more convincing had he demonstrated more elaborately the savage mind's presence in modern Euro-American societies.

36. See Delacampagne and Traimond (1997, 14–15), Lévi-Strauss (1981, 638–40; 1987a, 53–55, 61–62, 65–66), Lyotard (1979, 65), and Young (1990, 41–47). In a footnote charged with a rhetorical tone, Lévi-Strauss goes so far as to ethically and cross-culturally turn the tables on Sartre: "The price so paid for the illusion of having overcome the insoluble antinomy (in such a system) between my self and others, consists of the assignation, by historical consciousness, of the metaphysical function of Other to the Papuans. By reducing the latter to the state of means, barely sufficient for its philosophical appetite, historical reason abandons itself to a sort of intellectual cannibalism much more revolting to the anthropologist than real cannibalism" (Lévi-Strauss 1966, 257–58).

37. See Hénaff (1998, 150), Lévi-Strauss (1966, 263, 267, 269; 1969a, 496; 1977h, 335, 350; 1978c, 5–6, 17; 1995, xii), and Lévi-Strauss and Eribon (1991, 112, 117–18).

38. The French Revolution is Lévi-Strauss's favorite instance of this idea, for he considers it to be as much a mythological field of competing discourses as a set of factual events. Because of its signal role in French history, 1789 has been constructed rather than given, and thus shaped by the normative and social baggage of different paradigms (Lévi-Strauss 1966, 254–55; Lévi-Strauss and Eribon 1991, 117–18). See also Abélès (1999, 45–47, 55–56), Boon (1985, 161, 169–70), Clément (1985, 135–37), Delacampagne and Traimond (1997, 15–17), Derrida (1978b, 291), Fabian (1983, 57), Hénaff (1998, 219–20), Lévi-Strauss (1966, 257–58, 260–63; 1968f, 209; 1973, 354–55; 1977h, 354; 1978c, 40–43), Lévi-Strauss et al. (1970, 71), Lévi-Strauss and Bellour (1979, 192–93), Lyotard (1979, 55–57), Pace (1983, 114–15), Steiner (1970, 176), White (1978, 55–57, 90–91, 102–4), and Young (1990, 45–46).

39. See Lévi-Strauss (1955, 1188; 1968h, 335–36; 1985b, 8–11), Pace (1983, 83, 89–90), and Paz (1970, 99, 143–45).

40. Western modernity's belief in change for change's sake is one of its defining features: the expression "social whirlwind" *(tourbillon social)* captures this in Rousseau's writings (see chapter 1), whereas Marx's "all that is solid melts into air" serves

a similar function (see chapter 2). Baudelaire (1995 [1863], 12) has provided us with the locus classicus of the genre: "By 'modernity' I mean the ephemeral, the fugitive, the contingent, the half of art whose other half is the eternal and the immutable."

41. See Hénaff (1998, 34–35, 226), Lévi-Strauss (1977a, 28–29), Lévi-Strauss and Charbonnier (1969, 32–34, 38–42, 49–50), and Pace (1983, 52–53).

42. See Abélès (1999, 45–46), Hénaff (1998, 33–34, 215, 219–20, 225–27, 235–36), Lévi-Strauss (1966, 232–36; 1968c, 112, 117; 1969b, 15–16; 1977a, 28–29; 1977g, 321–22; 1977h, 335; 1981, 606–7; 1998, 66–69), Lévi-Strauss and Charbonnier (1969, 32–34, 38–39), Lévi-Strauss and Eribon (1991, 124–25), Paz (1970, 132–34), and Ricoeur (1974, 44).

43. See Hénaff (1998, 33–34, 235–36), Lévi-Strauss (1977h, 336–38; 1978a, 299–300, 408), Lévi-Strauss and Charbonnier (1969, 29–32), and Pace (1983, 104).

44. See Fabian (1983, 60), Lévi-Strauss (1973, 475; 1978a, 391; 1981, 694–95), and Lévi-Strauss and Eribon (1991, 125–26).

45. See Dosse (1997a, 262–63), Geertz (1973, 357–58; 1988, 39), Lévi-Strauss (1969a, 496–97; 1978a, 391–93; 1993, 176), Pace (1983, 69–70), and Sontag (1970, 196).

46. As will be discussed in the following chapter, Lévi-Strauss's and Foucault's projects are complementary in this respect: while Foucault undermines Western humanism through genealogy (historical estrangement), Lévi-Strauss does so ethnologically (cross-cultural estrangement).

47. See de Gramont (1970, 7), Derrida (1978b, 283), Hénaff (1998, 204–5), Honneth (1995c, 139–40), Leach (1989, 15–16), Lévi-Strauss (1966, 135–36, 257–258; 1969a, xxix–xxx; 1969b, 10–12; 1977i, 11; 1977f, 279–87; 1978a, 153; 1978b, 272–73, 431; 1981, 603–4, 625–30, 640, 650–51, 686–88; 1985d, 104–5, 114–15, 119–20; 1985f, 243; 1985h, 282–83), Lévi-Strauss and Charbonnier (1969, 71–72, 136–37), Lévi-Strauss and Eribon (1991, 115, 160–61, 175), Lyotard (1979, 62–63), Pace (1983, 52, 57–58), Paz (1970, 171–74), and Ricoeur (1974, 33).

48. See Lévi-Strauss (1963, 2–3, 103; 1977h, 328–29; 1978a, 390–92).

49. See de Gramont (1970, 16), Leach (1989, 31), Honneth (1995c, 139–48), Lévi-Strauss (1966, 90–95, 104; 1969b, 63, 94, 101–3, 105, 109, 113, 132, 151–53, 169, 173, 275, 316; 1973, 73, 108, 178, 211–13; 1977f, 283; 1977g, 320–21; 1978a, 150; 1978b, 75–79, 502–4; 1979, 95–120; 1981, 498–99; 1985b, 14), Lévi-Strauss and Bellour (1979, 158), Lévi-Strauss and Eribon (1991, 133, 136–37, 139–40), and Paz (1970, 102, 130).

50. Here, Lévi-Strauss is deliberately reversing Sartre's celebrated (and anthropocentric) phrase "hell is others" *("l'enfer, c'est les autres")* from the play *Huis clos.*

51. See Lévi-Strauss (1977b, 36–37; 1977f, 274; 1985d, 119–20), and Lévi-Strauss and Eribon (1991, 160–61).

52. See Clément (1985, 50–51), Dosse (1997b, 400), Hénaff (1998, 237–44), Honneth (1995c, 136, 148), Lévi-Strauss (1977b, 41–42; 1978c, 23–24; 1979, 130; 1985a, xvi; 1985h), Lévi-Strauss and Eribon (1991, 163), Merleau-Ponty (1960, 154–57), and Pace (1983, 71–72). Ricoeur (1974, 52) pejoratively classifies Lévi-Strauss's thinking as "a Kantianism without a transcendental subject"—a designation that Lévi-Strauss himself interprets positively (Lévi-Strauss et al. 1970, 61; Paz 1970, 170–72). Indeed, Lévi-Strauss's writings leave Kant's anthropocentrism *("the moral law within")* behind, while emphasizing the cosmological pole *("the starry heavens above")* of the latter's argument.

53. See Clément (1985, 23–24, 52–53), Hénaff (1998, 241–44), Honneth (1995c, 140–41, 145), Leach (1989, 36–37), Lévi-Strauss (1969a, xxix–xxx; 1977b, 41–42; 1977f, 273–74, 285–86), Lyotard (1979, 49–50), and Paz (1970, 105).

54. Allowing himself for a moment to glance back at the edifice of his four-volume *Mythologiques*, Lévi-Strauss muses: "I myself, in considering my work from within as I have lived it, or from without, which is my present relationship to it as it drifts away into my past, see more clearly that this tetralogy of mine, now that it has been composed, must, like Wagner's, end with a twilight of the gods; or, to be more accurate, that having been completed a century later and in harsher times, it foresees the twilight of man, after that of the gods which was supposed to ensure the advent of a happy and liberated humanity" (1981, 693). See also Boon (1985, 175), de Gramont (1970, 8), Dosse (1997a, 262–63), Lévi-Strauss (1978a, 413–15; 1993, 147, 176), and Lyotard (1979, 54).

6. An Ethnology by Other Means

1. Many prominent analysts have remarked on Foucault's ethnocentrism. See, inter alia, Lévi-Strauss and Eribon (1991, 72), Said (1988, 9–10), and Spivak (1988a, 280–81, 290–91). However, others, such as Stoler (1995) and Young (1995) have tempered this assessment by advancing two related arguments: first, that race and racism are important, though underestimated, categories within Foucault's own writings (notably in his 1976 lectures at the Collège de France and the first volume of *The History of Sexuality*); and second, that if recast in a broader geographical context, Foucault's work lends itself to critical analyses of colonial situations.

2. The translation is my own. On the importance of this statement, see Fuchs (1993, 109), Honneth (1991, 108), and Honneth and Joas (1988, 131).

3. See Fuchs (1993), Honneth (1991, 105–48), and Honneth and Joas (1988, 129–50). For Foucault, the modern age refers to the period between 1789 and the present. Reminiscent of both Weber and Baudelaire, one of his later essays, "What Is Enlightenment?" (1984a, 39), suggests that modernity should be seen as a cultural ethos rather than a historical epoch per se. Since my own use of the term "modernity" is historically broader (going back to the European intellectual Renaissance), I employ the adjective "postrevolutionary" to describe the period following the French Revolution throughout this chapter.

4. Dumont (1977, 1986, 1994) and Bourdieu (1979, 1988), Bourdieu, Chamboredon, and Passeron (1991), and Bourdieu and Wacquant (1992) have also contributed to the prominence of this inverted ethnology in France (see Fuchs 1993). In the United States, Rabinow (1996) and the *Late Editions* series edited by George Marcus (University of Chicago Press) are indicative of a similar trend.

5. This is not to say that Foucault's work is entirely free from exoticizing tendencies; see Kurasawa (1999). Foucault's ethnological historiography resembles the move made by some members of the Annales School in France, who began analyzing the European Middle Ages as a civilization embodying difference, even alterity, vis-à-vis the modern West—by contrast to conventional historiography, which treats the medieval era as modernity's direct ancestor. See, for instance, Le Goff's *Time, Work, and Culture in the Middle Ages* (1980), the original title of which, *Pour un autre Moyen Age* (For another Middle Ages), gives a better indication of such an anthropological tendency.

6. Although Foucault's first book is *Mental Illness and Psychology* (1976 [1954]), it is a minor work in his corpus. For some of his literary essays, see Foucault (1963, 1977b [1963], 1998b [1966], 1998c [1966]).

7. See Dreyfus and Rabinow (1983, 4, 11), Foucault (1965, ix–xii), Fuchs (1993, 111), Hacking (1986, 29), Harootunian (1988, 114–17), Honneth (1991, 111–12), and Honneth and Joas (1988, 133).

8. See Foucault (1965, 278, 281, 288–89; 1970, 383–84; 1977b, 32–34, 41–42; 1977c, 182, 185–86, 192; 1998b, 150–54, 166; 1998c, 174). Bataille's accursed share *(la part maudite)* epitomizes this otherness and excess. Foucault's "Introduction to Rousseau's *Dialogues*" (1998a [1961]) provides an excellent indication of his intellectual orientation in the early 1960s, since Rousseau's text represents for him another expression of an outside that lives beyond reason and its author, who has become other to himself.

9. *The Order of Things* (Foucault 1970, 383–84) refers to avant-garde literature as being outside Man as well as a vehicle of the death of Man through language—much like what Foucault believes is structural anthropology's drawing out of the cultural unconscious of Western modernity.

10. Foucault's (1994b) reply to Derrida's criticisms only addresses interpretive disagreements over Descartes' *Meditations,* leaving his other charges unanswered. Nevertheless, Foucault seems to have become aware of the untenable character of the position he held in *Madness and Civilization* since his subsequent work steers clear of the desire to let the Other speak.

11. Foucault does not haphazardly select these three disciplines, since they represented the strongholds of the structuralist paradigm in the French intellectual circles of the 1960s; behind them, one can read Lévi-Strauss, Lacan, and de Saussure, respectively. Dreyfus and Rabinow (1983, 17) point out that *The Order of Things* was originally to be titled *The Archaeology of Structuralism.*

12. See also Dreyfus and Rabinow (1983, 17–18, 57, 79, 125).

13. See Dreyfus and Rabinow (1983, 13), Foucault (1970, xxiv, 373), Fuchs (1993, 109–10), Honneth (1991, 105–10), and Honneth and Joas (1988, 135).

14. As Dreyfus and Rabinow (1983) convincingly argue, Foucault came to prefer genealogical over archaeological investigations in the wake of the epistemological and theoretical difficulties that he encountered after *The Archeology of Knowledge* (1972 [1969]). Nevertheless, it is a matter of shifting emphasis rather than complete rupture from one to the other.

15. See Foucault (1972; 1998d, 309–10).

16. See Davidson (1986, 225), Dreyfus and Rabinow (1983, 110, 203–4), and Foucault (1981, 70; 1984b, 78–82, 86–91; 1988b, 10–11).

17. On Foucault's technique of historical juxtaposition, see Hacking (1986, 29), Honneth and Joas (1988, 138–39), and Poster (1986, 208–9).

18. See Dreyfus and Rabinow (1983, 122–23, 256), Foucault (1970, xxiv; 1972, 4–6, 10; 1981, 68–69; 1984a, 46; 1984b, 83, 89; 1984c, 335–36; 1985, 3–4, 11; 1998f, 444–45), Flynn (1994, 32, 43–44), Honneth (1991, 126–27), Veyne (1978, 226), and Young (1990, 70–71, 74–75).

19. Foucault traveled once to Japan (April 2–29, 1978) and twice to Iran (September 16–24 and November 9–15, 1978), resulting in a series of interviews, lectures, and newspaper articles originally published in Japanese, Italian, and French (see Foucault 1994d to 1994v). The circumstances surrounding Foucault's involvement in the Iranian events are recounted in Eribon (1991, 281–91), whereas Defert (1994, 53–56) provides a useful chronology of both the Japanese and Iranian affairs. For an analysis of these writings, see Kurasawa (1999) and Stauth (1991).

20. His stated wish to launch a comparative project with Japanese and other Asian scholars on Christianity, Confucianism, and Zen Buddhism (Foucault 1994f, 592–93) never came to fruition. As for Iran, the publication of an article in *Le Nouvel observateur* (Foucault 1994k) and a discussion with two journalists (Foucault 1994r) were received with considerable hostility in France. He was criticized in a letter writ-

ten by an Iranian-French woman and attacked in *Le Matin* for supporting the Iranian Revolution and thereby overlooking the dangers of Shi'ite fundamentalism (notably the repression of women and the summary execution of political opponents by Khomeini's regime). To both, he replied harshly and defensively, accusing his interlocutors of bad faith (Foucault 1994o, 1994t). He also wrote an open letter to Mehdi Bazargan, then the prime minister of Iran, to appeal for the latter's intervention (Foucault 1994u), as well as a final article in *Le Monde* that constitutes an indignant reply to his critics (Foucault 1994v). Afterward, Foucault permanently closed the book on his Iranian experiences.

21. See Dreyfus and Rabinow (1983, 256), Foucault (1984c, 339; 1984d, 341, 343, 347–50; 1985, 7–8), and Poster (1986, 208–9).

22. Placing his own work in a tradition of critical reflection on modern Western rationality, Foucault (1998f, 441) comments: "I think that since Weber, in the Frankfurt School and anyhow for many historians of science such as Canguilhem, it was a question of isolating the form of rationality presented as dominant and endowed with the status of the one-and-only reason, in order to show that it is only *one* possible form among others." See also Foucault (1994g, 620).

23. See Harootunian (1988, 116–18, 124–25). In fact, what Clastres (1979, 34–35) terms the "ancient trinity" of the savage, the insane, and the child has consistently tested the bounds of Western rationalism. Nowhere are they more famously linked than in Freud's *Totem and Taboo* (1990 [1913]).

24. See Toulmin (1990).

25. See Foucault (1970, xxiii, 308–11, 317–18, 341–45, 386) and Hacking (1986, 32).

26. Although Foucault and Lévi-Strauss share this objective, their analyses nevertheless differ in that the former introduces a distinction between rationalism and anthropocentrism, which is less prominent in the latter's writings. Foucault accepts the conventional idea that the seventeenth century (what he terms the classical age) gradually substitutes human reason for divine will, yet challenges the notion that the coming into being of rationalism also implies a reflection on the essence of Man. He contends instead that the possibility of knowing Man only emerges in the late eighteenth and nineteenth centuries (what he terms the modern age, from which time originates anthropocentrism). By contrast, Lévi-Strauss traces back the sources of both rationalism and anthropocentrism to Renaissance humanism.

27. This encyclopedia, entitled the *Celestial Emporium of Benevolent Knowledge*, is described in Borges (1964, 103). On the importance of this trope for Foucault, see Jullien and Marchaisse (2000, 16–17).

28. See Foucault (1970, xv, xix).

29. See Clément (1985, 57–58), Foucault (1970, xxiv; 1998e, 335–38, 342), and Honneth and Joas (1988, 138). Bauman (1993, 163–65) has also extended Lévi-Strauss's concepts of anthropophagy and anthropemy to examine modern society, whereas Douglas's *Purity and Danger* (1966), which examines collective rites of purification from pollution, represents an interesting complement to Foucault's work.

30. See Dreyfus and Rabinow (1983, 3), Ewald (1995), Foucault (1981, 52–54, 70–71; 1988d, 146), and Hacking (1986, 30–31).

31. See Foucault (1965, 268; 1972, 41–42; 1977a, 80–82, 87, 92–93, 98, 104–5), and Harootunian (1988, 120).

32. See also Foucault (1989, 55).

33. See Foucault (1965, xi–xii, 3, 6, 35–39, 258–60; 1998e, 337–38, 341–42).

34. See also Foucault (1977a, 141–42, 198–99; 1989, 29–32).

35. See Foucault (1988a, 11; 1988c, 18–19; 1988d, 146).

36. Many commentators have remarked on the likeness between Foucault's and Weber's analyses of processes of rationalization. See Dreyfus and Rabinow (1983, 132–33, 165–66), O'Neill (1986), Owen (1994), and Smart (1983, 123–32).

37. See Foucault (1978, 42–44, 58, 65–68, 72).

38. See Foucault (1965, 70, 107, 246–47, 265; 1977, 98–99, 128–31, 168–69, 198–99, 308; 1983, 213–14; 1989, 123–24; 1998f, 443–44).

39. See Foucault (1983, 208, 211–12; 1984a, 43–44; 1988c, 18–19), Gordon (1987, 295–96), Honneth (1991, xxvii), and Honneth and Joas (1988, 136–37).

40. See Foucault (1994d, 527; 1994f, 592; 1994g, 618), Jullien and Marchaisse (2000, 16–33), and Kurasawa (1999).

41. See Foucault (1994j, 686–88; 1994k, 689–94; 1994l, 702–4; 1994p, 709–12; 1994q, 715–16; 1994r, 744–49; 1994s, 759–60; 1994v, 792–93), Kurasawa (1999), and Stauth (1991, 265–66, 269).

42. See Foucault (1984d, 341, 343, 347–50, 359; 1985, 9–10, 30, 92–93, 138–39; 1986, 68, 143–44, 239–40; 1988a, 2, 4–5; 1988c, 19).

43. See Foucault (1985, 65–70, 78–79, 138–39, 249–54; 1986, 39–41, 50–51, 65–68; 1989, 151, 159–60). In an interview with Dreyfus and Rabinow, Foucault (1984d, 359) schematically compares different civilizations' "formulas" for sexual behavior. They can be rendered as follows: Greek: *act*—pleasure—[desire]; Chinese: *pleasure*—desire—[act]; Christian: [desire]—act—[pleasure]; modern Western: [act]—desire—[pleasure]. It should be pointed out that ancient Greek aesthetics of life are reserved for male citizens, specifically excluding women, slaves, and most foreigners—a point of which Foucault is acutely aware. At another level, Hadot (1995) has criticized the rendition of his own concept of Greco-Roman "spiritual exercises" in Foucault's writings for being excessively focused on pleasure, aesthetics, and the self at the expense of both the Stoics' and the Epicureans' references to transcendentalism, universalism, and cosmology.

44. See Foucault (1984a, 41–42; 1984d, 350–51; 1985, 6, 10–11; 1988a, 2–3; 1988c, 18; 1988d, 146; 1989, 133–36). He mentions Baudelaire's (1995 [1863]) description of dandyism as an instance of the cultivation of a personal aesthetic asceticism.

Conclusion

1. On this topic, see Augé (1994), Chakrabarty (2000, 7–9), and Fabian (1983).

2. Here, I use "postcolonialism" less to refer to the school of thought of the same name (e.g., Said, Bhabha, Spivak) than to refer to the ongoing sociopolitical predicament of the world in the aftermath of decolonization—a predicament that includes both the Third World's formal political independence and its continued (and in some instances, intensified) socioeconomic dependence on the West. In other words, the postcolonial era is also one of neocolonialism brought about by transnational capitalism (Dirlik 1997, Miyoshi 1993, Spivak 1999).

3. See, inter alia, Appadurai (1996), Arnason (1997), Asad (1993), Augé (1994, 1998), Bhabha (1994), Bourdieu (1990), Chakrabarty (2000), Clifford (1988, 1997), Clifford and Marcus (1986), Dallmayr (1996), Dumont (1986, 1994), Friedman (1994), García Canclini (1995), Gilroy (1993, 2000), Inda and Rosaldo (2002), Kahn (1995), Marcus and Fischer (1999), Ong (1999), Papastergiadis (2000), Rabinow (1996, 1999), Rosaldo (1993), Said (1989, 1993), Spivak (1999), and Thomas (1991).

4. The situation is altogether different in the mainstream media, in popular

culture, and in the political sphere, where prejudices and flawed understandings of non-Western peoples continue to abound.

5. See Appadurai (1996, 65), Augé (1994, 1998), Bhabha (1994), Clifford (1988), Ellingson (2001), Fabian (1983), Fanon (1963), Hall (1991, 34–35), Kuper (1988), Rosaldo (1993), Said (1978, 1989, 1993), and Smith (1992, 9–10). Obviously, this is not to deny the resilience of exoticist imagery in popular culture (Ellingson 2001, Di Leonardo 1998, Torgovnick 1990).

6. This has been a central cross-cultural element of the interpretive turn in the social sciences for the past three decades, yet its importance remains undiminished today. See Geertz (1973, 1983) and Taylor (1985a, 1985b). Recently, Geertz (2000, 16) has elegantly restated the point: "This does not involve feeling anyone else's feelings, or thinking anyone else's thoughts, simple impossibilities. Nor does it involve going native, an impractical idea, inevitably bogus. It involves learning how, as a being from elsewhere with a world of one's own, to live with them."

7. Augé (1998, 34) makes a related point: "By trying too hard to avoid ethnocentrism, we have run the risk of removing all substance from the others' reality, of remaining unaware that their questions are also our questions (and vice versa) and that their responses are therefore not arbitrary or exotic in a way that might make them forever foreign or derisory to us."

8. See Appadurai (1996), Bhabha (1994), Clifford (1988, 1997), García Canclini (1995), Gilroy (1993, 2000), Hall (1990, 1991), Inda and Rosaldo (2002), Marcus (1998), Ong (1999), Papastergiadis (2000), Rosaldo (1993), Spivak (1999), and Tambiah (2000).

9. See Chakrabarty (2002), Marcus (1998), and Weiming (2000).

10. In addition, the internal diversity of these taxonomical categories should be acknowledged, so that "Western capitalism," for example, is a label that regroups the distinctive traditions of Anglo-American liberalism and Continental corporatism (Wittrock 2000).

Works Cited

Abélès, M. 1999. "Avec le temps." *Critique* 620–21: 42–60.

Ahmad, A. 1992. *In Theory: Classes, Nations, Literatures*. London and New York: Verso.

Alexander, J. C. 1982. *The Antinomies of Classical Thought*. Vol. 2 of *Theoretical Logic in Sociology*. Berkeley and Los Angeles: University of California Press.

———. 1987a. "The Dialectic of Individuation and Domination: Weber's Rationalization Theory and Beyond." In *Max Weber, Rationality and Modernity*, ed. S. Lash and S. Whimster, 185–206. London: Allen & Unwin.

———. 1987b. "The Centrality of the Classics." In *Social Theory Today*, ed. A. Giddens and J. H. Turner, 11–57. Cambridge, England: Polity Press.

———. 1988. "Introduction: Durkheimian Sociology and Cultural Studies." In *Durkheimian Sociology: Cultural Studies*, ed. J. C. Alexander, 1–21. Cambridge: Cambridge University Press.

Althusser, L. 1969 (1965). *For Marx*. Trans. B. Brewster. London: Verso.

Althusser, L., and E. Balibar. 1970 (1968). *Reading Capital*. Trans. B. Brewster. London: Verso.

Anderson, P. 1974. *Lineages of the Absolutist State*. London: Verso.

Appadurai, A. 1996. *Modernity at Large: Cultural Dimensions of Globalization*. Minneapolis: University of Minnesota Press.

Arendt, H. 1958. *The Human Condition*. Chicago: University of Chicago Press.

Aristotle. 1981. *The Politics*. Trans. T. A. Sinclair and T. J. Saunders. Harmondsworth: Penguin.

Arnason, J. P. 1982. "Rationalisation and Modernity: Towards a Culturalist Reading of Max Weber." *La Trobe University Sociology Papers* 9.

———. 1990. "Modernity as Project and as Field of Tensions." In *Communicative Action: Essays on Jürgen Habermas's "The Theory of Communicative Action,"* ed. A. Honneth and H. Joas, trans. J. Gaines and D. L. Jones, 181–213. Cambridge, Mass.: MIT Press.

———. 1992. "World Interpretation and Mutual Understanding." In *Cultural-Political Interventions in the Unfinished Project of Enlightenment*, ed. A. Honneth, T. McCarthy, C. Offe, and A. Wellmer, trans. B. Fultner, 247–67. Cambridge, Mass.: MIT Press.

———. 1997. *Social Theory and the Japanese Experience: The Dual Civilization.* London: Kegan Paul International.

Aron, R. 1970. "Le paradoxe du même et de l'autre." In *Echanges et communications: Mélanges offerts à Claude Lévi-Strauss à l'occasion de son 60ème anniversaire*, vol. 2, ed. J. Pouillon and P. Maranda. The Hague: Mouton.

Asad, T., ed. 1973. *Anthropology and the Colonial Encounter.* London: Ithaca Press.

———. 1993. *Genealogies of Religion: Discipline and Reasons of Power in Christianity and Islam.* Baltimore: The Johns Hopkins University Press.

Augé, M. 1994. *Pour une anthropologie des mondes contemporains.* Paris: Aubier.

———. 1998 (1994). *A Sense for the Other: The Timeliness and Relevance of Anthropology.* Trans. A. Jacobs. Stanford: Stanford University Press.

———. 1999. "Le triangle anthropologique: Mauss, Bataille, Lévi-Strauss." *Critique* 620–21: 4–12.

Bailey, A. M. 1981. "The Renewed Discussions on the Concept of the Asiatic Mode of Production." In *The Anthropology of Pre-Capitalist Societies*, ed. J. S. Kahn and J. R. Llobera, 89–107. London: Macmillan.

Ball, T. 1990 (1979). "Marx and Darwin: A Reconsideration." In *Karl Marx's Social and Political Thought: Critical Assessments*, ed. B. Jessop with C. Malcolm-Brown, 1: 334–46. London and New York: Routledge.

Barkan, E., and R. Bush. 1995, eds. *Prehistories of the Future: The Primitivist Project and the Culture of Modernism.* Stanford: Stanford University Press.

Bartra, R. 1994. *Wild Men in the Looking Glass: The Mythic Origins of European Otherness.* Trans. C. T. Berrisford. Ann Arbor: University of Michigan Press.

———. 1997. *The Artificial Savage: Modern Myths of the Wild Man.* Trans. C. Follett. Ann Arbor: University of Michigan Press.

Bauböck, R., A. Heller, and A. R. Zolberg, eds. 1996. *The Challenge of Diversity: Integration and Pluralism in Societies of Immigration.* Aldershot: Avebury.

Baudelaire, C. 1976 (1863). *Le peintre de la vie moderne.* In *Oeuvres complètes*, t. 2, ed. C. Pichois. Paris: Gallimard.

———. 1995 (1863). "The Painter of Modern Life." In *The Painter of Modern Life and Other Essays*, ed. and trans. J. Mayne, 1–41. London: Phaidon.

Baudrillard, J., and M. Guillaume. 1994. *Figures de l'altérité.* Paris: Descartes & Cie.

Bauman, Z. 1978. *Hermeneutics and Social Science: Approaches to Understanding.* London: Hutchinson.

———. 1987. *Legislators and Interpreters: On Modernity, Post-modernity and Intellectuals.* Cambridge: Polity.

———. 1989. *Modernity and the Holocaust.* Cambridge: Polity.

———. 1991. *Modernity and Ambivalence.* Cambridge: Polity.

———. 1993. *Postmodern Ethics.* Oxford: Blackwell.

Beilharz, P. 1992. *Labour's Utopias: Bolshevism, Fabianism, Social Democracy.* London and New York: Routledge.

Bellah, R. N., and P. E. Hammond. 1980. *Varieties of Civil Religion.* San Francisco: Harper & Row.

Bendix, R. 1960. *Max Weber: An Intellectual Portrait.* Garden City: Doubleday.

———. 1971. "Two Sociological Traditions." In *Scholarship and Partisanship: Essays on Max Weber*, ed. R. Bendix and G. Roth, 282–98. Berkeley and Los Angeles: University of California Press.

Benhabib, S. 1986. *Critique, Norm, and Utopia: A Study of the Foundations of Critical Theory*. New York: Columbia University Press.

———. 2002. *The Claims of Culture: Equality and Diversity in the Global Era*. Princeton, N.J.: Princeton University Press.

Bénichou, P. 1984 (1979). "Réflexions sur l'idée de nature chez Rousseau." In *Pensée de Rousseau*, ed. G. Genette and T. Todorov, 125–45. Paris: Seuil.

Benjamin, W. 1973 (1955). "Theses on the Philosophy of History." In *Illuminations*, trans. H. Zohn. London: Fontana.

Bennett, D., ed. 1998. *Multicultural States: Rethinking Difference and Identity*. London and New York: Routledge.

Berlin, I. 1969. "Two Concepts of Liberty." In *Four Essays on Liberty*, 118–72. Oxford: Oxford University Press.

———. 1997 (1976). "Herder and the Enlightenment." In *The Proper Study of Mankind: An Anthology of Essays*, ed. H. Hardy and R. Hausheer, 359–435. New York: Farrar, Straus and Giroux.

Berman, M. 1970. *The Politics of Authenticity: Radical Individualism and the Emergence of Modern Society*. New York: Atheneum.

———. 1988 (1982). *All That Is Solid Melts into Air: The Experience of Modernity*. Harmondsworth: Penguin.

Bernstein, R. J. 1978. *The Restructuring of Social and Political Thought*. Philadelphia: University of Pennsylvania Press.

———. 1992. "Incommensurability and Otherness Revisited." In *The New Constellation: The Ethical-Political Horizons of Modernity/Postmodernity*, 57–78. Cambridge, Mass.: MIT Press.

Besnard, P., ed. 1983. *The Sociological Domain: The Durkheimians and the Founding of French Sociology*. Cambridge: Cambridge University Press.

Beuchat, H., and M. Mauss. 1968 (1904–5). "Essai sur les variations saisonnières des sociétés eskimos." In *Sociologie et anthropologie*, 4th ed., ed. M. Mauss, 389–475. Paris: Presses Universitaires de France.

Bhabha, H. 1994. *The Location of Culture*. London and New York: Routledge.

Bloch, M. 1983. *Marxism and Anthropology: The History of a Relationship*. Oxford: Clarendon Press.

Boas, F. 1940. *Race, Language, and Culture*. New York: Free Press.

Boas, G. 1948. *Primitivism and Related Ideas in the Middle Ages*. Baltimore: The Johns Hopkins University Press.

Boon, J. 1985. "Claude Lévi-Strauss." In *The Return of Grand Theory in the Human Sciences*, ed. Q. Skinner, 159–76. Cambridge: Cambridge University Press.

Borges, J. L. 1964 (1952). "The Analytical Language of John Wilkins." In *Other Inquisitions, 1937–1952*, trans. R. L. C. Simms, 101–5. Austin: University of Texas Press.

Bourdieu, P. 1977 (1972). *Outline of a Theory of Practice*. Trans. R. Nice. Cambridge: Cambridge University Press.

———. 1979. *La distinction: Critique sociale du jugement*. Paris: Minuit.

———. 1988 (1984). *Homo Academicus*. Trans. P. Collier. Cambridge: Polity.

———. 1990 (1980). *The Logic of Practice*. Trans. R. Nice. Cambridge: Polity.

Bourdieu, P., and L. J. D. Wacquant. 1992. *An Invitation to Reflexive Sociology*. Chicago: University of Chicago Press.

Bourdieu, P., and J.-C. Passeron. 1967. "Sociology and Philosophy in France since 1945: Death and Resurrection of a Philosophy without Subject." *Social Research* 34, no. 1: 162–212.

Bourdieu, P., J.-C. Chamboredon, and J.-C. Passeron. 1991 (1968). *The Craft of*

Sociology: Epistemological Preliminaries. Ed. B. Krais, trans. R. Nice. Berlin and New York: de Gruyter.

Bunzel, R. L. 1966. Introduction to *How Natives Think*, ed. L. Lévy-Bruhl, trans. L. A. Clare, v–xviii. New York: Washington Square Press.

Calhoun, C. 1992. "Culture, History, and the Problem of Specificity in Social Theory." In *Postmodernism and Social Theory: The Debate over General Theory*, ed. S. Seidman and D. G. Wagner, 244–88. Oxford: Blackwell.

———, ed. 1994. *Social Theory and the Politics of Identity*. Oxford: Blackwell.

———. 1995. *Critical Social Theory: Culture, History, and the Challenge of Difference*. Oxford: Blackwell.

———. 1997. *Nationalism*. Minneapolis: University of Minnesota Press.

Camic, C., ed. 1997. *Reclaiming the Sociological Classics: The State of the Scholarship*. Malden, Mass.: Blackwell.

Canguilhem, G. 1966 (1943). *Le normal et le pathologique*. Paris: Presses Universitaires de France.

Carver, T. 1975. "Editor's Preface, Part 1." In *Karl Marx: Texts on Method*, ed. and trans. T. Carver. Oxford: Blackwell.

Cassirer, E. 1951 (1932). *The Philosophy of the Enlightenment*. Trans. F. C. A. Koelln and J. P. Pettegrove. Princeton: Princeton University Press.

———. 1954 (1932). *The Question of Jean-Jacques Rousseau*. Ed. and trans. P. Gay. Bloomington: Indiana University Press.

———. 1963 (1945). *Rousseau, Kant, and Goethe*. Trans. J. Gutmann, P. O. Kristeller, and J. H. Randall. New York: Harper & Row.

Castells, M. 1996. *The Rise of the Network Society*. Vol. 1 of *The Information Age*. Oxford: Blackwell.

———. 1997. *The Power of Identity*. Vol. 2 of *The Information Age*. Oxford: Blackwell.

———. 1998. *End of Millennium*. Vol. 3 of *The Information Age*. Oxford: Blackwell.

Castoriadis, C. 1987 (1975) *The Imaginary Institution of Society*. Trans. K. Blamey. Cambridge: Polity.

———. 1992 (1988). "Individual, Society, Rationality, History." In *Between Totalitarianism and Postmodernity*, ed. P. Beilharz, G. Robinson, and J. Rundell, 233–59. Cambridge, Mass.: MIT Press.

———. 1997a (1982). "Institution of Society and Religion." In *World in Fragments: Writings on Politics, Society, Psychoanalysis, and the Imagination*, ed. and trans. D. A. Curtis, 311–30. Stanford: Stanford University Press.

———. 1997b (1990). "Anthropology, Philosophy, Politics." Trans. D. A. Curtis. *Thesis Eleven* 49: 99–116.

C.E.R.M. (Centre d'études et de recherches marxistes). 1969. *Sur le "mode de production asiatique."* Paris: Editions sociales.

Chakrabarty, D. 2000. *Provincializing Europe: Postcolonial Thought and Historical Difference*. Princeton: Princeton University Press.

———. 2002. *Habitations of Modernity: Essays in the Wake of Subaltern Studies*. Chicago: University of Chicago Press.

Chinard, G. 1934. *L'Amérique et le rêve exotique dans la littérature française au XVIIe et au XVIIIe siècle*. Paris: Droz.

———. 1978 (1911). *L'exotisme américain dans la littérature française au XVIe siècle*. Geneva: Slatkine.

Clarke, J. J. 1997. *Oriental Enlightenment: The Encounter between Asian and Western Thought*. London and New York: Routledge.

Clastres, P. 1977 (1974). *Society against the State*. Trans. R. Hurley and A. Stein. Oxford: Blackwell.

——. 1979. "Entre silence et dialogue." In *Claude Lévi-Strauss,* ed. R. Bellour and C. Clément, 33–38. Paris: Gallimard.

Clément, C. 1985. *Claude Lévi-Strauss ou la structure et le malheur.* 2d ed. Paris: Seghers.

——. 1996. "De la structure à l'Europe." *Magazine littéraire* (hors-série): 8–11.

Clifford, J. 1988. *The Predicament of Culture: Twentieth-Century Ethnography, Literature, and Art.* Cambridge, Mass.: Harvard University Press.

——. 1997. *Routes: Travel and Translation in the Late Twentieth Century.* Cambridge, Mass.: Harvard University Press.

Clifford, J., and G. Marcus, eds. 1986. *Writing Culture: The Poetics and Politics of Ethnography.* Berkeley and Los Angeles: University of California Press.

Colletti, L. 1972 (1969). *From Rousseau to Lenin: Studies in Ideology and Society.* Trans. J. Merrington and J. White. London: New Left Books.

Collins, P. H. 1991. *Black Feminist Thought.* London and New York: Routledge.

——. 1998. *Fighting Words: Black Women and the Search for Justice.* Minneapolis: University of Minnesota Press.

Comte, A. 1975a (1830–42). *Cours de philosophie positive, leçons 1 à 45: Philosophie première.* Paris: Hermann.

——. 1975b (1830–42). *Cours de philosophie positive, leçons 46 à 60: Physique sociale.* Paris: Hermann.

Condorcet, A.-N. de. 1955 (1795). *Sketch for a Historical Picture of the Progress of the Human Mind.* Trans. J. Barraclough. London: Weidenfeld and Nicholson.

Dallmayr, F. 1996. *Beyond Orientalism: Essays on Cross-Cultural Encounter.* Albany: State University of New York Press.

Dallmayr, F., and T. A. McCarthy, eds. 1977. *Understanding and Social Inquiry.* Notre Dame, Ind.: University of Notre Dame Press.

Darwin, C. 1968 (1859). *The Origin of Species by Means of Natural Selection.* Ed. J. W. Burrow. Harmondsworth: Penguin.

——. 1981 (1871). *The Descent of Man, and Selection in Relation to Sex.* Princeton: Princeton University Press.

Davidson, A. I. 1986. "Archaeology, Genealogy, Ethics." In *Foucault: A Critical Reader,* ed. D. C. Hoy, 221–33. Oxford: Blackwell.

de Beauvoir, S. 1949. *Le deuxième sexe.* Paris: Gallimard.

de Brosses, C. 1988 (1760). *Du culte des dieux fétiches.* Paris: Fayard.

de Gramont, S. 1970. "There Are No Superior Societies." In *Claude Lévi-Strauss: The Anthropologist as Hero,* ed. E. N. Hayes and T. Hayes, 3–21. Cambridge, Mass.: MIT Press.

de Saussure, F. 1959 (1915). *Course in General Linguistics.* Ed. C. Bally and A. Sechehaye, trans. W. Baskin. New York: McGraw-Hill.

Defert, D. 1994. "Chronologie." In M. Foucault, *Dits et écrits, 1954–1988, t. I: 1954–1969,* ed. D. Defert and F. Ewald, 13–64. Paris: Gallimard.

Defoe, D. 1972 (1719). *Robinson Crusoe.* Ed. J. D. Crowley. Oxford: Oxford University Press.

Delacampagne, C., and B. Traimond. 1997. "La polémique Sartre/Lévi-Strauss revisitée: Aux sources des sciences sociales d'aujourd'hui." *Les temps modernes* 596: 10–31.

della Volpe, G. 1978 (1964). *Rousseau and Marx.* Trans. J. Fraser. London: Lawrence and Wishart.

Derathé, R. 1984 (1964). "L'homme chez Rousseau." In *Pensée de Rousseau,* ed. G. Genette and T. Todorov, 109–24. Paris: Seuil.

Derrida, J. 1976 (1967). *Of Grammatology*. Trans. G. C. Spivak. Baltimore: The Johns Hopkins University Press.

―――. 1978a (1967). "Cogito and the History of Madness." In *Writing and Difference*, trans. A. Bass, 31–64. London: Routledge.

―――. 1978b (1967). "Structure, Sign and Play in the Discourse of the Human Sciences." In *Writing and Difference*, trans. A. Bass, 278–93. London: Routledge.

Diamond, S. 1974. *In Search of the Primitive: A Critique of Civilization*. New Brunswick, N.J.: Transaction.

Diderot, D. 1972 (1796). *Supplément au voyage de Bougainville*. In *Le Neveau de Rameau et autres dialogues philosophiques*. Paris: Gallimard.

Di Leonardo, M. 1998. *Exotics at Home: Anthropologies, Others, American Modernity*. Chicago: University of Chicago Press.

Dirlik, A. 1997. "The Postcolonial Aura: Third World Criticism in the Age of Global Capitalism." In *Dangerous Liaisons: Gender, Nation, and Postcolonial Perspectives*, ed. A. McClintock, A. Mufti, and E. Shohat, 501–28. Minneapolis: University of Minnesota Press.

Dosse, F. 1997a (1991). *The Rising Sign, 1945–1966*. Vol. 1 of *History of Structuralism*. Trans. D. Glassman. Minneapolis: University of Minnesota Press.

―――. 1997b (1991). *The Sign Sets, 1967-Present*. Vol. 2 of *History of Structuralism*. Translated by D. Glassman. Minneapolis: University of Minnesota Press.

Douglas, M. 1966. *Purity and Danger: An Analysis of the Concepts of Pollution and Taboo*. London and New York: Routledge.

Dreyfus, H. L., and P. Rabinow. 1983. *Michel Foucault: Beyond Structuralism and Hermeneutics*. 2d ed. Chicago: University of Chicago Press.

Du Bois, W. E. B. 1995 (1903). *The Souls of Black Folk*. New York: Signet.

Dudley, E., and M. E. Novak, eds. 1972. *The Wild Man Within: An Image in Western Thought from the Renaissance to Romanticism*. Pittsburgh: University of Pittsburgh Press.

Dumont, L. 1972 (1966). *Homo Hierarchicus: The Caste System and Its Implications*. London: Paladin.

―――. 1977. *Homo aequalis I: Genèse et épanouissement de l'idéologie économique*. Paris: Gallimard.

―――. 1986. *Essays on Individualism: Modern Ideology in Anthropological Perspective*. Chicago: University of Chicago Press.

―――. 1994. *German Ideology: From France to Germany and Back*. Chicago: University of Chicago Press.

Dunayevskaya, R. 1981. *Rosa Luxemburg, Women's Liberation, and Marx's Philosophy of Revolution*. Sussex: Harvester.

Durkheim, E. 1927 (1895). *Les règles de la méthode sociologique*. 8th ed. Paris: Alcan.

―――. 1952 (1897). *Suicide: A Study in Sociology*. Trans. J. A. Spalding and G. Simpson. London: Routledge & Kegan Paul.

―――. 1956 (1922). *Education and Sociology*. Trans. S. D. Fox. Glencoe: Free Press.

―――. 1957 (1950). *Professional Ethics and Civic Morals*. Trans. C. Brookfield. London: Routledge & Kegan Paul.

―――. 1959 (1928). *Socialism and Saint-Simon*. Trans. C. Sattler. London: Routledge & Kegan Paul.

―――. 1960 (1953). *Montesquieu and Rousseau: Forerunners of Sociology*. Trans. R. Manheim. Ann Arbor: University of Michigan Press.

―――. 1965a (1924). "Individual and Collective Representations." In *Sociology and Philosophy*, trans. D. F. Pocock, 1–34. London: Cohen & West.

———. 1965b (1924). "The Determination of Moral Facts." In *Sociology and Philosophy*, trans. D. F. Pocock, 35–62. London: Cohen & West.

———. 1965c (1924). "Replies to Objections." In *Sociology and Philosophy*, trans. D. F. Pocock, 63–79. London: Cohen & West.

———. 1965d (1924). "Value Judgments and Judgments of Reality." In *Sociology and Philosophy*, trans. D. F. Pocock, 80–97. London: Cohen & West.

———. 1970a (1888). "Cours de science sociale: leçon d'ouverture." In *La science sociale et l'action*, 77–110. Paris: Presses Universitaires de France.

———. 1970b (1886). "Les études de science sociale." In *La science sociale et l'action*, 184–214. Paris: Presses Universitaires de France.

———. 1970c (1890). "Les principes de 1789 et la sociologie." In *La science sociale et l'action*, 215–25. Paris: Presses Universitaires de France.

———. 1970d (1893). "Sur la définition du socialisme." In *La science sociale et l'action*, 226–35. Paris: Presses Universitaires de France.

———. 1970e (1897). "La conception matérialiste de l'histoire." In *La science sociale et l'action*, 245–54. Paris: Presses Universitaires de France.

———. 1970f (1898). "L'individualisme et les intellectuels." In *La science sociale et l'action*, 261–78. Paris: Presses Universitaires de France.

———. 1970g (1906). "Internationalisme et lutte de classes." In *La science sociale et l'action*, 282–92. Paris: Presses Universitaires de France.

———. 1970h (1914). "L'avenir de la religion." In *La science sociale et l'action*, 305–13. Paris: Presses Universitaires de France.

———. 1970i (1914). "Le dualisme de la nature humaine et ses conditions sociales." In *La science sociale et l'action*, 314–32. Paris: Presses Universitaires de France.

———. 1973 (1925). *Moral Education: A Study in the Theory and Application of the Sociology of Education*. Ed. E. K Wilson and trans. E. K. Wilson and H. Schnurer. New York: Free Press.

———. 1975a (1895). "L'état actuel des études sociologiques en France." In E. Durkheim, *Textes, t. 1: Éléments d'une théorie sociale*, ed. V. Karady, 73–108. Paris: Minuit.

———. 1975b (1913). "Le problème religieux et la dualité de la nature humaine." In *Textes, t. 2: Religion, morale, anomie*, ed. V. Karady, 23–59. Paris: Minuit.

———. 1977 (1938). *The Evolution of Educational Thought: Lectures on the Formation and Development of Secondary Education in France*. Trans. P. Collins. London: Routledge and Kegan Paul.

———. 1978a (1889). "Review of Ferdinand Tönnies, *Gemeinschaft und Gesellschaft*." In *Emile Durkheim: On Institutional Analysis*, ed. and trans. M. Traugott, 115–22. Chicago: University of Chicago Press.

———. 1978b (1913). "Review of Lucien Levy-Bruhl, *Les fonctions mentales dans les sociétés inférieures* and Emile Durkheim, *Les formes élémentaires de la vie religieuse*." In *Emile Durkheim: On Institutional Analysis*, ed. and trans. M. Traugott, 145–49. Chicago: University of Chicago Press.

———. 1978c (1920). "Introduction to *Morality*." In *Emile Durkheim: On Institutional Analysis*, ed. and trans. M. Traugott. Chicago: University of Chicago Press.

———. 1984 (1893). *The Division of Labour in Society*. Trans. W. D. Halls. London: Macmillan.

———. 1995 (1912). *The Elementary Forms of Religious Life*. Trans. K. E. Fields. New York: Free Press.

Durkheim, E., and P. Fauconnet. 1975 (1903). "Sociologie et sciences sociales."

In E. Durkheim, *Textes, t. 1: Éléments d'une théorie sociale,* ed. V. Karady, 121–59. Paris: Minuit.

Durkheim, E., and M. Mauss. 1969a (1903). "De quelques formes primitives de classification: contribution à l'étude des représentations collectives." In M. Mauss, *Oeuvres, t. 2: Représentations collectives et diversité des civilisations,* ed. V. Karady, 13–89. Paris: Minuit.

———. 1969b (1913). "Note sur la notion de civilisation." In M. Mauss, *Oeuvres, t. 2: Représentations collectives et diversité des civilisations,* ed. V. Karady, 451–55. Paris: Minuit.

Eisenstadt, S. N., ed. 1986. *The Origins and Diversity of Axial Civilizations.* Albany: State University of New York Press.

———, ed. 1987a. *The West.* Vol. 1 of *Patterns of Modernity.* London: Pinter.

———, ed. 1987b. *Beyond the West.* Vol. 2 of *Patterns of Modernity.* London: Pinter.

———. 1991 (1971). "Some Reflections on the Significance of Max Weber's Sociology of Religions for the Analysis of Non-European Modernity." In *Max Weber: Critical Assessments,* ed. P. Hamilton, 4: 3–165. London and New York: Routledge.

———. 2000. "Multiple Modernities." *Daedalus* 129, 1: 1–29.

Eliade, M. 1960 (1957). *Myths, Dreams and Mysteries: The Encounter between Contemporary Faiths and Archaic Realities.* Trans. P. Mairet. New York: Harper & Row.

Elias, N. 1978 (1970). *What Is Sociology?* Trans. S. Mennell and G. Morrissey. London: Hutchinson.

———. 1987a. "The Retreat of Sociologists into the Present." *Theory, Culture & Society* 4, nos. 2–3: 223-47.

———. 1987b (1983). *Involvement and Detachment.* Trans. E. Jephcott. Oxford: Blackwell.

———. 1994a (1939). *The Civilizing Process.* Trans. E. Jephcott. Oxford: Blackwell.

———. 1994b (1987). *Reflections on a Life.* Trans. E. Jephcott. Cambridge: Polity.

Ellingson, T. 2001. *The Myth of the Noble Savage.* Berkeley and Los Angeles: University of California Press.

Engels, F. 1969 (1884). "The Origin of the Family, Private Property and the State." In K. Marx and F. Engels, *Selected Works,* 3: 191–334. Moscow: Progress Publishers.

Eribon, D. 1991 (1989). *Michel Foucault.* Trans. B. Wing. Cambridge, Mass: Harvard University Press.

Evans-Pritchard, E. E. 1988. Introduction to *The Gift: Forms and Functions of Exchange in Archaic Societies,* by M. Mauss. Trans. I. Cunnison. London: Routledge.

Evens, T. M. S. 1995. *Two Kinds of Rationality: Kibbutz Democracy and Generational Conflict.* Minneapolis: University of Minnesota Press.

Ewald, F. 1995. "Foucault: analytique de l'exclusion." *Magazine littéraire* 334: 22–24.

Fabian, J. 1983. *Time and the Other: How Anthropology Makes Its Object.* New York: Columbia University Press.

Fairchild, H. N. 1961 (1928). *The Noble Savage: A Study in Romantic Naturalism.* New York: Russell & Russell.

Fanon, F. 1963 (1961). *The Wretched of the Earth.* Trans. C. Farrington. New York: Grove Press.

Faubion, J. D. 2000. "Anthropology and Social Theory." In *The Blackwell Companion to Social Theory,* ed. B. S. Turner, 2d ed., 245–69. Malden, Mass.: Blackwell.

Ferrara, A. 1993. *Modernity and Authenticity: A Study of the Social and Ethical*

Thought of Jean-Jacques Rousseau. Albany, N.Y.: State University of New York Press.

Feuerbach, L. 1972a. "Towards a Critique of Hegel's Philosophy." In *The Fiery Brook: Selected Writings of Ludwig Feuerbach,* ed. and trans. Z. Hanfi, 53–96. New York: Anchor.

———. 1972b. Introduction to the *Essence of Christianity.* In *The Fiery Brook: Selected Writings of Ludwig Feuerbach,* ed. and trans. Z. Hanfi, 97–133. New York: Anchor.

Flynn, T. 1994. "Foucault's Mapping of History." In *The Cambridge Companion to Foucault,* ed. G. Gutting, 28–46. Cambridge: Cambridge University Press.

Foucault, M. 1963. *Raymond Roussel.* Paris: Gallimard.

———. 1965 (1961). *Madness and Civilization: A History of Insanity in the Age of Reason.* Trans. R. Howard. New York: Vintage.

———. 1970 (1966). *The Order of Things: An Archaeology of the Human Sciences.* Anonymous translation. New York: Vintage.

———. 1972 (1969). *The Archeology of Knowledge.* Trans. A. M. Sheridan Smith. New York: Harper & Row.

———. 1976 (1954). *Mental Illness and Psychology.* Trans. A. Sheridan. New York: Harper & Row.

———. 1977a (1975). *Discipline and Punish: The Birth of the Prison.* Trans. A. Sheridan. London: Allen Lane.

———. 1977b. "A Preface to Transgression." In *Language, Counter-Memory, Practice: Selected Essays and Interviews,* ed. D. F. Bouchard, 29–52. Oxford: Blackwell.

———. 1977c. "Nietzsche, Geneology, History." In *Language, Counter-Memory, Practice: Selected Essays and Interviews,* ed. D. F. Bouchard, 139–64. Oxford: Blackwell.

———. 1978 (1976). *The History of Sexuality, Volume 1: An Introduction.* Trans. R. Hurley. New York: Vintage.

———. 1981 (1971). "The Order of Discourse," trans. I. McLeod. In *Untying the Text: A Post-Structuralist Reader,* ed. R. Young, 48–78. London: Routledge & Kegan Paul.

———. 1983. "The Subject and Power." In *Michel Foucault: Beyond Structuralism and Hermeneutics* by H. L. Dreyfus and P. Rabinow, 2d ed., 208–26. Chicago: University of Chicago Press.

———. 1984a. "What Is Enlightenment?" In *The Foucault Reader,* ed. P. Rabinow, 32–50. New York: Pantheon.

———. 1984b (1971). "Nietzsche, Genealogy, History." In *The Foucault Reader,* ed. P. Rabinow, 76–100. New York: Pantheon.

———. 1984c. "Preface to *The History of Sexuality,* Volume 2." In *The Foucault Reader,* ed. P. Rabinow, 333–39. New York: Pantheon.

———. 1984d. "On the Genealogy of Ethics: An Overview of Work in Progress." In *The Foucault Reader,* ed. P. Rabinow, 340–72. New York: Pantheon.

———. 1985 (1984). *The History of Sexuality, Volume 2: The Use of Pleasure.* Trans. R. Hurley. New York: Vintage.

———. 1986 (1984). *The History of Sexuality, Volume 3: The Care of the Self.* Trans. R. Hurley. New York: Vintage.

———. 1988a (1984). "The Ethic of Care for the Self as a Practice of Freedom." In *The Final Foucault,* ed. J. Bernauer and D. Rasmussen, 1–20. Cambridge, Mass.: MIT Press.

———. 1988b. "Truth, Power, Self: An Interview." In *Technologies of the Self:*

A Seminar with Michel Foucault, ed. L. H. Martin, H. Gutman, and P. H. Hutton, 9–15. Amherst: University of Massachusetts Press.

——. 1988c. "Technologies of the Self." In *Technologies of the Self: A Seminar with Michel Foucault,* ed. L. H. Martin, H. Gutman, and P. H. Hutton, 16–49. Amherst: University of Massachusetts Press.

——. 1988d. "The Political Technology of Individuals." In *Technologies of the Self: A Seminar with Michel Foucault,* ed. L. H. Martin, H. Gutman, and P. H. Hutton, 145–62. Amherst: University of Massachusetts Press.

——. 1989. *Résumé des cours, 1970–1982.* Paris: Julliard.

——. 1994a (1967). "Qui êtes-vous, professeur Foucault?" In *Dits et écrits, 1954–1988, t. I: 1954–1969,* ed. D. Defert and F. Ewald, 601–20. Paris: Gallimard.

——. 1994b (1972). "Mon corps, ce papier, ce feu." In *Dits et écrits, 1954–1988, t. II: 1970–1975,* ed. D. Defert and F. Ewald, 245–68. Paris: Gallimard.

——. 1994c (1973). "De l'archéologique à la dynastique." In *Dits et écrits, 1954–1988, t. II: 1970–1975,* ed. D. Defert and F. Ewald, 405–16. Paris: Gallimard.

——. 1994d (1978). "Sexualité et politique." In *Dits et écrits, 1954–1988, t. III: 1976–1979,* ed. D. Defert and F. Ewald, 522–31. Paris: Gallimard.

——. 1994e (1978). "La philosophie analytique de la politique." In *Dits et écrits, 1954–1988, t. III: 1976–1979,* ed. D. Defert and F. Ewald, 534–51. Paris: Gallimard.

——. 1994f (1978). "La scène de la philosophie." In *Dits et écrits, 1954–1988, t. III: 1976–1979,* ed. D. Defert and F. Ewald, 571-95. Paris: Gallimard.

——. 1994g (1978). "Michel Foucault et le zen: un séjour dans un temple zen." In *Dits et écrits, 1954–1988, t. III: 1976–1979,* ed. D. Defert and F. Ewald, 618–24. Paris: Gallimard.

——. 1994h (1978). "L'armée, quand la terre tremble." In *Dits et écrits, 1954–1988, t. III: 1976–1979,* ed. D. Defert and F. Ewald, 662–69. Paris: Gallimard.

——. 1994i (1978). "Le chah a cent ans de retard." In *Dits et écrits, 1954–1988, t. III: 1976–1979,* edited by D. Defert and F. Ewald, 679–83. Paris: Gallimard.

——. 1994j (1978). "Téhéran: la foi contre le chah." In *Dits et écrits, 1954–1988, t. III: 1976–1979,* ed. D. Defert and F. Ewald, 683–88. Paris: Gallimard.

——. 1994k (1978). "A quoi rêvent les Iraniens?" In *Dits et écrits, 1954–1988, t. III: 1976–1979,* ed. D. Defert and F. Ewald, 688–94. Paris: Gallimard.

——. 1994l (1978). "Une révolte à mains nues." In *Dits et écrits, 1954–1988, t. III: 1976–1979,* ed. D. Defert and F. Ewald, 701–4. Paris: Gallimard.

——. 1994m (1978). "Défi à l'opposition." In *Dits et écrits, 1954–1988, t. III: 1976–1979,* ed. D. Defert and F. Ewald, 704–6. Paris: Gallimard.

——. 1994n (1978). "Les 'reportages' d'idées." In *Dits et écrits, 1954–1988, t. III: 1976–1979,* ed. D. Defert and F. Ewald, 706–7. Paris: Gallimard.

——. 1994o (1978). "Réponse de Michel Foucault à une lectrice iranienne." In *Dits et écrits, 1954–1988, t. III: 1976–1979,* ed. D. Defert and F. Ewald, 708. Paris: Gallimard.

——. 1994p (1978). "La révolte iranienne se propage sur les rubans de cassettes." In *Dits et écrits, 1954–1988, t. III: 1976–1979,* ed. D. Defert and F. Ewald, 709–13. Paris: Gallimard.

——. 1994q (1978). "Le chef mythique de la révolte de l'Iran." In *Dits et écrits, 1954–1988, t. III: 1976–1979,* ed. D. Defert and F. Ewald, 713–16. Paris: Gallimard.

———. 1994r (1979). "L'esprit d'un monde sans esprit." In *Dits et écrits, 1954–1988, t. III: 1976–1979*, ed. D. Defert and F. Ewald, 743–55. Paris: Gallimard.

———. 1994s (1979). "Une poudrière appelée islam." In *Dits et écrits, 1954–1988, t. III: 1976–1979*, ed. D. Defert and F. Ewald, 759–61. Paris: Gallimard.

———. 1994t (1979). "Michel Foucault et l'Iran." In *Dits et écrits, 1954–1988, t. III: 1976–1979*, ed. D. Defert and F. Ewald, 762. Paris: Gallimard.

———. 1994u. (1979) "Lettre ouverte à Mehdi Bazargan." In *Dits et écrits, 1954–1988, t. III: 1976–1979*, ed. D. Defert and F. Ewald, 780–82. Paris: Gallimard.

———. 1994v (1979). "Inutile de se soulever?" In *Dits et écrits, 1954–1988, t. III: 1976–1979*, ed. D. Defert and F. Ewald, 790–94. Paris: Gallimard.

———. 1998a (1962). "Introduction to Rousseau's *Dialogues*." In *Aesthetics, Method and Epistemology: Essential Works of Foucault, 1954–1984*, ed. J. D. Faubion, trans. R. Hurley, 2: 33–51. New York: New Press.

———. 1998b (1966). "The Thought of the Outside." In *Aesthetics, Method and Epistemology: Essential Works of Foucault, 1954-1984*, ed. J. D. Faubion and trans. R. Hurley, 2: 147–69. New York: New Press.

———. 1998c (1966). "A Swimmer between Two Words." In *Aesthetics, Method and Epistemology: Essential Works of Foucault, 1954-1984*, ed. J. D. Faubion and trans. R. Hurley, 2: 171–85. New York: New Press.

———. 1998d (1968). "On the Archaeology of the Sciences: Response to the Epistemology Circle." In *Aesthetics, Method and Epistemology: Essential Works of Foucault, 1954–1984*, ed. J. D. Faubion and trans. R. Hurley, 2: 297–333. New York: New Press.

———. 1998e (1970). "Madness and Society." In *Aesthetics, Method and Epistemology: Essential Works of Foucault, 1954–1984*, ed. J. D. Faubion and trans. R. Hurley, 2: 335–42. New York: New Press.

———. 1998f (1983). "Structuralism and Post-Structuralism." In *Aesthetics, Method and Epistemology: Essential Works of Foucault, 1954–1984*, ed. J. D. Faubion and trans. R. Hurley, 2: 433–58. New York: New Press.

Frazer, J. G. 1922 (1890). *The Golden Bough: A Study in Magic and Religion*. Abridged ed. London: Macmillan

Freud, S. 1990 (1930). *Totem and Taboo: Some Points of Agreement between the Mental Lives of Savages and Neurotics*. Trans. J. Strachey. In *The Origins of Religion*, vol. 13 of *The Penguin Freud Library*. Harmondsworth: Penguin.

———. 1994 (1930). *Civilization and Its Discontents*. Trans. J. Riviere. New York: Dover.

Friedman, J. 1994. *Cultural Identity and Global Process*. London: Sage.

Frisby, D. 1981. *Sociological Impressionism: A Reassessment of Georg Simmel's Social Theory*. London: Heinemann.

Frisby, D. 1987. "The Ambiguity of Modernity: Georg Simmel and Max Weber." In *Max Weber and His Contemporaries*, ed. W. J. Mommsen and J. Osterhammel, 422–33. London: Allen & Unwin.

Fuchs, M. 1993. "The Reversal of the Ethnological Perspective: Attempts at Objectifying One's Own Cultural Horizon: Dumont, Foucault, Bourdieu." *Thesis Eleven* 34: 104–25.

Fukuyama, F. 1989. "The End of History?" *The National Interest* 16: 3–18.

———. 1992. *The End of the History and the Last Man*. New York: Free Press.

Gadamer, H.-G. 1975. "Hermeneutics and Social Science." *Cultural Hermeneutics* 2, no. 4: 307–16.

——. 1976. *Philosophical Hermeneutics.* Ed. and trans. D. E. Linge. Berkeley and Los Angeles: University of California Press.

——. 1992. "The Historicity of Understanding." In *The Hermeneutics Reader,* ed. K. Mueller-Vollmer, 256–92. New York: Continuum.

——. 1994. (1960). *Truth and Method,* 2d ed. Trans. J. Weinsheimer and D. G. Marshall. New York: Continuum.

Game, A. 1991. *Undoing the Social: Towards a Deconstructive Sociology.* Toronto: University of Toronto Press.

Game, A., and A. Metcalfe. 1996. *Passionate Sociology.* London: Sage.

Gane, M. 1992a. "Introduction: Emile Durkheim, Marcel Mauss and the Sociological Project." In *The Radical Sociology of Durkheim and Mauss,* ed. M. Gane, 1–10. London and New York: Routledge.

——. 1992b. "Durkheim: The Sacred Language." In *The Radical Sociology of Durkheim and Mauss,* ed. M. Gane, 61–84. London and New York: Routledge.

Gaonkar, D. P. 1999. "On Alternative Modernities." *Public Culture* 11, no. 1: 1–18.

García Canclini, N. 1995. *Hybrid Cultures: Strategies for Entering and Leaving Modernity.* Trans. C. L. Chiappari and S. L. López. Minneapolis: University of Minnesota Press.

Garfinkel, H. 1967. *Studies in Ethnomethodology.* Englewood Cliffs, N. J.: Prentice-Hall.

Gay, P. 1954. Introduction to *The Question of Jean-Jacques Rousseau* by E. Cassirer. Ed. and trans. P. Gay. Bloomington: Indiana University Press.

——. 1963. Introduction to the Torchbook Edition. In *Rousseau, Kant and Goethe* by E. Cassirer, trans. J. Gutmann, P. O. Kristeller, and J. H. Randall, ix–xv. New York: Harper & Row.

——. 1966. *The Rise of Modern Paganism.* Vol. 1 of *The Enlightenment: An Interpretation.* London: Weidenfeld and Nicholson.

——. 1969. *The Science of Freedom.* Vol. 2 of *The Enlightenment: An Interpretation.* London: Weidenfeld and Nicholson.

Geertz, C. 1973. *The Interpretation of Cultures.* New York: Basic Books.

——. 1983. *Local Knowledge: Further Essays in Interpretive Anthropology.* New York: Basic Books.

——. 1988. "The World in a Text: How to Read 'Tristes Tropiques.'" In *Works and Lives: The Anthropologist as Author,* 25–48. Stanford: Stanford University Press.

——. 2000. *Available Light: Anthropological Reflections on Philosophical Topics.* Princeton: Princeton University Press.

Geras, N. 1972. "Marx and the Critique of Political Economy." In *Ideology in Social Science: Readings in Critical Social Theory,* ed. R. Blackburn, 284–305. London: Fontana.

Giddens, A. 1978. *Durkheim.* London: Fontana.

——. 1987. "Weber and Durkheim: Coincidence and Divergence." In *Max Weber and His Contemporaries,* ed. W. J. Mommsen and J. Osterhammel, 182–89. London: Allen & Unwin.

——. 1990. *The Consequences of Modernity.* Stanford, Calif.: Stanford University Press.

Gilroy, P. 1993. *The Black Atlantic: Modernity and Double Consciousness.* Cambridge, Mass.: Harvard University Press.

——. 2000. *Between Camps: Nations, Cultures and the Allure of Race.* Harmondsworth: Penguin.

Godelier, M. 1977 (1973). *Perspectives in Marxist Anthropology*. Trans. R. Brain. Cambridge: Cambridge University Press.

Goldberg, D. T., ed. 1994. *Multiculturalism: A Critical Reader*. Oxford: Blackwell.

Goldwater, R. 1987 (1938). *Primitivism in Modern Art*. Enlarged edition. Cambridge, Mass.: Harvard University Press.

Gombrich, E. H. 2002. *The Preference for the Primitive: Episodes in the History of Western Taste and Art*. London: Phaidon.

Gordon, C. 1987. "The Soul of the Citizen: Max Weber and Michel Foucault on Rationality and Government." In *Max Weber, Rationality and Modernity*, ed. S. Lash and S. Whimster, 293–316. London: Allen & Unwin.

Gouldner, A. W. 1973. "Emile Durkheim and the Critique of Socialism." In *For Sociology: Renewal and Critique in Sociology Today*, 369–91. London: Allen Lane.

Gramsci, A. 1971. *Selections from the Prison Notebooks*. Ed. and trans. Q. Hoare and G. Nowell Smith. New York: International Publishers.

Gunew, S., and A. Yeatman, eds. 1993. *Feminism and the Politics of Difference*. Boulder, Colo.: Westview.

Gutman, A., ed. 1994. *Multiculturalism: Examining the Politics of Recognition*. Princeton, N.J.: Princeton University Press.

Habermas, J. 1971 (1965). "Discussion on Value-Freedom and Objectivity." In *Max Weber and Sociology Today*, ed. O. Stammer and trans. K. Morris, 59–66. Oxford: Blackwell.

———. 1973 (1971). *Theory and Practice*. Trans. John Viertel. Boston: Beacon Press.

———. 1979 (1976). *Communication and the Evolution of Society*. Trans. T. McCarthy. Boston: Beacon Press.

———. 1984 (1981). *Reason and the Rationalization of Society*. Vol. 1 of *The Theory of Communicative Action*. Trans. T. McCarthy. Boston: Beacon Press.

———. 1986. *Autonomy and Solidarity: Interviews with Jürgen Habermas*. Ed. P. Dews. London: Verso.

———. 1987a (1968). *Knowledge and Human Interests*. Trans. J. J. Shapiro. Cambridge: Polity.

———. 1987b (1981). *Lifeworld and System*. Vol. 2 of *The Theory of Communicative Action*. Trans. T. McCarthy. Boston: Beacon Press.

———. 1987c (1985). *The Philosophical Discourse of Modernity: Twelve Lectures*. Trans. F. G. Lawrence. Cambridge, Mass.: MIT Press.

———. 1988 (1970). *On the Logic of the Social Sciences*. Trans. S. Weber Nicholsen and J. A. Stark. Cambridge, Mass.: MIT Press.

———. 1992. "Hermeneutics and the Human Sciences." In *The Hermeneutics Reader*, ed. K. Mueller-Vollmer, 293–319. New York: Continuum.

———. 1996 (1990). "Citizenship and National Identity." Appendix 2 in *Between Facts and Norms: Contributions to a Discourse Theory of Law and Democracy*, trans. W. Rehg, 491–515. Cambridge, Mass: MIT Press.

———. 2001. *The Postnational Constellation: Political Essays*, trans. M. Pensky. Cambridge, Mass.: MIT Press.

Hacking, I. 1986. "The Archaeology of Foucault." In *Foucault: A Critical Reader*, ed. D. C. Hoy, 27–40. Oxford: Blackwell.

Hadot, P. 1995 (1987). "Reflections on the Idea of the 'Cultivation of the Self.'" In *Philosophy as a Way of Life: Spiritual Exercises from Socrates to Foucault*, ed. A. I. Davidson and trans. M. Chase, 206–13. Oxford: Blackwell.

Hall, S. 1990. "Cultural Identity and Diaspora." In *Identity: Community, Culture, Difference*, ed. J. Rutherford, 222–37. London: Lawrence & Wishart.

———. 1991. "The Local and the Global: Globalization and Ethnicity." In *Culture, Globalization and the World-System: Contemporary Conditions for the Representation of Identity*, ed. A. D. King, 19–39. Binghamton, N.Y.: Department of Art and Art History, State University of New York at Binghamton.

Hannerz, U. 1992. *Cultural Complexity: Studies in the Social Organization of Meaning*. New York: Columbia University Press.

Haraway, D. 1991. "Situated Knowledges: The Science Question in Feminism and the Privilege of Partial Perspective." In *Simians, Cyborgs and Women: The Reinvention of Nature*, 183–201. London: Free Association Books.

Harootunian, H. D. 1988. "Foucault, Genealogy, History: The Pursuit of Otherness." In *After Foucault: Humanistic Knowledge, Postmodern Challenges*, ed. J. Arac, 110–37. New Brunswick, N.J.: Rutgers University Press.

Harvey, D. 1989. *The Condition of Postmodernity: An Enquiry into the Origins of Cultural Change*. Oxford: Blackwell.

Hegel, G. W. F. 1952 (1821). *The Philosophy of Right*. Trans. T. M. Knox. Oxford: Oxford University Press.

———. 1975 (1840). *Lectures on the Philosophy of World History: Introduction*. Trans. H. B. Nisbet. Cambridge: Cambridge University Press.

———. 1977 (1807). *The Phenomenology of Spirit*. Trans. A. V. Miller. Oxford: Oxford University Press.

Heller, A. 1976 (1974). *The Theory of Need in Marx*. Anonymous translation. London: Allison & Busby.

———. 1978 (1967). *Renaissance Man*. Trans. R. E. Allen. London: Routledge & Kegan Paul.

Hénaff, M. 1998 (1991). *Claude Lévi-Strauss and the Making of Structural Anthropology*. Trans. M. Baker. Minneapolis: University of Minnesota Press.

Hennis, W. 1988. *Max Weber: Essays in Reconstruction*. Trans. K. Tribe. London: Allen & Unwin.

Herder, J. G. 1966 (1784). *Outlines of a Philosophy of the History of Man*. Trans. T. Churchill. New York: Bergman.

Herodotus. 1996. *The Histories*. Trans. A. de Sélincourt. Harmondsworth: Penguin.

Hindess, B., and P. Q. Hirst. 1975. *Pre-Capitalist Modes of Production*. London: Routledge & Kegan Paul.

Hobbes, T. 1962 (1651). *Leviathan*. London: Fontana.

Hobsbawm, E. J. 1964. Introduction to *Pre-Capitalist Economic Formations* by Karl Marx. Ed. E. J. Hobsbawm and trans. J. Cohen, 9–65. New York: International Publishers.

———. 1977 (1962). *The Age of Revolution: Europe 1789–1848*. London: Abacus.

———. 1987. *The Age of Empire, 1875–1914*. London: Weidenfeld and Nicolson.

Hollier, D., ed. 1988 (1979). *The College of Sociology (1937–39)*. Trans. B. Wing. Minneapolis: University of Minnesota Press.

Honneth, A. 1985. "La Planète Lévi-Strauss: Allemagne." *Magazine littéraire* 223: 63.

———. 1991 (1985). *The Critique of Power: Reflective Stages in a Critical Social Theory*. Trans. K. Baynes. Cambridge, Mass.: MIT Press.

———. 1995a (1989). "Domination and Moral Struggle: The Philosophical Heritage of Marxism Reviewed." In *The Fragmented World of the Social: Essays in Social and Political Philosophy*, ed. C. W. Wright, 3–14. Albany, N.Y.: SUNY Press.

———. 1995b (1980). "Work and Instrumental Action: On the Normative Basis of Critical Theory." In *The Fragmented World of the Social: Essays in Social and Political Philosophy*, ed. C. W. Wright, 15–49. Albany, N.Y.: SUNY Press.

———. 1995c (1990). "A Structuralist Rousseau: On the Anthropology of Claude Lévi-Strauss." In *The Fragmented World of the Social: Essays in Social and Political Philosophy*, ed. C. W. Wright, 135–49. Albany, N.Y.: State University of New York Press.

———. 1995d (1992). *The Struggle for Recognition: The Moral Grammar of Social Conflicts*. Trans. J. Anderson. Cambridge: Polity.

Honneth, A., and H. Joas. 1988 (1980). *Social Action and Human Nature*. Trans. H. Meyer. Cambridge: Cambridge University Press.

Horkheimer, M. 1947. *Eclipse of Reason*. New York: Oxford University Press.

———. 1972 (1968). "Traditional and Critical Theory." In *Critical Theory: Selected Essays*, trans. M. J. O'Connell, 188–243. New York: Seabury Press.

Horton, R. 1995 (1973). "Lévy-Bruhl, Durkheim and the Scientific Revolution." In *Emile Durkheim: Critical Assessments*, ed. P. Hamilton, 7: 171–213. London and New York: Routledge.

Hubert, H., and M. Mauss. 1964 (1898). *Sacrifice: Its Nature and Function*. Trans. W. D. Halls. Chicago: University of Chicago Press.

———. 1968 (1902–3). "Esquisse d'une théorie générale de la magie." In M. Mauss *Sociologie et anthropologie*, 4th ed., 3–141. Paris: Presses Universitaires de France.

Huntington, S. 1993. "The Clash of Civilizations?" *Foreign Affairs* 72, no. 3: 22–49.

———. 1996. *The Clash of Civilizations and the Remaking of World Order*. New York: Simon & Schuster.

Inda, J. X., and R. Rosaldo, eds. 2002. *The Anthropology of Globalization: A Reader*. Malden, Mass.: Blackwell.

Irigaray, L. 1985a. *Speculum of the Other Woman*. Trans. G. Gill. Ithaca, N.Y.: Cornell University Press.

———. 1985b. *This Sex Which Is Not One*. Trans. C. Porter with C. Burke. Ithaca, N.Y.: Cornell University Press.

Jaspers, K. 1989. *On Max Weber*. Ed. J. Dreijmans and trans. R. J. Whelan. New York: Paragon House.

Jay, M. 1996 (1973). *The Dialectical Imagination: A History of the Frankfurt School and the Institute of Social Research, 1923–1950*. Berkeley and Los Angeles: University of California Press.

Jenkins, A. 1979. *The Social Theory of Claude Lévi-Strauss*. London: Macmillan.

Joas, H. 1996 (1992). *The Creativity of Action*. Trans. J. Gaines and P. Keast. Cambridge: Polity.

Jullien, F. 1989. *Procès ou création: Une introduction à la pensée chinoise*. Paris: Seuil.

———. 1995. *Dialogue sur la morale*. Paris: Grasset.

———. 1999. "A Philosophical Use of China: An Interview with François Jullien." *Thesis Eleven* 57: 113–30.

Jullien, F., and T. Marchaisse. 2000. *Penser d'un dehors (la Chine): Entretiens d'Extrême-Occident*. Paris: Seuil.

Kahn, J. S. 1995. *Culture, Multiculture, Postculture*. London: Sage.

Kalberg, S. 1994. *Max Weber's Comparative-Historical Sociology*. Cambridge: Polity.

———. 1997. "Max Weber's Sociology: Research Strategies and Modes of Analysis." In *Reclaiming the Sociological Classics: The State of the Scholarship*, ed. C. Camic, 208–41. Oxford: Blackwell.

Kant, I. 1991a (1784). "Idea for a Universal History with a Cosmopolitan Purpose." In *Political Writings*, 2d ed., ed. H. Reiss and trans. H. B. Nisbet, 41–53. Cambridge: Cambridge University Press.

———. 1991b (1784). "An Answer to the Question: 'What Is Enlightenment?'" In *Political Writings*, 2d ed., ed. H. Reiss and trans. H. B. Nisbet, 54–60. Cambridge: Cambridge University Press.

———. 1991c. "Conjectures on the Beginning of Human History." In *Political Writings*, 2d ed., ed. H. Reiss and trans. H. B. Nisbet, 221–34. Cambridge: Cambridge University Press.

———. 1996 (1787). *Critique of Practical Reason*. Trans. T. K. Abbott. Amherst, N.Y.: Prometheus.

Karady, V. 1968. "Présentation de l'édition." In M. Mauss, *Oeuvres, t. 1: les fonctions sociales du sacré*, ed. V. Karady, i–liii. Paris: Minuit.

———. 1995 (1988). "Durkheim et les débuts de l'ethnologie universitaire." In *Emile Durkheim: Critical Assessments*, ed. P. Hamilton, 8: 139-55. London and New York: Routledge.

Käsler, D. 1988 (1979). *Max Weber: An Introduction to His Life and Work*. Trans. P. Hurd. Cambridge: Polity.

Kögler, H. H. 1996 (1992). *The Power of Dialogue: Critical Hermeneutics after Gadamer and Foucault*. Trans. P. Hendrickson. Cambridge, Mass.: MIT Press.

Kozlarek, O. 2001. "Critical Theory and the Challenge of Globalization." *International Sociology* 16, no. 4: 607–22.

Krader, L. 1972. Introduction to *The Ethnological Notebooks of Karl Marx*. Edited and transcribed by L. Krader, 1–85. Assen: Van Gorcum.

———. 1975. *The Asiatic Mode of Production: Sources, Development and Critique in the Writings of Karl Marx*. Assen: Van Gorcum.

———. 1979. "The Ethnological Notebooks of Marx: A Commentary." In *Toward a Marxist Anthropology: Problems and Perspectives*, ed. S. Diamond, 153–71. The Hague: Mouton.

Kuper, A. 1988. *The Invention of Primitive Society: Transformations of an Illusion*. London and New York: Routledge.

Kurasawa, F. 1999. "The Exotic Effect: Foucault and the Question of Cultural Alterity." *European Journal of Social Theory* 2, no. 2: 147–65.

———. 2002. "A Requiem for the Primitive." *History of the Human Sciences* 15, no. 3: 1–24.

———. 2003. "Primitiveness and the Flight from Modernity: Sociology and the Avant-Garde in Interwar Paris." *Economy and Society* 32, no. 1: 7–28.

Kymlicka, W., and S. Mesure, eds. 2000. "Les identités culturelles." Thematic issue of *Comprendre: Revue de philosophie et de sciences sociales*, vol. 1.

Lacroix, B. 1981. *Durkheim et le politique*. Paris: Presses de la Fondation Nationale des Sciences Politiques.

Langer, M. 1984. "The Notion of 'Expression' in Marx." *Thesis Eleven* 8: 102–15.

Le Goff, J. 1980. *Time, Work, and Culture in the Middle Ages*. Trans. A. Goldhammer. Chicago: University of Chicago Press.

Leach, E. 1989 (1974). *Claude Lévi-Strauss*. Chicago: University of Chicago Press.

Lefebvre, H. 1968 (1966). *The Sociology of Marx*. Trans. N. Guterman. London: Allen Lane.

Lévi-Strauss, C. 1955. "Diogène couché." *Les temps modernes* 110: 1187–1220.

———. 1963 (1962). *Totemism*. Trans. R. Needham. Boston: Beacon Press.

———. 1966 (1962). *The Savage Mind*. Anonymous translation. London: Weidenfeld and Nicholson.

———. 1968a (1949). Introduction to *Structural Anthropology*. Trans. C. Jacobson and B. G. Schoepf, 1: 1–27. Harmondsworth: Penguin.

———. 1968b (1951). "Language and the Analysis of Social Laws." In *Structural Anthropology*. Trans. C. Jacobson and B. G. Schoepf, 1: 55–66. Harmondsworth: Penguin.

———. 1968c (1952). "The Concept of Archaism in Anthropology." In *Structural Anthropology*, trans. C. Jacobson and B. G. Schoepf, 1: 101–19. Harmondsworth: Penguin.

———. 1968d (1949). "The Sorcerer and His Magic." In *Structural Anthropology*, trans. C. Jacobson and B. G. Schoepf, 1: 167–85. Harmondsworth: Penguin.

———. 1968e (1949). "The Effectiveness of Symbols." In *Structural Anthropology*, trans. C. Jacobson and B. G. Schoepf, 1: 186–205. Harmondsworth: Penguin.

———. 1968f (1955). "The Structural Study of Myth." In *Structural Anthropology*, trans. C. Jacobson and B. G. Schoepf, 1: 206–31. Harmondsworth: Penguin.

———. 1968g (1953). "Social Structure." In *Structural Anthropology*, trans. C. Jacobson and B. G. Schoepf, 1: 277–323. Harmondsworth: Penguin.

———. 1968h (1958). Postscript to chapter 15. In *Structural Anthropology*, trans. C. Jacobson and B. G. Schoepf, 1: 324–45. Harmondsworth: Penguin.

———. 1968i (1954). "The Place of Anthropology in the Social Sciences and Problems Raised in Teaching It." In *Structural Anthropology*, trans. C. Jacobson and B. G. Schoepf, 1: 346–81. Harmondsworth: Penguin.

———. 1969a (1949). *The Elementary Structures of Kinship,* revised edition. Trans. J. H. Bell and J. R. von Sturmer and ed. R. Needham. Boston: Beacon Press.

———. 1969b (1964). *The Raw and the Cooked: Introduction to a Science of Mythology.* Vol. 1. Trans. J. and D. Weightman. London: Jonathan Cape.

———. 1970. "A Confrontation." *New Left Review* 62: 57–74.

———. 1971 (1945). "French Sociology." In *Twentieth Century Sociology*, ed. G. Gurvitch and W. E. Moore, 503–37. Freeport, N.Y.: Books for Libraries Press.

———. 1973 (1966). *From Honey to Ashes: Introduction to a Science of Mythology.* Vol. 2. Trans. J. and D. Weightman. New York: Harper & Row.

———. 1977a (1960). "The Scope of Anthropology." In *Structural Anthropology*, trans. M. Layton, 2: 3–32. Harmondsworth: Penguin.

———. 1977b (1962). "Jean-Jacques Rousseau, Founder of the Sciences of Man." In *Structural Anthropology*, trans. M. Layton, 2: 33–43. Harmondsworth: Penguin.

———. 1977c (1960). "What Ethnology Owes to Durkheim." In *Structural Anthropology*, trans. M. Layton, 2: 44–8. Harmondsworth: Penguin.

———. 1977d (1966). "The Work of the Bureau of American Ethnology and Its Lessons." In *Structural Anthropology*, trans. M. Layton, 2: 49–59. Harmondsworth: Penguin.

———. 1977e (1968). "Comparative Religions of Nonliterate Peoples." In *Structural Anthropology*, trans. M. Layton, 2: 60–67. Harmondsworth: Penguin.

———. 1977f (1973). "Answers to Some Investigations." In *Structural Anthropology*, trans. M. Layton, 2: 271-87. Harmondsworth: Penguin.

———. 1977g (1963). "Cultural Discontinuity and Economic and Social Development." In *Structural Anthropology*, trans. M. Layton, 2: 312-22. Harmondsworth: Penguin.

———. 1977h (1952). "Race and History." In *Structural Anthropology*, trans. M. Layton, 2: 323–62. Harmondsworth: Penguin.

———. 1977i. "Avant-propos." In *L'identité: Séminaire interdisciplinaire dirigé par Claude Lévi-Strauss,* 9–11. Paris: Presses Universitaires de France.

————. 1978a (1955). *Tristes Tropiques*. Trans. J. and D. Weightman. New York: Atheneum.

————. 1978b (1968). *The Origin of Table Manners: Introduction to a Science of Mythology*. Vol. 3. Trans. J. and D. Weightman. London: Jonathan Cape.

————. 1978c. *Myth and Meaning*. Toronto: University of Toronto Press.

————. 1979. "La famille." In *Claude Lévi-Strauss*, ed. R. Bellour and C. Clément, 93–131. Paris: Gallimard.

————. 1981 (1971). *The Naked Man: Introduction to a Science of Mythology*. Vol. 4. Trans. J. and D. Weightman. London: Jonathan Cape.

————. 1985a (1983). "Preface" to *The View from Afar*. Trans. J. Neugroschel and P. Hoss, xi–xvi. Oxford: Blackwell.

————. 1985b (1971). "Race and Culture." In *The View from Afar*, trans. J. Neugroschel and P. Hoss, 3–24. Oxford: Blackwell.

————. 1985c (1979). "The Anthropologist and the Human Condition." In *The View from Afar*, trans. J. Neugroschel and P. Hoss, 25–36. Oxford: Blackwell.

————. 1985d (1983). "Structuralism and Ecology." In *The View from Afar*, trans. J. Neugroschel and P. Hoss, 101–20. Oxford: Blackwell.

————. 1985e (1975). "Myth and Forgetfulness." In *The View from Afar*, trans. J. Neugroschel and P. Hoss, 186–91. Oxford: Blackwell.

————. 1985f (1983). "A Meditative Painter." In *The View from Afar*, trans. J. Neugroschel and P. Hoss, 243–47. Oxford: Blackwell.

————. 1985g (1977). "New York in 1941." In *The View from Afar*, trans. J. Neugroschel and P. Hoss, 258–67. Oxford: Blackwell.

————. 1985h (1976). "Reflections on Liberty." In *The View from Afar*, trans. J. Neugroschel and P. Hoss, 279–88. Oxford: Blackwell.

————. 1987a (1950). Introduction to *The Work of Marcel Mauss*. Trans. F. Baker. London: Routledge & Kegan Paul.

————. 1987b (1984). "The Future of Anthropology." In *Anthropology and Myth: Lectures 1951–1982*, trans. R. Willis, 11–24. Oxford: Blackwell.

————. 1988 (1985). *The Jealous Potter*. Trans. B. Chorier. Chicago: University of Chicago Press.

————. 1993. *Regarder Écouter Lire*. Paris: Plon.

————. 1995 (1991). *The Story of Lynx*. Trans. C. Tihanhi. Chicago: University of Chicago Press.

————. 1998. "Retours en arrière." *Les temps modernes* 598: 66–77.

Lévi-Strauss, C., and D. Eribon. 1991 (1988). *Conversations with Claude Lévi-Strauss*. Trans. P. Wissing. Chicago: University of Chicago Press.

Lévi-Strauss, C., and G. Charbonnier. 1969 (1961). *Conversations with Claude Lévi-Strauss*. Ed. G. Charbonnier and trans. J. and D. Weightman. London: Jonathan Cape.

Lévi-Strauss, C., and R. Bellour. 1979. "Entretien avec Claude Lévi-Strauss." In *Claude Lévi-Strauss*, ed. R. Bellour and C. Clément, 157–209. Paris: Gallimard.

Lévy-Bruhl, L. 1923 (1922). *Primitive Mentality*. Trans. L. A. Clare. London: Allen & Unwin.

————. 1965 (1927). *The "Soul" of the Primitive*. Trans. L. A. Clare. London: Allen & Unwin.

————. 1966 (1910). *How Natives Think*. Trans. L. A. Clare. New York: Washington Square Press.

————. 1975 (1949). *The Notebooks on Primitive Mentality*. Trans. P. Rivière. Oxford: Basil Blackwell.

————. 1983 (1935). *Primitive Mythology: The Mythic World of the Australian and Papuan Natives.* St. Lucia: University of Queensland Press.

Locke, J. 1924 (1690). *Two Treatises of Government.* London: Dent.

Lovejoy, A. O. 1948 (1923). "The Supposed Primitivism of Rousseau's *Discourse on Inequality.*" In *Essays in the History of Ideas,* 14–37. Baltimore: The Johns Hopkins University Press.

Lovejoy, A. O., and G. Boas. 1935. *Primitivism and Related Ideas in Antiquity.* Baltimore: The Johns Hopkins Press.

Löwith, K. 1982 (1932). *Max Weber and Karl Marx.* Trans. H. Fantel and ed. T. Bottomore and W. Outhwaite. London: Allen & Unwin.

Lukács, G. 1971 (1923). *History and Class Consciousness.* Trans. R. Livingstone. London: Merlin.

Lukes, S. 1977. "Alienation and Anomie." In *Essays in Social Theory,* 74–95. New York: Columbia University Press.

————. 1985 (1973). *Emile Durkheim, His Life and Work: A Historical and Critical Study.* Stanford, Calif.: Stanford University Press.

Lyotard, J.-F. 1979 (1965). "Les Indiens ne cueillent pas les fleurs." In *Claude Lévi-Strauss,* ed. R. Bellour and C. Clément, 49–92. Paris: Gallimard.

————. 1984 (1979). *The Postmodern Condition: A Report on Knowledge.* Trans. G. Bennington and B. Massumi. Minneapolis: University of Minnesota Press.

————. 1985. "Histoire universelle et différences culturelles." *Critique* 456: 559–68.

————. 1988 (1983). *The Differend: Phrases in Dispute.* Trans. G. Van Den Abbeele. Minneapolis: University of Minnesota Press.

Macpherson. C. B. 1962. *The Political Theory of Possessive Individualism: Hobbes to Locke.* Oxford: Oxford University Press.

Manganaro, M., ed. 1990. *Modernist Anthropology: From Fieldwork to Text.* Princeton: Princeton University Press.

Marcus, G. E. 1998. "Critical Anthropology Now: An Introduction." In *Critical Anthropology Now: Unexpected Contexts, Shifting Constituencies, Changing Agendas,* ed. G. E. Marcus, 3–28. Santa Fe, N.M.: School of American Research Press.

Marcus, G. E., and M. M. J. Fischer. 1999. *Anthropology as Cultural Critique: An Experimental Moment in the Human Sciences.* 2d ed. Chicago: University of Chicago Press.

Marcuse, H. 1971 (1965). "Industrialization and Capitalism." In *Max Weber and Sociology Today,* ed. O. Stammer and trans. K. Morris, 184–86. Oxford: Blackwell.

Márkus, G. 1978. *Marxism and Anthropology: The Concept of "Human Essence" in the Philosophy of Marx.* Trans. E. de Lacsay and G. Márkus. Assen: Van Gorcum.

————. 1980. "Four Forms of Critical Theory: Some Theses on Marx's Development." *Thesis Eleven* 1: 78–93.

————. 1982. "Alienation and Reification in Marx and Lukács." *Thesis Eleven* 5/6: 139–61.

Marouby, C. 1990. *Utopie et primitivisme: Essai sur l'imaginaire anthropologique à l'âge classique.* Paris: Seuil.

Marx, K. 1904 (1859). *A Contribution to the Critique of Political Economy.* Trans. N. I. Stone. Chicago: Charles H. Kerr.

————. 1964 (1857–58). *Pre-Capitalist Economic Formations.* Ed. E. J. Hobsbawm and trans. J. Cohen. New York: International Publishers.

———. 1967a (1885). *Capital.* Vol. 2. Ed. F. Engels. Anonymous translation. New York: International Publishers.

———. 1967b (1894). *Capital.* Vol. 3. Ed. F. Engels. Anonymous translation. New York: International Publishers.

———. 1968a (1853). "The British Rule in India." In *Karl Marx on Colonialism and Modernization,* ed. S. Avineri, 83–89. New York: Doubleday.

———. 1968b (1853). "The Future Results of British Rule in India." In *Karl Marx on Colonialism and Modernization,* ed. S. Avineri, 125–31. New York: Doubleday.

———. 1969a (1845). "Theses on Feuerbach." In K. Marx and F. Engels, *Selected Works,* 1: 13-80. Moscow: Progress Publishers.

———. 1969b (1850). "The Class Struggles in France, 1848 to 1850." In K. Marx and F. Engels, *Selected Works,* 1: 205–99. Moscow: Progress Publishers.

———. 1969c (1852). "The Eighteenth Brumaire of Louis Bonaparte." In K. Marx and F. Engels, *Selected Works,* 1: 394–487. Moscow: Progress Publishers.

———. 1969d (1859). Preface to *A Contribution to the Critique of Political Economy.* In K. Marx and F. Engels, *Selected Works,* 1: 507–16. Moscow: Progress Publishers.

———. 1969e (1871). "The Civil War in France." In K. Marx and F. Engels, *Selected Works,* 2: 178–244. Moscow: Progress Publishers.

———. 1969f (1875). "Critique of the Gotha Programme." In K. Marx and F. Engels, *Selected Works,* 3: 9–30. Moscow: Progress Publishers.

———. 1972 (1880–82). *The Ethnological Notebooks of Karl Marx.* Edited and transcribed by L. Krader. Assen: Van Gorcum.

———. 1973 (1857–58). *Grundrisse: Foundations of the Critique of Political Economy.* Trans. M. Nicolaus. New York: Vintage.

———. 1974a (1843). "Critique of Hegel's Doctrine of the State." In *Early Writings,* trans. R. Livingstone and G. Benton, 57–198. Harmondsworth: Penguin.

———. 1974b (1843). "Letters from the *Franco-German Yearbooks.*" In *Early Writings,* trans. R. Livingstone and G. Benton, 199–209. Harmondsworth: Penguin.

———. 1974c (1843). "On the Jewish Question." In *Early Writings,* trans. R. Livingstone and G. Benton, 211–41. Harmondsworth: Penguin.

———. 1974d (1843–44). "A Contribution to the Critique of Hegel's *Philosophy of Right.* Introduction." In *Early Writings,* trans. R. Livingstone and G. Benton, 243–57. Harmondsworth: Penguin.

———. 1974e (1844). "Excerpts from James Mill's *Elements of Political Economy.*" In *Early Writings,* trans. R. Livingstone and G. Benton, 259–78. Harmondsworth: Penguin.

———. 1974f (1844). "Economic and Philosophical Manuscripts." In *Early Writings,* trans. R. Livingstone and G. Benton, 279–400. Harmondsworth: Penguin.

———. 1974g (1844). "Critical Notes on the Article 'The King of Prussia and Social Reform.' By a Prussian." In *Early Writings,* trans. R. Livingstone and G. Benton, 401–20. Harmondsworth: Penguin.

———. 1975 (1842). "The Philosophical Manifesto of the Historical School of Law." In K. Marx and F. Engels, *Collected Works,* 1: 203–10. London: Lawrence & Wishart.

———. 1976a (1847). "The Poverty of Philosophy." Trans. H. Quelch. In K. Marx and F. Engels, *Collected Works,* 6: 105–212. London: Lawrence & Wishart.

———. 1976b (1867). *Capital.* Vol. 1. Trans. B. Fowkes. Harmondsworth: Penguin.

——— 1989a (1877). "Letter to Otechestvenniye Zapiski." Trans. B. Selman. In K. Marx and F. Engels, *Collected Works,* vol. 24. London: Lawrence & Wishart.

———. 1989b (1881). "Drafts of the Letter to Vera Zasulich." Trans. B. Selman. In K. Marx and F. Engels, *Collected Works,* vol. 24. London: Lawrence & Wishart.

Marx, K., and F. Engels. 1969 (1848). "Manifesto of the Communist Party." In *Selected Works*, 1: 98–137. Moscow: Progress Publishers.

———. 1975 (1844). "The Holy Family, or Critique of Critical Criticism." Trans. R. Dixon and C. Dutt. In *Collected Works*, 4: 5–211. London: Lawrence & Wishart.

———. 1976 (1845–46). "The German Ideology." Trans. C. Dutt, W. Lough, and C. P. Magill. In *Collected Works*, 5: 19–539. London: Lawrence & Wishart.

Mason, P. 1990. *Deconstructing America: Representations of the Other.* London and New York: Routledge.

———. 1998. *Infelicities: Representations of the Exotic.* Baltimore: The Johns Hopkins University Press.

Mathy, J.-P. 1993. *Extrême-Occident: French Intellectuals and America.* Chicago: University of Chicago Press.

Mauss, M. 1969a (1923). "Mentalité primitive et participation." In M. Mauss, *Oeuvres, t. 2: Représentations collectives et diversité des civilisations*, ed. V. Karady, 125–31. Paris: Minuit.

———. 1969b (1934). "Fragment d'un plan de sociologie générale descriptive." In M. Mauss, *Oeuvres, t. 3: Cohésion sociale et divisions de la sociologie*, ed. V. Karady, 303–58. Paris: Minuit.

———. 1969c (1913). "L'ethnographie en France et à l'étranger." In M. Mauss, *Oeuvres, t. 3: Cohésion sociale et divisions de la sociologie*, ed. V. Karady, 395–435. Paris: Minuit.

———. 1969d (1939). "Lucien Lévy-Bruhl (1857–1939)." In M. Mauss, *Oeuvres, t. 3: Cohésion sociale et divisions de la sociologie*, ed. V. Karady, 560–65. Paris: Minuit.

———. 1988 (1922–24). *The Gift: Forms and Functions of Exchange in Archaic Societies.* Trans. I. Cunnison. London: Routledge.

McGrane, B. 1989. *Beyond Anthropology: Society and the Other.* New York: Columbia University Press.

Meek, R. L. 1976. *Social Science and the Ignoble Savage.* Cambridge: Cambridge University Press.

Melotti, U. 1977 (1972). *Marx and the Third World.* Ed. M. Caldwell and trans. P. Ransford. Atlantic Highlands: Humanities Press.

Merleau-Ponty, M. 1953a. "Le philosophe et la sociologie." In *Éloge de la philosophie et autres essays*, 112–44. Paris: Gallimard.

———. 1953b. "Partout et nulle part." In *Éloge de la philosophie et autres essays*, 170–240. Paris: Gallimard.

———. 1960. "De Mauss à Claude Lévi-Strauss." In *Signes*, 143–57. Paris: Gallimard.

———. 1973 (1955). *Adventures of the Dialectic.* Trans. J. Bien. Evanston: Northwestern University Press.

Mestrovic, S. G. 1988. *Emile Durkheim and the Reformation of Sociology.* Totowa, N.J.: Rowman & Littlefield.

Mills, C. W. 1959. *The Sociological Imagination.* Oxford: Oxford University Press.

Miyoshi, M. 1991. *Off Center: Power and Culture Relations between Japan and the United States.* Cambridge: Harvard University Press.

———. 1993. "A Borderless World? From Colonialism to Transnationalism and the Decline of the Nation-State." *Critical Inquiry* 19, no. 4: 726–51.

Mohanty, C. T., A. Russo, and L. Torres. 1991. *Third World Women and the Politics of Feminism.* Bloomington, Ind.: Indiana University Press.

Molloy, S. 1980. "Max Weber and the Religions of China: Any Way out of the Maze?" *British Journal of Sociology* 31, no. 3: 377–400.

Mommsen, W. J. 1991 (1977). "Max Weber as a Critic of Marxism." In *Max Weber: Critical Assessments,* 1: 115–39. London and New York: Routledge.

Montaigne, M. de. 1948a (1578–80). "Of Cannibals." In *The Complete Works of Montaigne,* trans. D. M. Frame. Stanford: Stanford University Press.

———. 1948b (1578–80). "Of Coaches." In *The Complete Works of Montaigne,* trans. D. M. Frame, 150–59. Stanford: Stanford University Press.

Montesquieu, C. de S. 1952 (1748). *The Spirit of Laws.* Trans. T. Nugent and J. V. Prichard. Vol. 38 of *Great Books of the Western World.* Chicago and London: Encyclopedia Britannica.

———. 1973 (1721). *Persian Letters.* Trans. C. J. Betts. Harmondsworth: Penguin.

Morgan, L. H. 1964 (1877). *Ancient Society.* Ed. L. A. White. Cambridge, Mass.: Harvard University Press.

Morley, D., and K.-H. Chen, eds. 1996. *Stuart Hall: Critical Dialogues in Cultural Studies.* London and New York: Routledge.

Nelson, B. 1991a (1974). "Max Weber's 'Author's Introduction' (1920): A Master Clue to His Main Aims." In *Max Weber: Critical Assessments,* vol. 1, ed. P. Hamilton, 216–31. London and New York: Routledge.

———. 1991b (1969). "Conscience and the Making of Early Modern Culture: *The Protestant Ethic* Beyond Max Weber." In *Max Weber: Critical Assessments,* vol. 2, ed. P. Hamilton, 344–54. London and New York: Routledge.

———. 1991c (1976). "On Orient and Occident in Max Weber." In *Max Weber: Critical Assessments,* vol. 3, ed. P. Hamilton, 96–106. London and New York: Routledge.

Nietzsche, F. 1954 (1883–85). *Thus Spoke Zarathustra.* In *The Portable Nietzsche,* ed. and trans. W. Kaufmann. New York: Viking.

———. 1967 (1872). *The Birth of Tragedy.* In *The Birth of Tragedy and The Case of Wagner,* trans. W. Kaufmann. New York: Vintage.

———. 1974 (1882). *The Gay Science.* Trans. W. Kaufmann. New York: Vintage.

———. 1983 (1874). "On the Uses and Disadvantages of History for Life." In *Untimely Meditations,* trans. R. J. Hollingdale, 57–123. Cambridge: Cambridge University Press.

———. 1996 (1887). *On the Genealogy of Morals.* Trans. D. Smith. Oxford: Oxford University Press.

———. 1997 (1881). *Daybreak: Thoughts on the Prejudices of Morality.* Ed. M. Clark and B. Leiter and trans. R. J. Hollingdale. Cambridge: Cambridge University Press.

O'Neill, J. 1986. "The Disciplinary Society: From Weber to Foucault." *British Journal of Sociology* 37, no. 1: 42–60.

Ong, A. 1999. *Flexible Citizenship: The Cultural Logical of Transnationality.* Durham, N.C.: Duke University Press.

Ouellet, F. 2000. *Essais sur le relativisme et la tolérance.* Québec: Presses de l'Université Laval.

Owen, D. 1994. *Maturity and Modernity: Nietzsche, Weber, Foucault and the Ambivalence of Reason.* London and New York: Routledge.

Pace, D. 1983. *Claude Lévi-Strauss: The Bearer of Ashes.* London: Routledge and Kegan Paul.

Papastergiadis, N. 2000. *The Turbulence of Migration: Globalization, Deterritorialization and Hybridity.* Cambridge, England: Polity.

Park, R. E. 1950. *Race and Culture: The Collected Papers of Robert Ezra Park,* vol. 1. Glencoe, Ill.: Free Press.

———. 1952. *Human Communities: The Collected Papers of Robert Ezra Park,* vol. 2. Glencoe, Ill.: Free Press.

Parsons, T. 1937a. *Marshall, Pareto, Durkheim.* Vol. 1 of *The Structure of Social Action.* New York: Free Press.

———. 1937b. *Weber.* Vol. 2 of *The Structure of Social Action.* New York: Free Press.

Paz, O. 1970 (1967–68). "Claude Lévi-Strauss ou le nouveau festin d'Ésope." Trans. R. Marrast. In *Deux Transparents: Marcel Duchamp et Claude Lévi-Strauss,* 79–183. Paris: Gallimard.

Pietz, W. 1993. "Fetishism and Materialism: The Limits of Theory in Marx." In *Fetishism as Cultural Discourse,* ed. E. Apter and W. Pietz, 119–51. Ithaca, N.Y.: Cornell University Press.

Poggi, G. 1996. "*Lego Quia Inutile*: An Alternative Justification for the Classics." In *Social Theory and Sociology: The Classics and Beyond,* ed. S. P. Turner, 39–47. Oxford: Blackwell.

Polanyi, K. 1944. *The Great Transformation: The Political and Economic Origins of Our Time.* Boston: Beacon Press.

Poster, M. 1986. "Foucault and the Tyranny of Greece." In *Foucault: A Critical Reader,* ed. D. C. Hoy, 205–20. Oxford: Blackwell.

Postone, M. 1993. *Time, Labor, and Social Domination: A Reinterpretation of Marx's Critical Theory.* Cambridge: Cambridge University Press.

Prawer, S. S. 1976. *Karl Marx and World Literature.* Oxford: Oxford University Press.

Rabinow, P. 1996. *Essays on the Anthropology of Reason.* Princeton: Princeton University Press.

———. 1999. *French DNA: Trouble in Purgatory.* Chicago: University of Chicago Press.

Rabinow, P., and W. M. Sullivan. 1987. "The Interpretive Turn: A Second Look." In *Interpretive Social Science: A Second Look,* ed. P. Rabinow and W. M. Sullivan, 1–30. Berkeley and Los Angeles: University of California Press.

Richman, M. 1990. "Anthropology and Modernism in France: From Durkheim to the Collège de sociologie." In *Modernist Anthropology: From Fieldwork to Text,* ed. M. Manganaro, 183–214. Princeton, N.J.: Princeton University Press.

Ricoeur, P. 1974 (1969). "Structure and Hermeneutics." In *The Conflict of Interpretations: Essays in Hermeneutics,* ed. D. Ihde, 27–61. Evanston, Ill.: Northwestern University Press.

———. 1981a. "The Task of Hermeneutics." In *Hermeneutics and the Human Sciences: Essays on Language, Action and Interpretation,* ed. and trans. J. B. Thompson, 43–62. Cambridge: Cambridge University Press.

———. 1981b. "Hermeneutics and the Critique of Ideology." In *Hermeneutics and the Human Sciences: Essays on Language, Action and Interpretation,* ed. and trans. J. B. Thompson, 63–100. Cambridge: Cambridge University Press.

———. 1981c. "The Hermeneutical Function of Distantiation." In *Hermeneutics and the Human Sciences: Essays on Language, Action and Interpretation,* ed. and trans. J. B. Thompson, 131–44. Cambridge: Cambridge University Press.

Robertson, R. 1992. *Globalization: Social Theory and Global Culture.* London: Sage.

Roger, P. 1999. "Pour Claude Lévi-Strauss." *Critique* 620–21: 1.

Rorty, R. 1979. *Philosophy and the Mirror of Nature.* Princeton, N.J.: Princeton University Press.

————. 1991a. "Postmodernist Bourgeois Liberalism." In *Objectivity, Relativism, and Truth: Philosophical Papers,* vol. 1, 197–202. Cambridge: Cambridge University Press.

————. 1991b. "On Ethnocentrism: A Reply to Clifford Geertz." In *Objectivity, Relativism, and Truth: Philosophical Papers,* vol. 1, 203-10. Cambridge: Cambridge University Press.

————. 1991c. "Cosmopolitanism without Emancipation: A Response to Jean-François Lyotard." In *Objectivity, Relativism, and Truth: Philosophical Papers,* vol. 1, 211–22. Cambridge: Cambridge University Press.

Rosaldo, R. 1993. *Culture and Truth: The Remaking of Social Analysis.* Boston: Beacon Press.

Rosanvallon, P. 1989 (1979). *Le libéralisme économique: Histoire de l'idée de marché.* Paris: Seuil.

Rose, G. 1978. *The Melancholy Science: An Introduction to the Thought of Theodor W. Adorno.* London: Macmillan.

Roth, G. 1971a. "Weber's Generational Rebellion and Maturation." In R. Bendix and G. Roth, *Scholarship and Partisanship: Essays on Max Weber,* 6–33. Berkeley and Los Angeles: University of California Press.

————. 1971b. "Political Critiques." In *Scholarship and Partisanship: Essays on Max Weber,* by R. Bendix and G. Roth, 55–69. Berkeley and Los Angeles: University of California Press.

————. 1971c. "Sociological Typology and Historical Explanation." In *Scholarship and Partisanship: Essays on Max Weber,* by R. Bendix and G. Roth, 109–128. Berkeley and Los Angeles: University of California Press.

————. 1971d. "The Genesis of the Typological Approach." In *Scholarship and Partisanship: Essays on Max Weber,* by R. Bendix and G. Roth, 253–65. Berkeley and Los Angeles: University of California Press.

————. 1979. "Epilogue: Weber's Vision of History." In *Max Weber's Vision of History: Ethics and Methods,* by G. Roth and W. Schluchter, 195–206. Berkeley and Los Angeles: University of California Press.

Rousseau, J.-J. 1953 (1782). *The Confessions.* Trans. J. M. Cohen. Harmondsworth: Penguin.

————. 1959 (1782). *Rousseau Juge de Jean Jaques: Dialogues.* In *Oeuvres complètes,* t. 1, 657–992. Paris: Gallimard.

————. 1964a (1761). *Julie, ou La Nouvelle Héloïse.* In *Oeuvres complètes,* t. 2, 1–793. Paris: Gallimard.

————. 1964b (1776). *La Découverte du Nouveau Monde.* In *Oeuvres complètes,* t. 2, 811–41. Paris: Gallimard.

————. 1964c (1753). Préface à *Narcisse ou l'Amant de lui-même.* In *Oeuvres complètes,* t. 2, 959–74. Paris: Gallimard.

————. 1964d. *Ecrits sur l'Abbé de Saint-Pierre.* In *Oeuvres complètes,* t.3, 1540–74. Paris: Gallimard.

————. 1964e (1764). *Lettres écrites de la montagne.* In *Oeuvres complètes,* t. 3, 1575–1725. Paris: Gallimard.

————. 1964f (1861). *Projet de constitution pour la Corse.* In *Oeuvres complètes,* t. 3, 1726–32. Paris: Gallimard.

————. 1964g (1782). *Considérations sur le gouvernement de Pologne.* In *Oeuvres complètes,* t. 3, 1733–1804. Paris: Gallimard.

————. 1964h (1755). *Discours sur l'origine et les fondements de l'inégalité parmi les hommes.* Paris: Gallimard.

———. 1966 (1781). "Essay on the Origin of Languages." In J.-J. Rousseau and J. G. Herder, *On the Origin of Language*, trans. J. H. Moran and A. Gode, 1–83. New York: Frederick Ungar (English translation of Rousseau, 1995b).

———. 1969 (1762). *Émile ou De l'Éducation*. In *Oeuvres complètes*, t. 4, 245–877. Paris: Gallimard.

———. 1972 (1782). *Les Rêveries du promeneur solitaire*. Paris: Gallimard.

———. 1973a (1750). *A Discourse on the Arts and Sciences*. In *The Social Contract and Discourses*, trans. G. D. H. Cole. London: Dent.

———. 1973b (1755). *A Discourse on the Origin of Inequality*. In *The Social Contract and Discourses*, trans. G. D. H. Cole, 27–75. London: Dent (English translation of Rousseau, 1964h).

———. 1973c (1755). *A Discourse on Political Economy*. In *The Social Contract and Discourses*, trans. G. D. H. Cole, 115–53. London: Dent.

———. 1973d. *The General Society of the Human Race*. In *The Social Contract and Discourses*, trans. G. D. H. Cole, 155–62. London: Dent. Also known as the *Geneva Manuscript*.

———. 1973e (1762). *The Social Contract*. In *The Social Contract and Discourses*, trans. G. D. H. Cole, 164–310. London: Dent.

———. 1974 (1762). *Émile*. Trans. B. Foxley. London: Dent (English translation of Rousseau, 1969).

———. 1979 (1782). *Reveries of the Solitary Walker*. Trans. P. France. Harmondsworth: Penguin.

———. 1984 (1755). *A Discourse on Inequality*. Trans. M. Cranston. Harmondsworth: Penguin (English translation of Rousseau, 1964h).

———. 1995a (1758). *Lettre à d'Alembert*. In *Oeuvres complètes*, t. 5. Paris: Gallimard.

———. 1995b (1781). *Essai sur l'origine des langues*. In *Oeuvres complètes*, t. 5. Paris: Gallimard.

———. 1995c (1768). *Dictionnaire de musique*. In *Oeuvres complètes*, t. 5. Paris: Gallimard.

Rubin, W. 1984, ed. *"Primitivism" in Twentieth Century Art: Affinity of the Tribal and the Modern*. New York: Museum of Modern Art.

Rundell, J., and S. Mennell. 1998. "Introduction: Civilization, Culture and the Human Self-Image." In *Classical Readings in Culture and Civilization*, ed. J. Rundell and S. Mennell, 1–35. London and New York: Routledge.

Said, E. W. 1978. *Orientalism*. New York: Vintage.

———. 1988. "Michel Foucault, 1926–1984." In *After Foucault: Humanistic Knowledge, Postmodern Challenges*, ed. J. Arac, 1–11. New Brunswick, N.J.: Rutgers University Press.

———. 1989. "Representing the Colonized: Anthropology's Interlocutors." *Critical Inquiry* 15: 205–25.

———. 1993. *Culture and Imperialism*. New York: Knopf.

Sawer, M. 1977. *Marxism and the Question of the Asiatic Mode of Production*. The Hague: Nijhoff.

Scaff, L. A. 1989. *Fleeing the Iron Cage: Culture, Politics, and Modernity in the Thought of Max Weber*. Berkeley and Los Angeles: University of California Press.

Schiller, F. 1967 (1793–95). *On the Aesthetic Education of Man in a Series of Letters*. Ed. and trans. E. M. Wilkinson and L. A. Willoughby. Oxford: Oxford University Press.

Schluchter, W. 1979a. "The Paradox of Rationalization: On the Relation of Ethics and World." In *Max Weber's Vision of History: Ethics and Methods* by G. Roth and W. Schluchter, 11–64. Berkeley and Los Angeles: University of California Press.

———. 1979b. "Value-Neutrality and the Ethic of Responsiblity." In *Max Weber's Vision of History: Ethics and Methods* by G. Roth and W. Schluchter, 65–116. Berkeley and Los Angeles: University of California Press.

———. 1981. *The Rise of Western Rationalism: Max Weber's Developmental History.* Trans. G. Roth. Berkeley and Los Angeles: University of California Press.

———. 1987. "Weber's Sociology of Rationalism and Typology of Religious Rejections of the World." In *Max Weber, Rationality and Modernity,* ed. S. Lash and S. Whimster, 92–115. London: Allen & Unwin.

———. 1996. *Paradoxes of Modernity: Culture and Conduct in the Theory of Max Weber.* Trans. N. Solomon. Stanford: Stanford University Press.

Schnapper, D. 1998. *La relation à l'Autre: Au Coeur de la pensée sociologique.* Paris: Gallimard.

Schumpeter, J. A. 1950 (1942). *Capitalism, Socialism and Democracy.* 3rd ed. New York: Harper & Row.

Seidman, S. 1983. *Liberalism and the Origins of European Social Theory.* Berkeley and Los Angeles: University of California Press.

———. 1991a (1983). "Modernity, Meaning, and Cultural Pessimism in Max Weber." In *Max Weber: Critical Assessments,* vol. 4, ed. P. Hamilton, 153–65. London and New York: Routledge.

———. 1991b. "The End of Sociological Theory: The Postmodern Hope." *Sociological Theory* 9, no. 2: 131–46.

Shanin, T. 1983. "Late Marx: Gods and Craftsmen." In *Late Marx and the Russian Road: Marx and the Peripheries of Capitalism,* ed. T. Shanin, 3–39. New York: Monthly Review Press.

Shklar, J. N. 1969. *Men and Citizens: A Study of Rousseau's Social Theory.* Cambridge: Cambridge University Press.

Simmel, G. 1950 (1908). "The Stranger." In *The Sociology of Georg Simmel,* ed. and trans. K. H. Wolff, 402–8. New York: Free Press.

———. 1971 (1918). "The Conflict in Modern Culture." In *On Individuality and Social Forms: Selected Writings,* ed. D. Levine and trans. K. P. Etzkorn, 375–93. Chicago: University of Chicago Press.

———. 1990 (1900). *The Philosophy of Money.* Trans. T. Bottomore and D. Frisby. London and New York: Routledge.

Skinner, Q. 1969. "Meaning and Understanding in the History of Ideas." *History and Theory* 8: 3–52.

Smart, B. 1983. *Foucault, Marxism and Critique.* London: Routledge & Kegan Paul.

Smith, A. 1997 (1776). *The Wealth of Nations, Books 1–3.* Harmondsworth: Penguin.

Smith, B. 1989 (1960). *European Vision and the South Pacific.* 2d ed. Oxford: Oxford University Press.

———. 1992. *Imagining the Pacific in the Wake of the Cook Voyages.* Melbourne: Melbourne University Press.

———. 1994. "Modernism and Post-Modernism: Neo-Colonial Viewpoint—Concerning the Sources of Modernism and Post-Modernism in the Visual Arts." *Thesis Eleven* 38: 104–117.

Smith, D. E. 1987. *The Everyday World as Problematic.* Boston: Northeastern University Press.

————. 1990. *The Conceptual Practices of Power: A Feminist Sociology of Knowledge*. Toronto: University of Toronto Press.

Sontag, S. 1970 (1966). "The Anthropologist as Hero." In *Claude Lévi-Strauss: The Anthropologist as Hero*, ed. E. N. Hayes and T. Hayes, 184–96. Cambridge, Mass.: MIT Press.

Spencer, B., and F. J. Gillen. 1899. *The Native Tribes of Central Australia*. London: Macmillan.

Spencer, H. 1969 (1876–96). *The Principles of Sociology*. Ed. S. Andreski. London: Macmillan.

————. 1971. *Structure, Function and Evolution*. Ed. S. Andreski. London: Nelson.

————. 1972. *On Social Evolution: Selected Writings*. Ed. J. D. Y. Peel. Chicago: University of Chicago Press.

Spivak, G. C. 1988a. "Can the Subaltern Speak?" In *Marxism and the Interpretation of Culture*, ed. C. Nelson and L. Grossberg, 271–313. Urbana: University of Illinois Press.

————. 1988b. *In Other Worlds: Essays in Cultural Politics*. London and New York: Routledge.

————. 1993. *Outside in the Teaching Machine*. London and New York: Routledge.

————. 1999. *A Critique of Postcolonial Reason: Toward a History of the Vanishing Present*. Cambridge, Mass.: Harvard University Press.

Starobinski, J. 1971. *Jean-Jacques Rousseau: La transparence et l'obstacle*. Paris: Gallimard.

Stauth, G. 1991. "Revolution in Spiritless Times: An Essay on Michel Foucault's Enquiries into the Iranian Revolution." *International Sociology* 6, no. 3: 259–80.

Steiner, G. 1970. "Orpheus with His Myths." In *Claude Lévi-Strauss: The Anthropologist as Hero*, ed. E. N. Hayes and T. Hayes, 170–83. Cambridge, Mass.: MIT Press.

Stocking, G. W. 1968. *Race, Culture, and Evolution: Essays in the History of Anthropology*. Chicago: University of Chicago Press.

————. 1987. *Victorian Anthropology*. New York: Free Press.

Stoler, A. L. 1995. *Race and the Education of Desire: Foucault's "History of Sexuality" and the Colonial Order of Things*. Durham, N.C.: Duke University Press.

Symcox, G. 1972. "The Wild Man's Return: The Enclosed Vision of Rousseau's *Discourses*." In *The Wild Man Within: An Image in Western Thought from the Renaissance to Romanticism*, ed. E. Dudley and M. E. Novak, 223–47. Pittsburgh: University of Pittsburgh Press.

Tambiah, S. J. 2000. "Transnational Movements, Diaspora, and Multiple Modernities." *Daedalus* 129, no. 1: 163–94.

Tanaka, S. 1993. *Japan's Orient: Rendering Pasts into History*. Berkeley and Los Angeles: University of California Press.

Taussig, M. T. 1980. *The Devil and Commodity Fetishism in South America*. Chapel Hill: University of North Carolina Press.

Taylor, C. 1985a (1971). "Interpretation and the Sciences of Man." In *Philosophy and the Human Sciences: Philosophical Papers 2*, 15–57. Cambridge: Cambridge University Press.

————. 1985b (1981). "Understanding and Ethnocentricity." In *Philosophy and the Human Sciences: Philosophical Papers 2*, 116–33. Cambridge: Cambridge University Press.

————. 1985c (1979). "What's Wrong with Negative Liberty." In *Philosophy and the Human Sciences: Philosophical Papers 2*, 211–29. Cambridge: Cambridge University Press.

———. 1989. *Sources of the Self: The Making of the Modern Identity.* Cambridge, Mass.: Harvard University Press.

———. 1991. *The Ethics of Authenticity.* Cambridge, Mass.: Harvard University Press.

———. 1994. "The Politics of Recognition." In *Multiculturalism: Examining the Politics of Recognition,* ed. A. Gutman, 25–73. Princeton, N.J.: Princeton University Press.

———. 1998 (1996). "From Philosophical Anthropology to the Politics of Recognition: An Interview with Charles Taylor." Trans. S. Rothnie. *Thesis Eleven* 52: 103–12.

———. 1999. "Two Theories of Modernity." *Public Culture* 11, no. 1: 153–74.

Tenbruck, F. H. 1980. "The Problem of Thematic Unity in the Works of Max Weber." *British Journal of Sociology* 31, no. 3: 316–51.

Testard, A. 1985. *Le communisme primitif, t. 1: Economie et idéologie.* Paris: Editions de la Maison des sciences de l'homme.

Thomas, N. 1991. *Entangled Objects: Exchange, Material Culture, and Colonialism in the Pacific.* Cambridge, Mass.: Harvard University Press.

Thompson, J. B. 1981. *Critical Hermeneutics: A Study in the Thought of Paul Ricoeur and Jürgen Habermas.* Cambridge: Cambridge University Press.

Thompson, K. 1982. *Emile Durkheim.* London and New York: Tavistock.

Thorner, D. 1990 (1966). "Marx on India and the Asiatic Mode of Production." In *Karl Marx's Social and Political Thought: Critical Assessments,* ed. B. Jessop with C. Malcolm-Brown, 2: 436–65. London and New York: Routledge.

Tiryakian, E. A. 1995. "Emile Durkheim." In *Emile Durkheim: Critical Assessments,* ed. P. Hamilton, 7: 88–138. London and New York: Routledge.

Todorov, T. 1984. *The Conquest of America: The Question of the Other.* Trans. R. Howard. New York: Harper & Row.

———. 1993 (1989). *On Human Diversity: Nationalism, Racism, and Exoticism in French Thought.* Trans. C. Porter. Cambridge, Mass.: Harvard University Press.

Tolstoy, L. 1934 (1886). *What Then Must We Do?* Trans. A. Maude. Oxford: Oxford University Press.

Tönnies, F. 1957 (1887). *Community and Society.* Trans. and ed. C. P. Loomis. New York: Harper & Row.

Torgovnick, M. 1990. *Gone Primitive: Savage Intellects, Modern Lives.* Chicago: University of Chicago Press.

Toulmin, S. 1990. *Cosmopolis: The Hidden Agenda of Modernity.* Chicago: University of Chicago Press.

Touraine, A. 1992. "Is Sociology Still the Study of Society?" In *Between Totalitarianism and Postmodernity,* ed. P. Beilharz, G. Robinson, and J. Rundell, 173–98. Cambridge, Mass.: MIT Press.

———. 1995 (1992). *Critique of Modernity.* Translated by D. Macey. Oxford: Blackwell.

———. 1997. *Pourrons-nous vivre ensemble? Égaux et différents.* Paris: Fayard.

Trilling, L. 1972. *Sincerity and Authenticity.* Cambridge, Mass.: Harvard University Press.

Trinh, T. M. 1989. *Woman, Native, Other: Writing Postcoloniality and Feminism.* Bloomington, Ind.: Indiana University Press.

Turner, B. S. 1974. *Weber and Islam.* London: Routledge & Kegan Paul.

———. 1978. *Marx and the End of Orientalism.* London: Allen & Unwin.

Tylor, E. B. 1974a (1871). *Primitive Culture: Researches into the Development of*

Mythology, Philosophy, Religion, Art, and Custom. Vol. 1. New York: Gordon Press.

———. 1974b (1871). *Primitive Culture: Researches into the Development of Mythology, Philosophy, Religion, Art, and Custom.* Vol. 2. New York: Gordon Press.

van der Sprenkel, O. B. 1964. "Max Weber on China." *History and Theory* 3, no. 3: 348–70.

Veyne, P. 1978. "Foucault révolutionne l'histoire." In *Comment on écrit l'histoire*, 2d ed. Paris: Seuil.

Vico, G. 1984 (1744). *The New Science.* Trans. T. G. Bergin and M. H. Fisch. Ithaca, N.Y.: Cornell University Press.

Vogt, W. P. 1976. "The Use of Studying Primitives: A Note on the Durkheimians, 1890–1940." *History and Theory* 15, no. 1: 33–44.

Voltaire, F.-M. A. de. 1947 (1759). *Candide or Optimism.* Trans. J. Butt. Harmondsworth: Penguin.

———. 1954 (1767). *L'Ingénu.* In *Romans et contes.* Paris: Gallimard.

———. 1956 (1764). *Philosophical Dictionary.* Trans. P. Gay. New York: Harcourt, Brace & World.

———. 1963a (1756). *Essai sur les moeurs et l'esprit des nations*, t. 1. Paris: Garnier Frères.

———. 1963b (1756). *Essai sur les moeurs et l'esprit des nations*, t. 2. Paris: Garnier Frères.

———. 1995 (1755). "Letter to Jean-Jacques Rousseau." In *The Portable Enlightenment Reader*, ed. I. Kramnick, 375–78. Harmondsworth: Penguin.

Wacquant, L. J. D. 1995. "Durkheim et Bourdieu: le socle commun et ses fissures." *Critique* 579–80: 646–60.

Wada, H. 1983. "Marx and Revolutionary Russia." In *Late Marx and the Russian Road: Marx and the Peripheries of Capitalism*, ed. T. Shanin, 40–75. New York: Monthly Review Press.

Wagner, P. 1994. *A Sociology of Modernity: Liberty and Discipline.* London and New York: Routledge.

Wallerstein, I., chair. 1996. *Open the Social Sciences: Report of the Gulbenkian Commission on the Restructuring of the Social Sciences.* Stanford: Stanford University Press.

———. 2000. *The Essential Wallerstein.* New York: New Press.

Walzer, M. 1987. *Interpretation and Social Criticism.* Cambridge, Mass.: Harvard University Press.

Warnke, G. 1993. *Justice and Interpretation.* Cambridge, Mass.: MIT Press.

Weber, M. 1930a (1920). Introduction to *The Protestant Ethic and the Spirit of Capitalism.* Trans. T. Parsons, 13–31. London: Allen & Unwin.

———. 1930b (1904–5). "The Protestant Ethic and the Spirit of Capitalism." In *The Protestant Ethic and the Spirit of Capitalism*, trans. T. Parsons, 33–292. London: Allen & Unwin.

———. 1946a. "Politics as a Vocation." In *From Max Weber: Essays in Sociology*, trans. and ed. H. H. Gerth and C. Wright Mills, 77–128. New York: Oxford.

———. 1946b (1919). "Science as a Vocation." In *From Max Weber: Essays in Sociology*, trans. and ed. H. H. Gerth and C. Wright Mills, 129–56. New York: Oxford University Press.

———. 1946c (1915). "The Social Psychology of the World Religions." In *From Max Weber: Essays in Sociology*, trans. and ed. H. H. Gerth and C. Wright Mills, 267–301. New York: Oxford University Press.

———. 1946d (1922–23). "The Protestant Sects and the Spirit of Capitalism." In *From Max Weber: Essays in Sociology,* trans. and ed. H. H. Gerth and C. Wright Mills, 302–22. New York: Oxford University Press.

———. 1946e (1915). "Religious Rejections of the World and Their Directions." In *From Max Weber: Essays in Sociology,* trans. and ed. H. H. Gerth and C. Wright Mills, 323–59. New York: Oxford University Press.

———. 1949a (1917). "The Meaning of 'Ethical Neutrality' in Sociology and Economics." In *The Methodology of the Social Sciences,* ed. and trans. E. A. Shils and H. A. Finch, 1–47. Glencoe, Ill.: Free Press.

———. 1949b (1904). "'Objectivity' in Social Science and Social Policy." In *The Methodology of the Social Sciences,* ed. and trans. E. A. Shils and H. A. Finch, 49–112. Glencoe, Ill.: Free Press.

———. 1949c (1905). "Critical Studies in the Logic of the Cultural Sciences." In *The Methodology of the Social Sciences,* ed. and trans. E. A. Shils and H. A. Finch, 113-88. Glencoe, Ill: Free Press.

———. 1951 (1915). *The Religion of China: Confucianism and Taoism.* Trans. H. H. Gerth. New York: Free Press.

———. 1952 (1917–19). *Ancient Judaism.* Trans. and ed. H. H. Gerth and D. Martindale. New York: Free Press.

———. 1958 (1916). *The Religion of India: The Sociology of Hinduism and Buddhism.* Trans. H. H. Gerth and D. Martindale. New York: Free Press.

———. 1971 (1896). "The Social Causes of the Decay of Ancient Civilization." Trans. C. Mackauer. In *Max Weber: The Interpretation of Social Reality,* ed. J. E. T. Eldridge, 254–75. London: Michael Joseph.

———. 1972 (1908). "Georg Simmel as Sociologist." Trans. D. N. Levine. *Social Research* 39, no. 1: 155–63.

———. 1976 (1909). *The Agrarian Sociology of Ancient Civilizations.* Trans. R. I. Frank. London: New Left Books.

———. 1978a (1921–22). *Economy and Society: An Essay in Interpretive Sociology,* 2 vols., ed. G. Roth and C. Wittich. Berkeley and Los Angeles: University of California Press.

———. 1978b (1910). "Anticritical Last Word on *The Spirit of Capitalism.*" Trans. W. M. Davis. *American Journal of Sociology* 83, no. 5: 1105–31.

———. 1979 (1894). "Developmental Tendencies in the Situation of East Elbian Rural Labourers." *Economy and Society* 8, no. 2: 177–205.

———. 1980. "The National State and Economic Policy (Freiburg Address)." *Economy and Society* 9, no. 4: 428–49.

———. 1981 (1919–20). *General Economic History.* Trans. F. H. Knight. New Brunswick, N.J.: Transaction.

———. 2002. *The Protestant Ethic and the Spirit of Capitalism.* Trans. S. Kalberg. Los Angeles: Roxbury.

Weber, Marianne. 1988 (1926). *Max Weber: A Biography.* Ed. and trans. H. Zohn. New Brunswick, N.J.: Transaction.

Weil, E. 1984 (1952). "Rousseau et sa politique." In *Pensée de Rousseau,* ed. G. Genette and T. Todorov, 9–39. Paris: Seuil.

Weiming, T. 2000. "Implications of the Rise of 'Confucian' East Asia." *Daedalus* 129, no. 1: 195–218.

Wellmer, A. 1985. "Reason, Utopia, and the *Dialectic of Enlightenment.*" In *Habermas and Modernity,* ed. R. J. Bernstein, 35–66. Cambridge: Polity.

White, H. 1978. *Tropics of Discourse: Essays in Cultural Criticism.* Baltimore: The Johns Hopkins University Press.

Whitney, L. 1934. *Primitivism and the Idea of Progress in English Popular Literature of the Eighteenth Century.* Baltimore: The Johns Hopkins Press.

Wieviorka, M. 1996, ed. *Une société fragmentée? Le multiculturalisme en débat.* Paris: La Découverte.

Winch, P. 1970 (1964). "Understanding a Primitive Society." In *Rationality,* ed. B. R. Wilson, 78–111. Oxford: Blackwell.

Wittfogel, K. A. 1957. *Oriental Despotism: A Comparative Study of Total Power.* New Haven: Yale University Press.

Wittrock, B. 2000. "Modernity: One, None, or Many?" *Daedalus* 129, no. 1: 31–60.

Wolf, E. R. 1974. Foreword to *In Search of the Primitive: A Critique of Civilization,* by S. Diamond, xi–xiii. New Brunswick, N.J.: Transaction.

———. 1982. *Europe and the People without History.* Berkeley and Los Angeles: University of California Press.

Young, I. M. 1990. *Justice and the Politics of Difference.* Princeton, N.J.: Princeton University Press.

Young, R. 1990. *White Mythologies: Writing History and the West.* London and New York: Routledge.

Young, R. J. C. 1995. "Foucault on Race and Colonialism." *New Formations* 25: 57–65.

Zerzan, J. 1994. *Future Primitive and Other Essays.* Brooklyn, N.Y.: Autonomedia.

Index

FUYUKI KURASAWA is assistant professor of sociology at York University in Toronto, Canada, as well as a faculty associate of the Yale Center for Cultural Sociology. He was named a "Young Canadian Leader" by *The Globe and Mail* newspaper in 2000.